Blistered Feet
Blissful Mind

Tim Price

with illustrations by

Victor Lunn-Rockliffe

HEADHUNTER BOOKS
www.headhunterbooks.co.uk

D1146453

First published in July 2010 by Head-Hunter Books

Copyright © 2009 Tim Price (author)
and
Victor Lunn-Rockliffe for the illustrations.
The moral right of the author has been asserted.

ISBN 978-1-906085-17-9

Head-Hunter Books
www.headhunterbooks.co.uk

Printed in Poland by
Opolgraf S.A.

Contents

Foreword

Many of us have come to a stage in our lives when we ask ourselves why we are doing what we are doing. The world tells us that if we are wealthy and successful, if we have fame and fortune, then we will be happy.

In my own personal experience, I was never particularly wealthy but I worked for people who were. I was never famous but I rubbed shoulders with those who were. I had a taste of what success could be like and it seemed pretty empty to me. I was working all sorts of hours, making others rich but they didn't seem particularly contented either.

Then it happened to me. I came across somebody who seemed to be really genuine, bright and contented. A Buddhist monk, who it so happened was going on the same train as me, was standing in Waterloo train station. I was always interested in Buddhism; I loved the tales of enlightened masters, wise and gentle beings who seemed to have beautifully simple answers to complicated questions. But most of it I could not understand. The books I had read really only entertained me. I was still confused. I had not met anyone who really practiced the path. Meeting this monk really changed my life.

We sat together for just an hour or so. I loved every moment. We talked about many things but the Ajahn was continually bringing me back to the present, pointing to the obvious in ways that I found extraordinarily liberating. We laughed together and sometimes I cried, just relieved to find someone who really seemed to understand me. This was almost 30 years ago.

I was young, ambitious and competent in my work but the memory of the monk had stuck in my mind. Shortly after our first meeting, I went to meet him at the monastery that he had recently established. On first impression, the strict discipline of the monks living there both inspired me and terrified me. I could see that it essentially involved giving up a lot and I was certainly not ready for it. Success was eluding me but I was still hungry for it. I kept going back to see him, my first Ajahn, usually in times of crisis! After a while I came to know other monks and nuns who lived there and then travelled to branch monasteries as the community expanded and moved around.

Most significantly a growing faith in the efficacy of meditation practice led me away from seeking what I had come to see as pointless entertainment and the taste for a profound peace grew in my heart. I regularly joined meditation retreats when my partners were going to paradise beaches for their holidays. At the same time, a business life was developing about me. I was giving it less and less ambitious input as time passed. It seemed to be happening to me rather than by me. The job simply bored me. I felt I was wasting my time. Then some years later, noticing a growing rift between myself and my business partners and associates, I simply quit. I told them I was taking early retirement. Some of them thought I was crazy; some even believed I was rolling in money both of which could not have been further from the truth!

I joined the monastic community because I was aware of an intense internal frustration which I could not satisfy and an almost constant feeling of grief for the illusory and deluded world which seemed to surround me. This overwhelming dissatisfaction is a common experience. Rebellion is a response for those of us who truly feel imprisoned in an alien or hostile environment.

Perhaps the alms mendicant monk is the ultimate rebel. Living in the world but not of the world. Choosing to go against it but learning to live in harmony with it at the same time. The teachings are like a key, which opens the door to our prison cell. We have to follow the instructions and use it to open the lock. Painting the key gold and offering it flowers and incense is not going to set us truly free.

The Bhikkhu life is a particular form which some Buddhist men adhere to for a while. Few do it for a lifetime. Most Buddhists are not monks or nuns of course but the Buddha offered a system of training for those who are inclined to follow it. The rules and observances are intended to give a firm framework which is used for reflection and contemplation. As the practice is applied, the very restrictions and boundaries we have chosen for ourselves act as tools, mirrors or skilful means by which we develop a particular kind of wisdom. It helps us to wake up, to see things as they are in a way which brings unconditional freedom from suffering, enlightenment or, using the Buddha's own word, Nibbäna.

The teachings are intended to be applied. In the same way, if the doctor gives us a medicine, he expects us to take it, not to put it on a shrine and worship it. He encourages us to complete the course and not stop because it might not taste wonderful at first and he advises us to go back to the doctor regularly so that doses and alterations can be made. This way the remedy will work.

Our teachers help us understand the principal cause of our troubled minds. When we understand the reason behind it all, we can see a way to be free. This we realise for ourselves, nobody can do it for us, which can be a liberating and empowering discovery when we see it is possible to find the way independently. Teachers grow old, sick and die but the teaching can be trusted. It continues to work regardless.

Few follow the path to completion but in my experience those I know who have followed it for a while, have benefited greatly and I am grateful to all those who have practiced it well.

This book is offered to give readers a taste of Buddhist practice in action. There are those beings who endeavour to walk this path. It was the very sight of a monk which played a significant part in motivating the historical Buddha to follow his path leading to his discovery. He made it clear that this sign of the mendicant monk or nun should be a visible presence in the world. He made sure that his monastic disciples were not hidden away.

Dhamma books in this tradition are usually distributed free of charge as the teachings are considered priceless and asking money for them would naturally exclude some people from gaining access to them. Those who visit the monastery can take what they need. This storybook is commercially published simply because it is going to reach a much wider circulation. It is intended to give those who may not already have had the chance to see it before, a glimpse into another way of life, perhaps encouraging the reader to investigate the Noble Eightfold Path a little more for themselves. Any profits are to be simply recycled into making it more available for those who are interested.

The monk's needs are few. I am appreciative for all the support received. I rejoice in having the opportunity to have lived for a number of years in this way and to be able share some of it with you. With special gratitude to my teachers whose example will always provide me with food for the heart.

All of these stories have actually happened, quite separate little snapshots of meetings between worlds, from personal experience or as related to me by my friends. The names, places and some of the backgrounds have been altered to give the story a kind of thread and, like beautiful beads on a necklace, they have found their own natural order and place.

For my personal dedications:

I am always grateful to my wonderful parents, undoubtedly my first teachers who brought me up to recognise a beautiful thing when I see one. To my brother who continues to inspire me and my former wife who sacrificed a great deal to support my wellbeing. Bless them.

I also dedicate any merit following the production of this book to my wider Sangha family, brothers and sisters, near and far who have helped me on The Way.

Special thanks to Victor Lunn-Rockliffe for his amazing illustrations and all the enjoyable time we spent together working on them.

Not forgetting little Edward, or whatever his name was, wherever he is now.

May we all realise Nibbäna.

"I don't live like this all the time;
it's a special practice.
Besides I don't have the stamina
for it anymore....

I live in a monastery
where things are still very chaotic...

I rarely get what I want
but I do get what I need.

Although I don't always
recognise it at the time!"

Guardian Pirate

The Ajahn and his companion stood restfully, leaning lightly on the wooden fence as they checked the map. The footpath had taken them exactly to the point they expected, just a mile from the edge of town. The last hour or so had been hard going. They were both a little tired and hungry. Now time was running short and the daily Alms Round presented itself with an uncomfortable edge of uncertainty for the young monk. The Ajahn, however, has been through this many times. Looking upon his young friend, he suggests he prepare his bowl, robes and bag now before they enter the outskirts of town. They walk a few steps off the muddy, well trodden trail to a grassy patch where they can sort out their equipment with care.

Their alms bowls take up a significant amount of space, not just in the simple shoulder bag they carry but in their lives. It is the robes and the bowl which transform the traveller from an odd stranger into a monk, at least as far as outward appearance goes. The Ajahn carefully releases his bowl from a draw-cord at the bottom of his bag, removes the extra tee shirt, thermal vest, bathing cloth and some other utensils from inside the bowl. Everything is carefully folded and wrapped in cloth to prevent anything scratching the inside. He removes the beautifully woven wicker stand, fastened by the shoulder strap, tidies the cords and crochet cover and puts his bowl onto a cloth in the long grass that has been laid there for the purpose. Putting his gear back into the bowl-less container from underneath, the cloth bag eases and relaxes, its tight and slick shape sags as the bones of the bowl have been removed. The bag won't stand so neatly on the ground now. It's become all soft and lumpy. The Ajahn steadies it and glances over to his friend.

"Oh no! Now look at this!" mutters his younger companion, spreading his things on the grass. "Tooth paste everywhere!" Various plastic bags are stuffed and unfolded as he fumbles about. "The tube has split. Well, I guess it's not too bad," he continues to himself. He goes on to mouth a silent commentary as he stuffs things away.

Remembering how the Ajahn showed him the way of putting on his huge robe without dragging it on the ground, he stood awkwardly as the cloth was twisted and ravelled, then held between his legs, his arms extended full length upwards, then while twiddling his fingers to form a long roll, his head had become concealed inside the huge robe so he missed seeing the old man walking past with his dog. The passer-by looked a little dazed, maybe hung over or perhaps rather shy of taking a closer look or a little fearful of strangers on his routine dog exercise run or perhaps half waking from a dream. He hesitates for a second. Then preferring the old and the familiar, he dreams on striding through the mud. His tiny canine friend takes a quick sniff at the young monk's bag, then trots along behind.

Blistered Feet, Blissful Mind

With the bag pulled high on his left shoulder, bowl strap over his neck and shoulder, the Ajahn had stepped over the stile into the lane and was surveying the way ahead, formerly obscured by the hedge and trees. It was a narrow lane with just enough for two cars to pass, then a steep bank with long grass and some wild flowers, flanked by wild hedgerows and bushes. As the road curved away, he saw a row of cottages pressed tight against the lane with neat flowerbeds, cars parked in front and great green wheel-along dustbins that announced the arrival of suburbia. This was a small country town in South East England. A landscape familiar to the Ajahn as it is close to the place in which he grew up.

His friend, however, was from a different part of the world. No cute little footpaths through forests, fields and farms in America. No winding lanes that he knew of. He was surprised to be walking past houses in a street without a sidewalk and everything seemed so small and quaint to him.

The stylish country cottage and farm building conversions of new and wealthy professional families gave way to some new council house flats or perhaps they were retirement homes. Great expanses of concrete and tarmac, trees and plants framed in brick plinths, handsome yet cut off from each other. Now they are back in the town. They cross a busy road. Although there are many vehicles moving about, there was hardly anyone out walking in the street. They passed a small park which was lined with large houses with manicured gardens and expensive cars on gravel driveways. The monks were heading for the market or shopping areas, only their map was not going to tell them where to look. Instinctively, they head for the centre and soon find themselves in a supermarket car park. There is a clear strategy in locating a good place to stand and the Ajahn positions himself just off the entrance to the main street not directly in front of the supermarket entrance but in its view and in a place wide enough for people to walk past at a comfortable distance. His trusted companion stands beside him, shuffling his feet a little before settling down.

The last few hours of concerted effort has focused the minds of these two venerable monks into a full-on march towards one of the principal goals for the day, mealtime. However carefully they plan their route and select their resting place the previous night, it is often a push to get to the market place in good time. Now they stand still, perhaps a little dazed, minds not yet attuned to the people's busy energy as they bustle along on their familiar shopping venture. The monks' discipline means they have to be finished with their food before noon of that day. They cannot receive alms food until after dawn, neither can they keep any food and store it away for the next day. This is a rule set down by The Lord Buddha some 2,500 years ago for monks following his training. Each day they have to make contact with the laity; this means they cannot live secluded from the world, yet they live divorced from much of its worldliness.

Venerable Suñño was born in a comfortable family in California. He described himself as a West Coast 'beach bum' when he first ventured into the monastery. Now he is surfing a different kind of wave. The long stares, pointed fingers from passing children and the stolen glances from their parents unnerve him. He tries to offer a friendly smile, which seems to touch the stranger for a second then bounces off as they quickly look away, striding past as if nothing was seen at all. How weird that they could be standing in such a public place, so strangely dressed and yet feeling almost invisible.

Alms Round is still an unfamiliar challenge for Venerable Suñño who had been out to a local town near the monastery a few times before when he was a novice. But that was different. Then it felt close to home. There was always someone who knew the monastery, an old friend or devotee who knows the form and offers something to eat. Now he is on a special adventure several days walk from familiar territory. These people probably have never seen Buddhist monks in their town and have no idea what brings them here. Maybe they feel these strange men will try and sell them something or try to persuade them to accept something they don't want. So they pass at a safe distance.

The usual worrisome thoughts arise for the young monk. "This is no good. We'll never get anything here. Let's go somewhere else." Then receiving another cold stare. "Why don't we stand over there? They won't see us here." Waves of hunger well up inside as his mind fantasises about warm pizza or a Danish pastry. "Oh please, can't you see I am hungry?" The mad mind rambles on as he shuffles a little, maybe to relieve the shivers from the cold. Feelings of frustration and agitation coming partly from excited anticipation. Having no idea what to expect. On another level he really loves the uncertainty.

Now the Ajahn just stands looking at the ground in front of him. His face bears a gentle smile. Sometimes he looks up, scans the windows and rooftops and then opens to the passers-by with a broad gaze. He peacefully receives the hustle and bustle of shoppers and workers as they go about their business with an air of amusement. Just being here. There is nowhere else to go but be right here. When it is time to move, we will.

Now we wait and see what happens.

Ten minutes pass without a visible flicker of interest. Standing still feels much harder on the body than walking. Energy wavers in a dull ache, feelings and emotions have become distant by a weariness which ebbs and flows. The wanderers gently calm their minds with simple contemplation of the body, easing tension, supported by each other's willingness to endure the discomfort. Suñño's head jerks up in surprise as he is aware of polished shoes, baggy grey trousers, a stripey tee shirt and waist coat, one step in front of him. "Oh... sorry... what?" he mutters as he realises he has missed the first words of his questioner who had strode up to him without any preamble.

"Is there a monastery near here?" he says again. "Are you Shaolin?" He continues, now nervously glancing from one monk to the other. "Are you from India? Wow, I love the drums, do you play?"

"We are from a monastery in West Sussex, Hartwood. Do you know it?" replies the Ajahn.
"No" he replies abruptly, then spins round on the spot and walks quickly away just as Suñño was trying to explain.
 "We are Buddhist from..." and then he was gone. "Wow, what was that?" turning to the Ajahn. "Where did he come from? So rude."
"Nervous," said the Ajahn. "Let's walk a little."
"Drums!" exclaimed Suñño "and what about his crazy hat and moustache! He looked like a mad pirate!"

He falls in behind the Ajahn as they continue silently along the pedestrian street which linked the supermarket car park to the main High Street. There are a lot more people here. The pavement is not so wide and there is a constant stream of cars, vans and occasional buses rolling along in both directions. The street is lined mostly with banks, fashion and shoe shops, gift shops and vendors of consumables; various objects providing numerous entertainment outlets for all the family. Bright plastic colours and a mixed medley of pop music and perfume invade the senses as the brown-robed wanderers glide through as if they had just stepped out of a time machine.

After negotiating their way a few yards down the street they come across a small square with a war memorial in the centre - a small island of swept and well-worn stone slabs with iron bollards painted black about its shores, keeping the cars from parking there. Facing the square on one side is a church, rising high upon a flight of steps. The other side is a bakery and between them a rustic looking Tudor style building with a sign, 'Health Foods' in old-fashioned script.
The Ajahn turns and looks to his companion who returns an enthusiastic nod, then several more nods as they positioned themselves in front of the lone soldier statue. As they stand side-by-side, they can study the old post office, which now looms in front of them. There is a large clock almost two floors up which says it is fifteen minutes past eleven. The pirate came pacing boldly towards them from the post office. This time the wanderers are more prepared and they greet each other with warm smiles. From the pirate's pocket came a tightly closed fist, which he carefully opens to reveal a few coins. Without looking up, he chooses a couple of coins and offers them to the Ajahn who makes no movement to receive them. The pirate waves his hand about as if looking for a slot in a piggy bank.

"That is very kind and generous but we don't receive money," said the Ajahn. "It is a lovely offer but I cannot accept it."

The pirate almost reeled back in surprise "Oh, sorry, sorry I, I didn't realise. I didn't know, sorry, sorry." He looked disbelievingly at the coins in his hand, swaying back and forward. Feeling embarrassed and yet very intrigued, his body language said it all, shy then curious, shaken but not frightened off. "So... what are you doing? I mean where do you come from?... Sorry, sorry I don't know what..."

"That's ok. We are Buddhist monks and we are on a kind of pilgrimage, walking across the country."
"Oh wow and why are you standing here?"
"We are on our daily Alms Round, collecting our food for the day."
"I didn't know, sorry. Monks eh? So what do you do all day? Do you play music?"
"No, we don't play music. We don't have radios or TV either! We meditate, look after the monastery, try to help each other and support the people who visit us."
"Amazing! You walked here from where?" said the pirate as he took a long and very close look at the Ajahn's alms bowl. "So what is this for?"
"My alms bowl." He opens the lid.
"There is nothing in it!" The pirate's peculiar gait unnerves Venerable Suñño as the pirate swings around and bends over to point his nose at the other monk's bowl. The lid opens in return. "Right!" he exclaims and stands up straight. Staring expressionless, right into the young monk's eyes, his face just a few inches away. Then in a moment he is gone.

A few seconds later an elderly lady made her tentative approach, coin in hand. She stood still and listened to the familiar explanation, her face lighting up. She puts her purse away and draws up her wheelie basket in front. "Do you like apples?" she asks.
"Apples are fine!" said the Ajahn. She places an apple in each bowl.
"What about these?" as she holds up a packet of chocolate biscuits. A broad smile and an open bowl lid is all the monk needs to do to express approval.
"Bless you," says the Ajahn.
"Bless you too," replies the lady. "Are you Buddhist?" she continues.
"Yes."
"I am Church of England... Born and bred!" she smiles. "Jesus loves you."

Suñño is deeply moved by her sincerity. Maybe her bright eyes and clear Christian faith sparks up some deep memories from his childhood. He swallows hard as a tear wells up and runs down his cheek. He watches her walking purposely away with her thick grey winter coat and floral headscarf, skinny legs with tiny red court shoes and a battered wheelie basket - everyone's favourite auntie.

The constant melee of shoppers passing by felt a little more distant as the profound beauty of recent events resonated in the hearts of our wanderers. They stand in a silent thought bubble, contemplating blessings, glowing warm again. There seem to be more people watching them now from a distance. A bright young face studies them from the bakery window as she wraps fresh loaves in paper. They catch an occasional brief glance of the pirate as he seemed to weave about the crowds, appearing to enjoy a little conversational sparring with many folks. Two young women step forward and smile, standing a few paces in front of the monks, both shy and giggly.

"Can we take a picture?" asks one. The Ajahn looks over to Suñño who glances back, tight-lipped, tilting his head from side to side.
"Well?" replied the Ajahn with a strained looking smile. A mobile phone was whipped out, then held out in front of her face for a few seconds and then gone.
"Thanks" said one young woman. Turning away to her friend, they both studied the tiny plastic image she had made, then giggling again as they moved off.
"Thanks," added Suñño, shaking his head. He watched them slink off with their skin-tight jeans and provocative walk wobbling through his mind.

After a few more minutes, the Ajahn turned about and they slowly walked back towards their first spot by the car park. Just as they are about to cross the busy road, a young girl appears in front with some oranges in an orange plastic net. She awkwardly tips them into the young monk's bowl and runs off without a word. Surprised, the monk steps backwards off the pavement and receives a cautionary hoot from a passing car. At this moment, he spots the pirate again, grinning from a shop doorway.

Once they are back by the supermarket, they quickly receive offers of food. First they are offered money but people quickly seem to understand what the monks need. It appears that the word is out and others soon join in. This quickly becomes a problem as some shoppers have asked them to wait so that they can go into the supermarket to buy something whilst others have already brought quite enough for them to eat for today. In just twenty minutes, the doubts about having sufficient food are replaced with concerns about the need to desert some of the generous folks who have made offers but have not yet materialised such as a posh postman and a woman with two children. Maybe they won't come back at all. However, they have too much food now and time is running out.

The Ajahn had seen a little cemetery on the way into town. It is raised up with a stone wall, stone steps and an iron gate. The wanderers go swiftly through, now moving with extra care. Apart from their precious alms bowls they now have shopping bags and large bottles of fizzy drink to carry. This together with their other shoulder bags is quite a balancing act.

The monks exchange few words as they find a quiet corner between the gravestones. They lay down plastic sheets and sitting cloths on the ground and prepare their bowls. They silently lay out their offerings, opening bags and spreading them out with care so that everything is presented. The contents of their bowls are also laid out and Venerable Suñño begins by choosing a bag of bread rolls. He tears it open and offers them to his senior as if on a tray with both hands. As the Ajahn takes them, Suñño puts his hands together and slightly lowers his head in a beautiful salute. A couple of rolls are taken and the remainder are given back. The junior takes three and puts them in his bowl. Then the French bread stick is broken in two and shared. The tin of sardines is briefly considered by the Ajahn but returned, then accepted by his companion. Their mixed fare consists of cakes, cheese, a bag of sugar, chocolate, bananas, biscuits, potato chips, a large tin of tomatoes, oranges, apples, a small tin of baked beans, two meat pies, a small bag of uncooked lentils, two loaves of sliced bread, a carton of orange juice, two bottles of Pepsi, a bag of peanuts, two raw eggs and a jar of marmalade.

"A handsome spread," said Suñño as he wipes his can opener clean on a piece of bread. The Ajahn smiles and raises his hands, palms together in front of his chest and looks upwards into the great yew tree towering above. Together they chant the blessings in an ancient Indian tongue. A few moments of silent appreciation ensues then they consume their alms food without a word.

"Sure it is easier for you
if I accept your money
but I want you to feel
and know better than that.

Money is cheap
but your loving attention is priceless."

Man's Best Friend

Walking long distances is a challenging practice in itself as the monks travel as lightly as possible - they don't go with specialised camping equipment. The Ajahn chose to walk in sandals and his companion followed suit. The shoulder bag is very simple, homemade in brown robe-coloured cloth. The Ajahn folds a rain poncho and ties it under the shoulder strap to act as padding. However light it seems at first, after a few hours it appears to gain weight and it is often necessary to change shoulders as they walk. For the first few days, the body wants to complain at almost every step. The shoulder stiffens and tension steadily grows, pulling the neck and lower back muscles into knots. Although the feet are well accustomed to wearing sandals, the steady pounding for hours on end eventually produces a few blisters. By mid afternoon, every stile stepped over is a strain. The warm sun beats down on shaven heads and the sweat means that plasters, protecting blistered feet, won't stay stuck for long.

They follow an ancient footpath, which snakes along the crests of hills stretching East and West for miles across the countryside. The trail is clearly marked with wooden signposts and a small carved and coloured design which points the way through woodlands, fields with sheep or cows grazing, farmyards and villages. The ancient rights of way precede the tarmac roads, farm tracks and fences which sometimes run along its route and sometimes cross it heading in a different direction. Our wanderers will need to negotiate a series of gates, step over stiles and often have to stop and identify which direction the path takes as it meanders across a ploughed field or gets lost in an orchard.

Venerable Suñño had completely lost interest in the countryside for the past couple of hours as his mind is locked in physical pain. He keeps the faint figure of his companion in his sight, grits his teeth and grinds on. The trail now follows a farm track used mostly by tractors and off-road vehicles. There are deep parallel ruts with a grassy ridge in the middle. The ruts are rocky with potholes and loose stones. There are few level places to put his feet, even the seemingly grassy middle hides obstacles on which it is easy to stub a toe or twist an ankle. All concentration is on the ground as one could easily injure oneself on a track like this. His bag was refusing to stay on his shoulder the way it was before and the horsefly bite on the side of his neck means that the right shoulder is no good for bag hauling for a while. Focused in the body, he could not see any point which didn't hurt except perhaps for the fingers of his left hand. His right hand steadies the bag as it bounces against his sore hip. He knew this journey was not going to be so easy and he was ready to accept a challenge but right now he knows he is coming close to breaking point! His mind's voice screaming, 'Oh please stop! I really need to stop... How much further... I can't stand it anymore!' And on... And on it went ...

They walk through an open gate into a field. The grass is cropped short by the teeth of a thousand sheep and a great grey log lies invitingly in front of them. Swinging his bag onto his lap, the Ajahn sits down. He pats the log and invites his friend to sit beside him which he does, collapsing in a heap then looking at his friend with a groan and a great sigh.

"Well," said the Ajahn, "I am completely exhausted. Aching all over!" With a bright smile, almost a look of delight he continues, "I reckon I'm getting too old for all this!" and laughs.

His young friend doesn't understand the joke and stares barefaced. The Ajahn continues to chuckle, then the chuckle turns into a full belly laugh; holding his stomach he begins to roll about his waist. He points a finger at Suñño with such a loving eye and cackles on. Moved by this extraordinary behaviour Suñño starts to smile.

"And you know what?" continues the Ajahn, "I haven't a clue where we are going!" and roars with laughter.

At this point his tense and worried friend lets go, he reaches out to touch his teacher's hand as his belly starts to quiver and shake. In a moment the pain is forgotten.

"We must be mad," says Suñño. "This is killing me!" He grins and waves his hands about his face.

A few moments later all is calm. Water bottles are taken out and they take in the enormous vista before them. This hilltop is free of trees and a great green landscape of chequered fields lined with hedges reveals itself in front of them. Scattered amongst them are farmhouses with red tiled roofs. Way in the distance they can make out the shapes of larger buildings, a church steeple and the brightly coloured specks of cars lined up in rows. They rest for a while. The sky begins to glow orange as the sun sets.

"Do you see kind and generous people down there?" said the Ajahn. "I say we start looking for a place to rest for the night and head over there tomorrow for pindapat[1]."
"Looks good to me. I could do with a rest and it's not too far to walk in the morning," said Suñño, "but where do we spend the night?" He holds up an empty water bottle. "I could use a refill and a roof would be nice... Oh wow and a shower would be fantastic!"
"How about a cup of tea?" said the Ajahn putting on a posh English upper class accent and laughed.

They strolled slowly back to the footpath and stopped at the gate. The Ajahn pointed one finger left, the other right and wagged his head quizzically. Suñño shrugged his shoulders and the teacher went left, onwards into unexplored

[1] pindapat - Alms Round

territory. They kept looking for paths which turned left again, down the hill in the direction of the town. But no left turn came for a long while. All routes seemed to turn them down the other side of the hill. They walked on, keeping a downhill preference which led them further and further into dense woodland. There was a clear public footpath sign at the entrance to the woodland but now they were in there, many other paths opened up before them. The light was beginning to fade and it was clear they were lost. The map came out but it had been a while since they had looked at it. Was it this forested area? Or this?

They chose to make these walking pilgrimages in the summer months. The weather is bearable (the winter would mean carrying tents, back packs and sleeping bags for sure) but the unpredictable English climate means even the summer can be pretty cold. Last night was spent sleeping out in the open, hidden by a clump of bushes at the edge of a field. It seemed ideal in the early evening but once it became dark, the temperature dropped considerably. Neither of them had much sleep. The Ajahn seemed to walk up and down most of the night or sat wrapped up with his robes and his poncho over his head. In the morning everything was wet with dew and they did not stop shivering until hours after dawn. Around summer solstice, it is light from 3:30 in the morning until after 10:00 at night. They both carry a tiny flashlight which helps them to find, say the insect repellent when it rolls out of their bag in the dark but is hopeless for following a narrow track in dense woodland at night.

Suñño takes it upon himself to find a way out and strides out ahead, Ajahn following behind. The path becomes more and more difficult to see and then, it is gone. They look backwards and try to retrace their steps only to find branches blocking the way in every direction. In the poor light they need to hold one hand in front of their face to prevent small branches from poking them in the eye. Then they stumble as their feet fall into rabbit holes or as they trip over branches. A certain air of panic creeps in and the Ajahn begins to chuckle. They both stop simultaneously and listen. A dog barks, not far away.

"Dog," whispers the Ajahn, "Man's best friend." They wait a moment more and another bark.
"This way" says Suñño as they follow the sound. Then a tearing sound is heard. "Damn it, now I have a robe to fix." Some more cussing continues, punctuated by giggles and wry comments from the Ajahn.

The light increases as they near the edge of the wood. They come to a halt at a barbed wire fence and an open field. They lift their things carefully over the wire then, by pressing the lower wire down with a foot and lifting the top wire with a hand, our wanderers get through without further damage to their robes. As they gather themselves, some very large dark creatures move towards them. Almost silently at first but once they are quite close, one of these huge animals stamps a very heavy hoof and snorts gruffly.

"Oh shit!" says an American whisper. Then more heavy hoofs from an enormous beast which seems to be charging straight towards them.

"Run!" came an American cry.

"Where?" came a cool reply as one robed figure makes a dash into the open. Suddenly the runner drops like a stone and cries out again in broad Californian;

"Oh shit, damn... Oh no!"

The Ajahn turns his flashlight on and walks up to his friend who is lying spread-eagled in a pile of ...

"Shit. Yes, horse shit," said the Ajahn.

He makes reassuring noises and reaches out to stroke the long snout of a beautiful grey mare as they both look down upon the miserable young monk. The Ajahn tries hard to suppress his amusement as they continue across the field towards the farmhouses down the hill. Right now a good laugh is probably not going to help!

It is quite dark as the monks approach the farm buildings from the fields. They are looking for a way to open the gate when a small girl with long blonde hair walks backwards out of a barn with a large box in her arms. Catching a glance of two shadowy and ghostly figures she screams and drops the box. The terrified stable girl's mood soon changed once she heard the monks' voices. She took an immediate shine to the American and led them straight to her boss in the large house. Within a few minutes, the stinking Californian was showered, his robes were churning around in a machine and our wanderers were grinning at each other over hot cups of tea in an old caravan surrounded by horses.

"Buddhists are you?" said the old man standing in the caravan door. "Not Hare Krishna? My cousin got Hare Krishna and went a bit nutty in India. He's all right now. He sells herbs in London." He calls over the stable girl. "Fetch these good fellows some biscuits or a sandwich or something!"

"They don't want anything!" came a distant reply from the shed nearby. "I already asked 'em. They won't eat 'til mornin' but they'll 'ave breakfast with us. They'll come to the house at 7:00!" She walks towards them in the darkness with a flashlight. "Come on Tom, let 'em rest. They've walked all the way from Midhurst."

"Midhurst? That's where Cowdray Park is isn't it? Where your Uncle Brian broke his leg playing polo?" Their voices paled in the distance and there was peace at last.

"Lovely people," said the Ajahn. "I'll go and get your robes from the house in a little while. The woman said she would put them in a tumble dryer for you!"

"Is it ok to let her do it for me?" said Suñño. Believing that having a woman washing your robes is an offence against the monk's rule.

"Given the situation, it was hard to refuse. Besides, we thought the old man was doing it." He poured out the last of the hot water from a thermos flask.

"I'll get my stuff from the dryer," said Suñño wrapping a small blanket around his shoulders.

"It's ok. You stay here. Maybe it's not a good idea to go about half dressed. We don't want to give the girl the wrong idea eh?"
"Of course. I wasn't thinking. Thank you Ajahn".

The young monk was woken at 4:30 by the sound of his companion shaking the dog hair from his robes. The light showed that they were both covered in dog hair and both severely bitten by fleas but Suñño was so tired that he had slept like a log. They both like to begin the day with an hour or so of meditation. Having had enough of the fleas, they were sitting outside on wooden palettes which they found under the caravan when the stable girl came across with cups of hot tea at 6:30. She stood at a distance, a little nervous. She had been thinking of their new visitors all night and had been very excited at the idea of seeing them again in the morning. From 5:30 she had been preparing a special breakfast in the kitchen, silently rehearsing all the questions she had for them. Walking across the field with her eyes on the teacups, trying not to spill too much, she had come quite close to the monks before she saw they were sitting motionless outside. Cross-legged and with eyes closed, they were certainly looking very peaceful. Dare she disturb them now?

Hovering for a while she had just decided to say, in a quiet and friendly voice, "Excuse me" when the older monk opened his eyes and looked straight at her. She stepped back in surprise and tea slopped down her front.

"Hello," he said. "Oh, is it time already?"
"I've brought tea," she spluttered out. Then hands him both cups and turns to make a quick get away.
"Bless you," said the monk in a beautiful quiet tone.
As she reaches the gate she calls out, "Breakfast in half an hour, up at the house. Come round the back door, round by the green horse box!"

Just then another voice comes screaming from the house, "Stop! Damson, come here! Here!... Damson here! Damson... DAMSON!!" A tall, thin older woman ran out from behind the house, shrieking in a high-pitched voice. This upper class voice, usually reserved and well mannered, begins to lose its cool. "Naughty girl!" she barks. Old Tom appears at the other side of the house, running full speed. As he turns the corner, a huge black dog, almost as wide as it is tall, appears from behind a wall and bolts down the track with Tom in hot pursuit. "Damson!" The girl joins in; "Damson!" As the dog comes blundering towards the caravan, its great jowls flapping, spattering saliva from its mouth, she has mad looking eyes which stare fixedly at the strangers. Our young friend takes up his needle, thread and robe and stands very slowly. Keeping his eyes on the mad hound, he backs into the caravan doorway. Damson, the great black monster takes up a strong position in front of the seated monk. Barking and snarling the dog lurches back and forth, stepping sideways only to avoid the grasping hand of the girl. She takes hold of the dog's collar for a second but the animal is much too strong; it probably weighs more than her. Certainly heavier than the older lady of the house who now stands shouting hysterically to one side. Tom joins in and the three of them hop about yelling, "Damson! Damson!" The dog leaps back and forth, people leap up and down in a growing frenzy. A young man comes running from the house with a length of chain, deftly sweeps down on an extremely revved up Damson and slips the chain noose about the neck and pulls hard. The animal rears up, takes a few steps back, lowers her centre of gravity and charges towards the monk who remains seated and remarkably calm. The lad can barely hold on but is quickly helped by Tom who also grabs the chain.

The Ajahn slowly stands as the cries for Damson quieten. The chain tightens about the poor dog's throat. Damson can't bark now but the chain hasn't weakened her determination. She continues to lunge forward, then tries weaving sideways in a attempt to break loose.

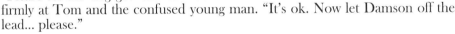

"I'm dreadfully sorry!" cries the older woman. "Bad girl Damson!" she waves a finger at the dog. "She was on the kitchen table, eating everything."
"Oh Damson!" cries the stable girl "That was special food for the monks. Bad girl!" she waves a finger at the dog. "She is only a puppy really!"
"Let go of the chain" said the monk, now standing close.
"She bites!" said Tom.
"Please" said the Ajahn in a quiet and calm tone.
"Please let the dog go." He looked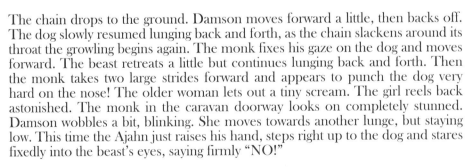
firmly at Tom and the confused young man. "It's ok. Now let Damson off the lead... please."

The chain drops to the ground. Damson moves forward a little, then backs off. The dog slowly resumed lunging back and forth, as the chain slackens around its throat the growling begins again. The monk fixes his gaze on the dog and moves forward. The beast retreats a little but continues lunging back and forth. Then the monk takes two large strides forward and appears to punch the dog very hard on the nose! The older woman lets out a tiny scream. The girl reels back astonished. The monk in the caravan doorway looks on completely stunned. Damson wobbles a bit, blinking. She moves towards another lunge, but staying low. This time the Ajahn just raises his hand, steps right up to the dog and stares fixedly into the beast's eyes, saying firmly "NO!"

Damson goes weak in the legs and her belly flops to the ground. Her eyes change and her facial expression is immediately transformed into complete submission. Then, in a moment, she rolls onto her back. The Ajahn crouches down and takes the chain off. He presses the dog's great broad chest with an open palm and speaks gently. Nobody hears his words. The Ajahn and the dog stand up together, look at each other then re-join the group. Silence prevails for a while. The monk dusts himself down, goes back to his seat on the wooden palette, takes up his tea and drinks. All eyes are on him. He looks about smiling. Then the great black beast saunters over to him, lays belly down in front, staring at her new master.

"Good!" says the monk. "Now we have peace!" and he begins to laugh.

Stares of disbelief turn to smiles and everyone relaxes. The stable girl comes over to her canine friend and puts an arm about its neck.

"Poor old Damson." She exclaims and takes a long look at the monk but gets no response.
"Please come and have something to eat, you must be starving," said the woman of the house. "The dog has eaten the bacon and eggs but I am sure we can have toast or porridge. Do you like porridge?"
"Sounds great," adds Suñño.
"Good, lets go."

They move together towards the gate. Even the old horses have come to join the party. Damson wags a stubby tail.

"Damson is a lovely dog," said the older woman, "but so naughty!"
"Seems a bit confused," said the Ajahn. "Would be happier with some training."
"She is just a puppy, a year and a half. She's not that bad, you know."
"A great dog, just confused. She needs to know where she stands. Right now, you don't own the dog, the dog owns you. It is only a baby and it needs boundaries. In fact we all need boundaries, don't we?" and laughs.
"He's right, Elizabeth," said Tom, now introducing the lady of the house. "The dog rules the place!" He turns to the Ajahn. "Drove her husband away!"
"Not quite," said Elizabeth, the older woman.
"Pretty much," said the stable girl and the woman begins to cry.
"The dog is much happier with some discipline. Dogs are essentially pack animals. They depend on some hierarchy. She'd be more contented if she has a definite place, things she can do to be of service. She's too young and foolish to be the leader!"
"But do we need to hit her?" asks the young girl.
"Dog language," the monk snarls, bares his teeth and then laughs.
"Seems a bit rough," said the other monk.
"How else do you teach it? Give it a book to read?" replies the Ajahn. Now everyone laughs. They gather at the back door. The monks stand aside to let the others in first. Damson comes up to the Ajahn's side and nuzzles up to him, then licks his hand.

"Oh look! She is saying sorry," says the girl.

Breakfast is a long and drawn out affair. The Ajahn spends a long time talking to Elizabeth about boundaries, about generosity, mutual understanding and loving kindness. She talks mostly about her husband, his work, their distant children and her domineering mother. Her marriage is certainly on the rocks. She listens attentively to the teacher's every word. She is very emotional, sometimes smiling, sometimes tearful but always asking questions.

"Just trust in that natural goodness," he says to her as they part a couple of hours later.
"Oh, you are wonderful. Thank you so much," she said with tears in her eyes. As the monks walked down the lane the great black beast started to howl! Damson broke loose and ran after them. The Ajahn has to turn back and bring the dog home. By the time they hit the road, they are getting hungry again. The girl had said that the town is four or five miles away and it is nearly ten o'clock. So much for their plans. It's another forced march to town.

The Catalyst

The Alms Round had been very slow to begin with. They had only made contact with one woman who was doubtful and hesitant at first but once she had understood the reason for the monks' visit to their little village, she had been very big-hearted and provided all. She then vanished. Our friends have finished their meal and they are putting away their things when their generous donor returns. The monks have hidden themselves in the Churchyard, one of the Ajahn's favourite places. She had been frantically looking all over for them so she arrives breathless and anxious.

"Oh, there you are! I was afraid I had missed you," she said gasping. She stands over the two monks who are kneeling on the ground. "I really want to talk to you... is that ok?" she paused. "To talk, I mean. You do talk don't you?"
"Sure!" said the Ajahn. "Perhaps we could find a good place to sit down. We are comfortable on the ground but I guess you would prefer a seat?"
"Oh yes, there is a bench over there," she points a finger.
"Let's go and see," adds Suñño.

They go over to the edge of the graveyard where a bench is sited looking out over the fields beyond. The woman marches purposely over to the bench, sits down and motions the monks to sit beside her. A few feet or so in front of the bench is a low wall. The monks sit on the wall and face the woman who at first looks a little agitated. She pats the bench beside her with her hand in a welcoming gesture.

"That's ok, we'll sit here thank you, I can see you better this way," said the Ajahn who leans forward to greet the woman. He signals to his friend to move a little further along the wall so as not to overcrowd her. Suñño moves a couple of paces away and she visibly relaxes.
"So, let me get this straight," she begins again. "You are walking to where?"
"East, I think.." the Ajahn turns to his friend.
"More North-East," came Suñño's reply.
"Nowhere in particular then. So why do you do it? I mean, no money, look at you... you hardly have anything! The poor lad, look at his feet! It must be so hard... why do you do it?" She turns her attention to the younger monk.
"Good question!" he smirks. It is a good question for him. He has been suffering all morning. The pain shines clear on his face. He looks at his teacher for a good reply.
"Well it is a kind of a test," said the Ajahn.
"A test! Of what? You could die out here! I mean, what if nobody gave you anything? What happens if you get sick?" She waved her hands about in dismay.
"I mean what is it all about?" she said in an almost angry tone of voice.
"Giving," said the Ajahn.

"I mean, why don't you put a sign out instead of just standing there. How are we to know you want food? At least you could put a sign to say you want food and not money. I am sure people would give much more then."

"We may get more from it, that is true but you wouldn't."

"I don't understand. I would feel happier if you have a sign. People won't understand you!"

"So far, so good! Some days are leaner than others, but so far we haven't gone without, have we?" the Ajahn said turning to his friend who shakes his head in agreement.

"But you turned down my money and still you didn't say you wanted food. What kind of crazy game are you playing?" At this point the young monk giggles again. She looks over baffled but now a little amused. Smiling, they both look at the Ajahn.

"Now you are anxious but a few minutes ago by the supermarket, you were very happy, weren't you?" said Ajahn.

"Yes, it was wonderful!"

"You gave us a lot of good food, carefully chosen and individually packaged! You put it into our bowls and then you said 'thank you' to us!" the Ajahn reminded her. "You were glowing with delight!"

"I did!" she nodded. "It felt great working out what to buy, then putting it into your empty bowls!"

"So you scored 100%!" the Ajahn laughed. She looks on, puzzled and yet intrigued.

"I don't get it."

"You see, I wanted you to be the one who wins all the merit," he continues. "If I had asked you for something, hinted or directed you, I would have interfered and you would have only scored, say, 60% and the other 40% is taken off my account. This way you have done all the good work and we both win!" The Ajahn roars and almost falls backwards off the wall.

"So you deliberately won't ask?" she said rather incredulously.

"That's it." He cups his hands in front of him to demonstrate the point. She leans forward. "I trust in the natural goodness of human nature. When we walk out into the world, we find we attract goodness and generosity by making ourselves truly vulnerable. We live this way to show that goodness and generosity really exist in this world and we act as a kind of catalyst which can make it happen. This morning, I am delighted to see it working once again. In fact it has been working for monks in this tradition for more than 2,500 years. First in India, now in East Sussex!"

"Wow, that's beautiful," she slides off the bench and kneels on the ground.

"You see it makes me so happy to see you working it out all on your own!" The Ajahn beams. "I had a strong feeling you would come back. Most people do. It is very rare to meet anyone who refuses money! Your natural generosity was glowing all along. When you came back, you made an invitation 'Can I get you something?' So I have an invitation from you and I respond. Each time you took another step in a generous direction, the happier you became. Is that right?"

"It's the best thing in ages!" she presses her hands to her chest.

"So, you understand that I love the chance to make people happy too! I help to reveal the beauty they already have. It's like being a mirror! They give to me, thank me and shine! And the truth is that I am only a part of the equation. They discover it for themselves. I am only the catalyst. It is a beautiful life!" The Ajahn put his hands together in front of his chest. "The Buddha said that a generous person is a happy person. And now you can see it for yourself!"

For a few moments the woman took on the appearance of a little child as she sat there on the ground. The Ajahn began chanting the blessing in the Pāli language and after a few lines, the other monk joined in a harmonious duet. The woman, fleetingly looking like a little child, started to cry with pure joy. Then there was a few moments silence.

"What were you chanting?"
"The Buddha's words in praise of generosity. Blessings bringing you long life, good health, prosperity and good looks."
"Good looks? I think it's a bit late for me!" she laughs. Although Suñño noticed immediately that this lady had visibly changed during the course of their conversation, she definitely looked at least ten years younger now. She stood up, actually more like springing up into life. Then she walked twice around the bench, stopping with both hands on the backrest, nodding at the monks.

"Please, will you come and see my father-in-law? He is really sick. We live next to the vicarage. Please, if you can spare the time, I think he would love to see you. I am sure you could help him, he is very miserable." She walks up to Suñño "We can do something to dress your feet, maybe you would like a bath? Yes, that's a point, what do you do for a bath?"
"Jump in the river!"
"No?"
"At a push!" grinned Suñño who is now beaming.
"Would you like to rest up for a few days? We have spare rooms." She reached out a gesturing hand to the Ajahn. "My husband works from home, he saw you in the village. I am sure he'd be interested to meet you."
"Let's see," said the Ajahn. Remaining seated, he stretches round to gaze over the fields. "One thing at a time... The weather looks good." The woman looks anxious again.
"Ok, let's go and see the old man first."
"Oh great, wonderful, thank you! Would you like some coffee? I have Pete's coffee from California?" She smiles at the young monk who looks as if he has just won the lottery.
"Things are looking up!" adds the Ajahn raising his head and shaking it in a teasing way towards his friend. "That certainly moved the mind, didn't it?" They grin at each other.

The night before the Ajahn was talking about some of the benefits of living this way of renunciation. Being able to simply follow our wishes, often leads to a restless and agitated mind. So much of our attention becomes occupied in looking for something else to satisfy us. Then when we get it, there is a momentary sense of satisfaction, which we barely notice because the mind is already off chasing the next little hit! We train ourselves to be content with whatever we are offered, not in a forceful way, but by means of wise reflection. If we lay ourselves open to simply receiving the gifts of others, everything becomes a blessing and contentment arises naturally. Having the opportunity to manipulate the situation and thinking we can have what we want, gives the mind good reason to become disturbed. Choosing choice-less-ness makes everything so much easier. The monks take this practice upon themselves in order to support a tranquil mind and to better understand what drives them. This way they develop wise understanding and live with an untroubled mind. Suñño begins to see that although this adventure seems to be physically quite strenuous, his mind is becoming quite calm. That was until the coffee arrived!

He had consumed a whole jug of strong black coffee with loads of sugar and was very much enjoying the company of the woman's husband Nigel and their son Frank in their workshop.

"Pat rushed in to tell us that she had seen you by the 'Bull' and went off again, half crazy looking for you!" said Nigel.
"She said she thought you had just disappeared into the heavens!" laughed Frank. "She got the van out and drove about like a maniac and nearly knocked the vicar over!"

The father and son have a small cabinet making business in a beautifully converted barn. It is all quite muddled. There are half finished kitchen units and cupboard doors spewing out into the little yard which barely separates the workshop from their living quarters. 'Rex', an elderly Labrador lies in a pile of wood shavings chewing an old bone. 'Dusty' the cat is curled up in a plastic bowl, which is perched on the top shelf of a cupboard containing a fascinating collection of old tools, tins of varnish, magazines and very dusty cassette tapes. There is a big 'Frank Zappa' poster on the wall, looking remarkably like young Frank who has long hair  and wearing a vest. Frank casually rolls a cigarette as they speak. For a moment, the young Californian feels very much at home!

"Yeah, I had a girlfriend from San Francisco when I was in college," said Frank. "I went there a couple of times, nearly moved in. Then we fell out." He flops into a dusty armchair. "I help dad most of the year but go off to India or somewhere hot in winter when things are quiet and I'm not too broke."

"I did the same when I was young," says Nigel. "Drove an old parcels van across Africa with Pat. We lived in the back."

He points to a faded photo of two long-haired hippies and a small child standing beside a brightly coloured van and a figure riding a camel in the distance. They exchanged some travel stories for half an hour. Then it is time to get back to work; they have a deadline to meet. As he was leaving, Suñño noticed that Nigel's right hand was shaking as he picked up a paintbrush. He was rather overweight, his skin very pale and sweaty and he was having difficulty breathing.

The living area across the yard wasn't quite so dusty. The Ajahn is upstairs sitting beside the bed of an old man who looks like a corpse. His eyes are sunken so far, he must be very close to death. The room smells of stale urine and Dettol. Pat bustles in and out, bringing tea which is not touched.

The Ajahn holds the old man's hand. He whispers something into his ear and the old man closes his eyes for a moment and smiles a toothless smile. He squeezes the Ajahn's hand with what little strength he has then his whole body relaxes and he sleeps. They returned to the kitchen and sit at the table.

"It's terrible isn't it, poor fellow," said Pat. "It's not right is it?"
"He's all right," said the Ajahn. "He's just dying, that's all." Pat is quite startled at his openness and fidgets uncomfortably, then opens to it.
"I guess so," she looks to the floor. "Guess we all do."
"You are looking after him beautifully."
"Thank you," she said, visibly moved. "Nigel really can't cope with it."
"He knows he is going soon and really appreciates your care. He hated the hospital. Go and be with him. You don't need to say anything. He is ready. No need to pretend any more."
"You will come for tea at 5:00?" she asks, feeling choked.
"Ok, maybe better later ... 6 o'clock?" She nods and nips upstairs.
"Let's go and chill out for a while," said Ajahn turning to his friend. "We could go off to the river bank and the woods behind for a few hours... Good idea?"
"Great," replies his friend. They place their bags in the hall then leave quietly, agreeing to meet back at the churchyard before 6:00.

Suñño finds a magic spot by the river. There is a footpath which runs alongside but nobody came by. Wired by the coffee, he paces up and down doing walking meditation for some time. This is a full day. Pat is an angel and it is truly inspiring to see her in action. Nigel and Frank seem really quite lost and dazed, both quite sickly. 'They put on a confident face but underneath they are really in a mess,' thinks the young monk. The coffee lets him down with a crash. He sits down to meditate for a few seconds then flops to one side and falls asleep in the warm sun.

* * *

The Ajahn waited by the church for twenty minutes or so, then returned to the barn. The workshop is deserted; only Rex comes out to greet the monk. There is no sign of anyone in the lower floor of the house either. It is all open plan with a large glass window opening to the yard. He puts his head through the door and calls out gently,

"Anyone home?" ....silence.

He sits for a while, on a packing crate outside the workshop, listening. Half an hour later, a battered white van comes screeching into the yard and Pat climbs out. She doesn't notice the monk sitting there and dashes straight into the house. The Ajahn waits for a moment then moves towards the door. Pat is speaking on the phone. She sees him and waves him in. He waits in the doorway.

"Yes, yes all right I'll pick him up later, thank you." She hangs up. "Oh my goodness Ajahn! Nigel cut himself badly this afternoon. Instead of going to the hospital, he patched himself up and went to the Bull with Frank. Now they are both too drunk to drive and I've have to take him to the hospital." She flops her hands by her sides. "These men are hopeless!" She fumbles through her handbag, "Can you make yourself tea?" she hands the monk a key.
"If you give me the tea things, yes, I can," he says.
"This is the key to the store room out back. Frank used to use it to entertain friends so there are camp beds and stuff in there. You can use the outside toilet and shower - I think it still works. Please make yourselves at home. Sorry, must dash." She heads for the van. "Oh yes, Dad is much more settled now, thanks. Go up and see him!" The van starts with a roar and she is gone. Rex looks up as if to say, "They're a mad lot, but I love 'em!"

* * *

The cold damp air finally gets to our other hero as he begins to stir by the river. Two teenage boys see him and creep up from behind. Giggling, they toss a few berries into the air, trying to have them fall on the stranger's head. Then suddenly, plop!
 "Good shot! I think it went in his ear!" more giggles.

The monk sits bolt upright, confused for a second and then staggers to his feet. He barely pays any attention to the boys before walking briskly off towards the church.
"Wow, what was that!" cried one.
"Weirdo!" said the other
"Yeah, weirdo, should be locked up!"

* * *

Suñño arrived at the barn to find the place unnervingly quiet, and very dark. Alarmed to notice their bags had gone, he felt a slight panic. Then the Ajahn called him from the old man's bedroom. There was a single light in the room, the only light in the place.

"Come and see," came a whisper.
"I am sorry Ajahn, I fell asleep...." Then a resonating silence which seemed to fill the house.... "Is he dead?" whispered an American voice.
"Ten minutes ago"
"Wow, beautiful... So peaceful... So white... like a doll." The young monk comes really close to the body, covered only from the waist down. The old man's ribs stand out, the belly is sunken and remarkably still. The eyes and mouth are still just a little open. For a moment his mind seems to play tricks with him and he imagines it breathing but it remains still as if made of wax. "I have never seen a dead body before."
"Study it for a while, you will learn a lot." The older monk pulls up a chair so his friend can sit down. The Ajahn encourages him to reflect on death. His own death and others around him. He speaks gently for a few minutes until the all-consuming silence envelops the space and they just sit. "Seeing the end so clearly really helps us to appreciate the wonder of life. And the peace of letting go," said the Ajahn.

* * *

Two or three hours later, the family returned and the silence was briefly shattered. The Ajahn greeted them and told them what had happened. Then the perpetual air of panic, which seemed quite normal to these folks, devastated the peace which our monks had been enjoying. The men were both pretty drunk. Frank came upstairs and barely poked his head through the door. He was as white as a sheet and very shaky. Then vanished quickly. Nigel came into the room, stared at his  father's body for a few moments and slumped down to sit on the floor, propped against the wall. He stayed there motionless, one hand in bandages, muttering something about mum and funerals. Pat was lifted by the calm she received from the dark robed figures standing by the bed. Her attention moving from the monk looking at the corpse to her own looking at the corpse. Back and forth. A kind of silent transmission took place and she understood. She smiled feeling happy. She could see the struggle was over.

"It doesn't matter to me what I receive, if anything at all.

I do this for them, not for me."

Little Redhead

"Alms Round... wow what a trip!" said Suñño as they walked out of town. The Ajahn could not help but notice the powerful emotions on his companion's face, his eyes welling up with tears, mouth a quiver. "What ever happened there? What changed so quickly? I don't get it!" Suñño added.

There is enough time this morning to walk a mile or so more before finding a place to eat. Something quite miraculous had happened, somehow the Ajahn needed to walk it off for a few minutes, quite quickly and silently. The footpath heading north was a short way out of town, clearly marked with a wooden sign, over a stile and into an apple orchard. It would be the perfect place to take their daily meal. They prepare their seats in silence as usual and place the plastic carrier bags before them with some reverence. These bags are special. Still without speaking, they gazed upon them. The Ajahn looked inside. A well thought out meal with sandwiches, pie, chips, biscuits, apple, orange and a can of milky coffee. The two bags are identical. Some careful thought had gone into preparing these and they must have cost a few pounds. Together they pieced together their impressions of what had happened, and the story emerged.

They were definitely dazed and a little spaced out when they arrived in the High Street. This was a small town. Almost all the shopping and business took place in the one street which turned a sharp corner by the medieval church. At one end of the street was a large school, which had an annexe at the other. Most of the pedestrian traffic on weekday mornings was school children in dark navy blue uniforms, as they moved about from class to class. Between classroom changes, the street was very quiet. There were few shoppers out that morning and mostly people were passing in their cars. It seemed very likely that it was going to be a long wait but the monks had reasonable time for Alms Round that day.

Some teenage kids, who had grouped together, were most amused to see these two weird looking fellows standing on the pavement. Safety in numbers allowed them to show off confidently. They often poked fun at the monks, laughing and joking about them. However, they chose to do this from the opposite side of the road, still nervous about coming too close. The monks noticed several elderly ladies with shopping carts, who would also cross the road and pass by at a safe distance. If anyone came close, they would keep their eyes close to the ground. 'This is a wealthy neighbourhood, people seemed much more up tight and shy', thought Suñño, 'the poorer places seem to be so much more friendly and generous than this'. But they definitely weren't all wealthy. In stark contrast, they noticed a few others, travelling families perhaps, possibly farm workers, moving about with children who were clearly not at the fancy school. They were more shabbily dressed and grubby.

The Ajahn noticed her first, from quite a distance, just as they turned the corner by the church gate. The woman was screaming at a little girl as she dragged her along by the neck of her sweater. She was surrounded by a small gang of scruffy and mischievous youngsters, aged maybe eight to sixteen. They swayed about the street, often jay walking in the road, swaggering along with a well-rehearsed act, which says 'I don't give a damn!'

"No you bloody well don't!" she yells again to another offspring. "If you don't shut up right now, you'll get a slap!" The kids stop for a second as they spot the monks a few yards ahead. Fingers point; whispers, giggles and great mocking laughs ring out. "Oh my God!" some child jeers, "What is THAT!" The gang stand still for another moment then their red face mother cries "Stupid bloody....!" and muttering, she marches straight towards the monks. The gang hang back a little and fall quiet as mum glances back and glares at them. Standing so close to Ajahn, sometimes pressing against his alms bowl, she lets loose a barrel of abuse, spit from her mouth actually speckles his face.

"Well, I am telling you I am not giving you anything! Look at you...what a bloody mess! What do you look like! Stupid!... I am not giving you anything. Who the HELL do you think you are!" She comes very close to striking the monk with her hand but he made no move to defend himself. "What are you up to?" she prods his chest. "Well I don't f..king well want to know!" and then she marches off, the gang in tow. Wide-eyed and open-mouthed, the Ajahn turns to his friend who was literally hiding behind his teacher during the assault.

"Vicious!" said Suñño. "Did she hit you?"
"Close."
"What now?"
"We wait," said the Ajahn, smiling. He adds, "Very interesting. This is a good teaching for us. Don't you think so?"

They wait some more but not for long. A gentleman stops to say 'Hello'. He is friendly and courteous. A small dog held by a lead weaves about the man's legs, getting in a tangle. He talks about his dog; about its breed, its diet, its habits and then struggles to unwind the long cord which binds them.

"He's a good friend," says the monk who is finding it difficult to understand the personal details.
"My wife is dead. We are alone now," adds the gentleman and his four-legged friend takes him up the hill. He walks with a stoop and steps to one side as the angry woman strides back towards the monks with her gang. They pass each other but the old man is forced off the pavement. The red-faced mother is grossly overweight but her hands and wrists are fine and delicate. She could be anywhere between 30 and 50 years old. This time she is coming back down the street and crosses over to make a second confrontation. Without a second's hesitation, she demands,

"What do you want here?... I don't care, 'coz I'm not giving you anything!... ok?" She shakes her fist at the young monk who has again retreated behind his teacher. "You should know better... Go and get a proper job! Do something decent! Wasters... both of you! You are both a bloody disgrace and I am not giving you anything, I TELL YOU!"

"We are not asking for anything." The Ajahn finally gets a word in. She stops for a moment and glowers at him but meets an expressionless but gentle face, eyes slightly lowered.

"Well, f..k off then!" she cries. The gang snigger and they scatter a little before moving further down the street. At the same time the pavement fills with small blue uniforms, white shirts and matching ties.

"Charming," adds Suñño, his face is white.

"Wakes you up though!" replies the elder. "Suddenly I'm not tired anymore. Poor woman, imagine living with a mind like that?"

The mood changes for a while and becomes playfully up-tempo. Some of the passing kids are coming close. They receive the odd dry remark from some boys, which is playfully retuned by the Ajahn who is familiar with such banter.

"Hare Krishna!" cries one.

"Harry who?" came the reply which was greeted by a wry smile. Suñño laughed at this one.

"Looking cool" said a girl.

"It's a way of life!" replies the Ajahn and they laugh. Just then one of the boys slides through the growing crowd and tosses a tiny penny coin which lands on the Ajahn's bowl lid. The others cheer and begin to move away.

"Nice one!" said the monk. "I love the gift but we don't receive money." He offers the penny back.

"What do you mean?" asks another boy.

"We don't accept money, we don't use it. But thanks for the offer, nice thought."

"You don't use money? Wow that's crazy!"

"Neat!" calls another. "Never heard of it."

One boy takes the coin from the monk and throws it at another boy, hitting him on the head. The boy then howls. This foolish playfulness breaks down barriers of uncertainty and leads to more questions as the ever-changing number of the group, which now surround the monks, ebbs and flows past. A girl takes out a pound coin and offers it to the handsome American monk who smiles and shakes his head.

This little melee results in a few sticky sweets, an apple and a bar of chocolate between them. One of the girls offered to get something from the shop during her next break, which was encouraging. A scruffy little redhead with a green dress came up from behind them and put a half empty plastic pack of peppermints into the young monk's bowl. Then she disappeared in a flash. Our wanderers were left alone for a while. They crossed the street and walked a little way but the pavement was narrow there so they chose to return quickly to this same spot, a couple of doors down from the little grocery store which was the best place to stand. One of the schoolboys ran out and gave the Ajahn a large Cornish pasty. "Buddhism is pretty neat eh?" he said and dashed back to class.

"Bless you my friend," called the Ajahn. The boy stopped for a moment, turned around and made a sweet bow, Chinese style, then waves and runs away.

The red-faced mother and gang leader made her way back up the street. Both monks were aware of her coming and kept a low profile. She walked quickly on the other side of the road, jabbing remarks to the gang who were more subdued than before. Just a few paces past them, she began crossing to their side and headed into the store. 'Dangerously close,' thinks Suñño. Her gang are looking out of the window, strangely quiet. The monks decide to move down the hill and check out the area past the church. They begin to move off when Suñño recognises the redhead and the green dress looking out of the store window. 'Was she part of the gang?' Meanwhile the church ladies have set up a stall selling home made cakes, bread, jam and other goodies outside the great porch. The monks stand at a respectful distance whilst the church folks watch from behind their proudly homemade produce. The customers at the stall seem to be identical - church ladies with permed hairdos and poodles who keep their backs to the monks as if hiding from them. Eventually, the vicar comes over and makes polite conversation with the monks. Reaching out nervously by keeping to the weather, funds for the church roof and reassuring the monks that, 'We all believe in the same God really. Don't we?' Then rejoined the ladies saying, "Would you like a cup of tea?"

Just at that moment the red-faced mother appeared with the gang standing well back this time except for the little redhead with a green dress who held onto her mother's belt. A few seconds passed. The church ladies were visibly unsure of the grubby gang and their leader, who stood on one side, and the brown-robed and shaven-headed 'freaks' on the other. Their heads were moving from one group to the other. Stalemate is broken when the mother pulls out two shopping bags she was concealing behind her, shakes off the little girl and makes straight for the young monk who finds himself standing on the wrong side of his teacher. She reaches out with a bag and waves it at the monk who opens his bowl lid in amazement.

"Here!" she said. "Take it." The bag won't fit in the bowl so he reaches out and he takes it in his hand. She turns to the Ajahn and begins to tremble. "Please .... take." As the bag is received, she loses control and weeps. She tries to suck in a couple of sobs but is speechless. With tears now streaming down her face she looks directly into the Ajahn's eyes and cries, "I am so sorry!" Untangling her fingers from the plastic bag, she immediately whirls around, her great pleated skirt swept up, she beats a hasty retreat, making a beeline for the gang who open up their ranks to receive her and then turn to move away. She leaves behind the little redhead in a green dress who stands alone for a moment with the biggest smile in the whole world.

"Thank you," she said to the Ajahn and ran off after her mum.
"Extraordinary," said a church lady. And then there was silence.

* * *

"I don't care if I never get another thing to eat," said Suñño as they prepared to give the blessing. That morning was special. They added some verses of protection to their chanting. The Ajahn's voice continued for a while with the rhythmic Pāli passages, which were familiar to his friend but not yet memorised. Rather than pulling out his chanting book from his bag, he just listened to savour the occasion, keeping his palms pressed together in front of his heart.

"The ignorant mind just sees what it wants to see," said the Ajahn after the food was finished.
"What do you mean?"
"Without the ability to reflect, the mind is completely influenced by its memories; the conditioning it has received from the past. Many of these memories are mixed up or based on false assumptions. When there is no stability in the mind, having nothing to trust or rest in, it is natural that it has to keep hunting for something else to hold on to, something outside of ourselves. Like views, opinions or just the idea of being right, being OK in a world which questions this right-ness and OK-ness all the time."
"She must have had some bad experiences with religious people before?"
"Possibly. There was a lot of fear in her eyes."
"And hatred. She was really scary to me!" Suñño looked at his teacher. "You were impressive. How did you stay so cool?"
"She was good to the kids," the Ajahn continues "Pretty firm but very fair, they trusted her and loved her. She must be struggling to support such a large family. I stayed cool because it was necessary. She wanted a fight for sure. But I wasn't giving her one. This broke up some of her habitual perceptions or beliefs and it rattled her! I really confused her!"
"Did you think she was going to hit you?"
"I wasn't even thinking about it really, I could feel her pain, see her fear. I just kept offering her kindness in my mind, wishing her well in my heart."
"Well what a change?!" Suñño shakes his head with a look of delight.
"The girl must have been behind us, watching and listening to our session with the school kids."

"Yeah, she gave me these." Suñño picks up the little plastic box of mints and hands it to the Ajahn, who receives it with tenderness.

"Then she went off to tell her mum what she had seen... I guess."

"Then what a turnaround!"

"A fine and beautiful woman," added the Ajahn. "She knows a good thing when she sees one, only she gets confused under pressure. She's had a tough life but the angel still shines through when it gets a glimpse of light. I am very grateful to her. She has shown me the real beauty of human nature at its best. The ability to transform."

"I will never forget her face," adds Suñño.

"Wonderful woman."

"And the little girl?"

"Takes after her mum."

The Pink One

One of the great benefits of living a disciplined life is that it keeps everything nice and simple. Setting a deadline of midday for completing the food-finding mission means that once it is done with, the rest of the day is free of concerns about eating. At least that is the idea. The Lord Buddha said that he was content with eating once a day and encouraged his monks to follow with the same practice. This cut off time of 1:00pm (noon in English summer time) was coming as a relief to Suñño as he becomes used to this way of life.

"That's it!" he sighed and packed up the left over bits and pieces into one bag. The bag of uncooked rice he kept separate. There was no way they could use it but he hoped he could find a good place to leave it on the way out of town. These monks do not keep food overnight so it all has to go, be given away or thrown away. But care and respect is given to these remainders. After all, it was rightly blessed and should be treated as such.

"I could use some water," said the Ajahn as they left the park.
"There's a faucet by the gate," he said pointing his finger. "Hey, let me fill that for you?" Suñño took the Ajahn's water bottle and went off to the tap. He took the 'trash' as he called it, with him in search of a 'rubbish bin'. They often joked about the English and American expressions they used. When he returned with the water, it was quickly consumed and then refilled. That day's meal was almost all dry bread, cake and potato 'crisps' or 'chips'.

The Ajahn told a story about a time when he was going on Alms Round in a small city in California. He was staying at a new branch monastery in Mendocino County. One morning he was walking with two or three other monks on a weekly Alms Round in the town close to the monastery. This was still a fairly new adventure for them. The locals were used to seeing a few freaky characters about but the monks sure were strange. The streets in the American town were very different from here. They were wide! The sidewalks were also wide and almost deserted. Hardly anyone walks anywhere in that neighbourhood. They drive from store to store. That morning they came across an ageing hippy, clearly 'high' on something. He bowled up to the monks as they walked towards him, bent over a little, his head craning upwards and an expression on his face which suggested his eyesight wasn't too good. One hand reached forward;

"Hey man, got any change man?"
"Err change... you mean money?" said the English monk.
"Just a few cents, man? Spare us some change, man?"
"Sorry friend. I don't have any money. We don't use it." The Ajahn smiled and the hippy took a step backwards.
"Shit man! What do you mean? You don't use it?" The hippy stared back in

bewilderment.

"No I don't use money," confirms the monk. Then the hippy took a few moments to take stock of the situation. Standing with his feet spread wide apart and swaying as if on the deck of a moving ship he 'checked these guys out, ...real careful.'

"You don't use it, huh?" he said with his head scanning the monk up and down. "Well, what are you, some kind of dumpster diver or something?!" The Ajahn took a few seconds to work out what this guy was talking about. Then he replies;

"Friend... do I look like a dumpster diver!"

"I love it, 'dumpster diver'!" they laughed together. The Ajahn went on to say that the old hippy ended up giving him some food the following week when they returned for another Alms Round. He offered them some very stale pizza.

From the beginnings of their tradition, at the time of the Buddha, the monks would collect small pieces of abandoned cloth and sew them together to make their robes. Going to charnel grounds and collecting discarded cloth which had been used for dressing corpses. Some monks still like to do this as a special ascetic practice, then they dye the cloth with natural dye made from wood bark or leaves. They would also make use of other discarded items for making a bowl, sandals or fastenings for a bag. Perhaps mend a broken flashlight or penknife. Our monks considered this for a while. This meant they could describe themselves as dumpster divers after all! However if they take anything, even if it is regarded as almost worthless but knowing it belongs to another and taking it deliberately without permission with the mind of a thief, that monk is considered to be defeated, no longer in communion. The monk's life is over from that moment onwards and there can be no return. Having acknowledged their fault, they take off their robes and return to lay life. Their possessions are therefore, usually meticulously cared for; all received as gifts from lay supporters or happened upon by chance. Hence, they are difficult to replace if they are lost.

* * *

Suñño was not feeling well. Maybe it was something he ate. It could have been the water from the tap in the park although the Ajahn seemed unaffected.

"When you have lived on alms food for a while, especially in Asia, your digestive system gets used to a fair amount of rough treatment," said the Ajahn. "Sometimes we refer to food poisoning as 'noble stomach', it kind of goes with the life style!"

"It's not too bad," is Suñño's comment as he climbs out from behind the bushes, having relieved himself. "At least I still have some paper!" he holds up a flattened cardboard roll with a few layers of screwed up toilet paper rolled around it. Then it is back to walking again.

The path they have chosen is quite a famous ancient trail, originally dating back to the early Christian pilgrims who came this way. As it is the weekend and the beginning of a school holiday period, there are several families out for a walk. There are young backpackers with huge heavy bags, and elderly couples with dogs. There are some mountain bikers, sweating and grunting up the hills, then flying down again chased by yapping dogs and shouts of joy. Definitely holiday time.

However for the young monk the world has become very small again, all pain and perplexing, a long way from a holiday. First it was his back, then the blisters, followed by the sunburn and now the belly ache. To top it all, the next section of the trail seems to be constantly climbing up hill, which appeared steep and uneven, without shade or even a cool breeze. All his attention is fixed on the small area just a metre or two in front as sweat runs into his eyes and makes them sore. Then his nose begins to burn and he touches rock bottom. His hay fever begins to come on strong! He stops and looks up. His companion is nowhere in sight. The path stretches a long way ahead and there is no sign of another brown robe, anywhere.

No map, lost and completely fed up, he steps a few paces off the path and collapses, sprawled out on the ground like he'd just been shot. Lying on his back, he can see a tiny speck in the sky, way up high. Suddenly he is aware of the skylark, beating its tiny wings with incredible energy and singing its little heart out, absolutely beautifully. In a few seconds, his eyes fill with tears, his nose is ablaze with a blinding itch and fluids flow down his face. Sitting up, his tissue supply is exhausted in five minutes and he chooses to mop his face with a smelly sock - the only thing he can find handy at the time. Fumbling about deep in the middle of his tightly packed bag, he eagerly pulls out a crumpled pack of antihistamine tablets, washes one down with the last few precious drops of water and feels all his energy is exhausted. At the same time, he senses his bodily fluids draining away and sits slumped and dejected for over an hour. Still no sign of his friend.

The skylark barely gives up for a minute. Hovering above, its joyful song rings out and helps to slowly soothe the furrowed brow of our shaven-headed, pink skinned and not so lesser-spotted-monk. Frustration turns to anger. 'How can he just walk off and leave me behind! He knows I am sick. How can he be so heartless! Pushing on and on. Never takes a break. Never, ever looks back to see if I need help. I really trusted him and now he has really blown it. When I see him again I am going to tell him how thoughtless and self-centred he is!' thought Suñño. Getting up again, he is feeling quite dizzy. Pulling himself together he continues upwards. After a few minutes his energy is returning but everything narrows down again at the top of the hill. He meets a 'T' junction and no sign to point the way. 'Now what?'

Back at the footbridge for the third time, the Ajahn pulls out the map from inside his belt. The paper is becoming weak and frayed, damp with sweat, folds are beginning to tear and the corner indicating the spot he seems to be located, is no longer readable. He is a little amused to be finding himself quite distressed. There are a number of possibilities, he considers with one finger on the map.

41

'If Suñño has gone down this one, and has continued walking for the last two hours or so, there would be little hope of catching him now.' He had asked a number of people who were following along the pilgrims' way if they had seen another monk. No reported sightings at all. So he had retraced his steps all the way back, asking almost everyone he met. Nothing. The best option now seemed to be to just stay put. This was about the last place he had seen his friend. Eventually he must make his way back, mustn't he? 'Patience,' he said to himself, 'something will turn up.' Then something did.

"Ajahn, would you like some tea?" Startled to hear a woman's voice the Ajahn looked up as if it came from above. Was this a dream?

"Tea?" he said.

"Or apple juice, or perhaps you would just like some water?" continued a young woman as she approached from behind. She looked a little familiar to the monk who was still quite dazed. "John said he had seen you sitting up here when he was walking the dog. What a wonderful surprise! But he didn't tell me it was you. What are you doing in our part of the country?" She sat down, opened a bag and produced a thermos flask, two cartons of fruit juice and a bottle of water. Two children came running up the river bank screaming and shouting. "You remember Lilly and Richard?" She continued, "They must have grown since you last saw them?"

"Mummy, mummy" cried the little girl, pulling on her sleeve as the young woman continued to remind the Ajahn of the ceremony in London three years before when she attended a short talk given by him.

"Mummy, mummy," the child wouldn't be quietened.

"What is it dear?" says mummy.

"It's the wrong monk mummy!" cries the girl.

"No dear, you would be too young to remember Ajahn."

"No, no! Not the same monk, mummy. We saw a pink one." Then pointing a finger, "Up there!" They all look in the direction her finger was pointing as John, a much older fellow, comes wheezing along the river bank behind them.

"Ajahn! Great, you are here as well. We should have brought refreshments enough for two. Are you on tudong[2]?"

"Yes, good to see you John. It must be what... ten years since you disrobed."

The Ajahn is surprised to see his old friend. John used to live with him in the

[2] *Tudong - Austere practice, usually referring to this kind of walking pilgrimage.*

monastery for a couple of years. He was an excellent novice and well trained in monastic conventions. John came up close to the monk, kneels in front of him and bows three times, slowly and beautifully, placing both palms and his forehead to the ground each time.

"Wow, I am so pleased to see you!" said John "You are looking really well. Is there anything we can do for you?"
"Have you seen my friend?" the Ajahn continues.
"Yes, yes! Over there!" the children call out again in unison this time. "He's up there!" and their attention is once more brought to the hill above them.
"A pink one?" said the Ajahn looking at the little girl with a wry smile.
"He was sleeping in the long grass, up there." Little Lilly looked so endearing in baggy shorts and what must be one of mummy's blouses with rolled up sleeves and a scarf for a belt. Her white top had ragged and muddy tails which dragged on the ground.
"He had a brown skirt on, just like you. And his head is really pink!" she giggled.

The children took some fruit juice, a bottle of water and mummy to go in search of 'the pink one'. Venerable Suñño had realised after waiting at the 'T' junction for a while that he must have wandered off the pilgrims' way. He was quickly retracing his steps and only a few minutes away from his teacher when he met the children bearing refreshments.

"Lilly said you were dead" said the little boy. "I said you were just resting."
"Uncle John sent us home to get mummy," added Lilly, "and to get you some orange juice. Here!" she offers the very spaced-out monk, who can hardly believe his eyes, a carton of warm orange juice, well shaken. The boy gives him the water. The monk downs the juice and most of the water in a few seconds. The children look on attentively, chatting on about how their dog found him. How they were so quiet, and how fast they could run.

"He doesn't speak mummy," said young Richard when their mother caught up with them.
"How do you feel Bhante[3]?" asked mummy.
"Terrible," said the monk.
"We live about twenty minutes walk away. Would you like to rest for a while at our place?" She speaks gently with her palms together, held up in front of her chest. The monk closes his eyes and nods a silent reply.

Back at the bridge, the Ajahn and John were chatting about 'the good old days' and laughing together when the children came screaming back to join them. There followed some playfulness, more jokes about the bright pink monk, which the Ajahn found very entertaining. As soon as they saw Suñño approaching, all conversation ceased and the two men were galvanised into action. John carried Suñño's bag and the Ajahn provided a steady shoulder to hold onto as they

[3] *Bhante is the polite particle used to refer to Buddhist monks in the Theravada tradition. Bhante literally means 'Venerable Sir'.*

followed the little river, crossed another footbridge and along a narrow lane towards John's house.

"I lost you," said the Ajahn as they walked. "I turned around and you had vanished! Are you ok? I've been looking for hours. Thought you had been carried away by a monster or something!" cracking the little joke he put a friendly arm on Suñño's shoulder.
"I was," said Suñño. "A nasty mean and very ugly monster."
"Really?" said the Ajahn, his eyes open wide, his shaved eyebrows raised, "Curious indeed, what kind of monster?"
"One of the worst kind," said Suñño. Now the children draw close as the young monk continues to explain. "I didn't recognise it at first, it kind of crept up on me, really slowly."
"I am scared," cried little Richard as he holds fast to the Ajahn's hand, "Where did it go?"
"It is still here, only now it is much smaller!" Suñño smiles. The children's intervention begins to amuse him as things become clearer in his own mind. The youngsters begin to look around nervously for the monster. Then Suñño begins to laugh. "It's getting smaller all the time!"

Just at that moment, our six weary walkers arrive at John's cottage. There are some chairs, a bench, a small wooden police car and a rocking horse in the garden. John invites them all to sit down;

"Please Bhante, tell us about this monster?" Now everyone wants to hear his story.
"Well, let me see," said Suñño rising to the occasion.

Richard is in his police car, ready to chase off after this monster. Lilly straddles her rocking horse, escape route ready. The Ajahn and the grown-ups take the chairs and Venerable Suñño sits high on the bench cross-legged. He pauses for a while. In the minds of the children, the silence is electric.

"Where did you meet this monster?" asks mummy.
"It was very sneaky," Suñño looks at the children and smiles, his face lighting up. "It started as a little niggle, then it became a grumble, then slowly the problem was overpowered by sheer ANGER!" The kids both straighten up, startled. Suñño laughs and the tension drops instantly.
"Go on," prompts the Ajahn.
"I was getting very hot and bothered. Then I was fed up and wanted to stop but the Ajahn kept on going. This made me more and more cross until I started to blame the Ajahn for all my aches and pains. Then I started to blame him for everything. I really started to HATE him!" Both the children looked shocked and glanced at the Ajahn who seemed to be really enjoying the story too!
"That's not nice!" adds Lilly, rocking feverishly.
"No it is not nice," agrees Suñño. "It is a poisonous monster and the more you play with these monsters, the worse they get. The more I blamed, the more angry

and hateful I became until I was almost blinded by ugly thoughts. So I stopped looking where I was going, followed the wrong path and became lost!"

"Then what?" asks Lilly.

"I started to hate myself for being so stupid. Then the monster's poison started to make me really sick, it took away all my energy. Anger is like that isn't it? So I collapsed in a mess, beaten down by my own foolish thinking!"

"Then what?"

"When I woke up, a little bird started to sing, way up high in the sky. It seemed happy to see me so I felt a little better about myself."

"Sky lark!" cried Lilly as she hops off her horse dancing about flapping her wings.

"So, I soon realised that I was lost and tried to find my way back. I was still a bit angry with myself because I had run out of water and I had lost my friend too.... Then two little angels came along. They gave my monster a real fright."

"They did?" said Lilly.

"They gave it lovely drinks and said nice things to it."

"We did. It was us wasn't it?" said Richard.

"Yes it was. You were so kind and friendly!"

"It's all right," sang Lilly, "We will always be your friend!"

"Yes," said Richard, "no need to be afraid anymore."

"Friendliness frightened the monster away!" Suñño concluded, fanning the air with the backs of his hands, his face bright pink and radiant.

"Sadhu[4] Sadhu" exclaims the Ajahn. Mummy and John join in and they all pronounce SADHU loudly together, expressing their appreciation of Suñño's lesson.

"I don't think the kids quite understood the significance but it was an excellent teaching for me!" said John. "Spot on, just what I needed!"

Suñño turns to his teacher with palms together, "Sorry Ajahn." And he makes a little bow.

" Sorry for what?" said the Ajahn. "It seems like your practice is going well. I am very proud of you!"

"I am very proud of him too!" adds little Lilly with her hands on her hips and her tummy extended. "I think he is very clever."

"He is getting wise," said the Ajahn. "Now he knows the monsters in his mind a little better, maybe they won't find it so easy to deceive him next time."

"We'll see!" said Suñño.

[4] *Sadhu is a Sanskrit and Päli term used as an exclamation for something well done.*

"Yes, in some traditions,
they have the practice of doing
one hundred thousand prostrations.

Our style is much the same,
only we have
one hundred thousand frustrations!"

Just A Wind Up

"This seems like a non-starter to me," said Suñño, "We are too late now. It is gone 11:30 already and there's practically nothing here." The Ajahn didn't move.

"Ok, I won't say another word," muttered the young monk.

They stood waiting in an almost deserted street with just a few shops, in a small town in the middle of nowhere. This was much more of a tourist place with gift shops and restaurants which don't normally do much trade until early in the afternoon. Surrounded by ancient timber framed buildings, cobbled roads and pavements, the monks were not looking quite so out of place as they usually do in an English country town. The pub in the middle of town advertised medieval banquets and there were posters in the town hall entrance advertising a medieval jousting tournament with exciting action drawings of knights on horseback. A small van was parked across the street and a large fellow with stripey trousers, frilly shirt and a headscarf started off-loading a number of theatrical looking articles, piling them against a lamp post. Two large drums, a loudspeaker, a small electronic keyboard on two wooden boxes. He looked over at the monks and called out, "Alright fella's!" Then he climbed into his van and drove off. Passers-by studied the heap of instruments and things as they passed but studiously avoided looking at the monks. They would steal a glance but pretend they were not really looking at all. Meanwhile the streets were becoming more crowded.

Five minutes later the same colourful street performer, now carrying a guitar, returned to set up his gear which he did with remarkable skill and speed. Within a couple more minutes, he was sitting on a box, strumming joyful melodies with one hand, positioning a microphone with another and beating a drum with his foot pedal.

'This is the second pirate on this trip,' thought Suñño, wondering if he was likely to be as helpful as the other one. As the musician completed his set-up, he began telling a few silly jokes and introduced himself as 'the bringer of the balmy ballad'. The Ajahn decided at this point to change their standing place and moved down the street. As they walked away, the ballad rang out with a familiar guitar riff from Bob Marley. "No woman, no cry!" he sang, then called out, "Alright boys?!"

Standing again for a little while, a cyclist stopped and stared at the monks. He reached into his saddlebag and took out a camera, took a picture of them and peddled off up the street. A man of about 60 years old with a bright pink silk shirt, baggy black silk trousers and a large belly came straight towards the monks and began nudging the Ajahn's alms bowl against his tummy.

"Hello boys!" he said "Are you monks?"

"Buddhist monks," said the Ajahn, "We are on a pilgrimage."

"Do you have girlfriends?" said the man bringing his sweaty face right up to Suñño.

"No girlfriends, nope we've given up all that!" said Suñño.

"Oh I see, well I expect you have each other though eh? Know what I mean? You help each other out then!" said the old man winking at the young monk and pouting his lips.

"We are totally celibate!" exclaimed Suñño obviously offended, "It is a monks' privilege."

"You mean no sex at all? None, not even to help yourself?" said the man with a grin.

"Not even!" said Suñño.

"Oh you poor things!" the old man cried, "I couldn't do without it." Rubbing himself against Suñño's bowl, he went on "I love sex, oh yes, sex is best." He turned to the older monk, "What about you?"

"Leave it out," said the Ajahn.

"I mean, what do you do early in the morning when it's so hard? You can't do nothing, can you? You must have sex. We all need sex," the old man looked directly into the Ajahn's face.

"Like scratching a mosquito bite, the more you scratch the more it itches," said the monk.

"You're right there!" said the man with a smirk.

"Then you end up with a painful bloody mess and never feel satisfied! Wind yourself up and throw it down the drain, a lot of fuss over nothing, driving yourself mad and end up feeling like a fool eh?" said the monk looking straight back at the man.

"Oh but I couldn't do without sex," said the old man.

"If you don't scratch, it soon stops itching," sighed the monk as the man walked away, stiff legged and stooping with a rounded back.

"Was he for real?" said Suñño, "I could suddenly understand what it must feel like to be a young woman who is pursued by a sex maniac! Horrendous!"

Just then, two people walking their dogs on leads passed each other right in front of the monks. As they paused to allow their pets to introduce themselves, both of the monks were most amused at the way both animals went straight to sniff at the others rear end.

"Real animal realm stuff!" laughed Suñño then directing his attention to the old man who was still only a few yards down the street.

"I am afraid he's stuck lower than that," said the Ajahn, "A hungry ghost that fellow."

"I reckon," said Suñño.

The town was milling with people, time was running out and nobody showed any more interest in the hungry monks until suddenly a voice came from behind.

"Hello Bhante! Are you from Hartwood?" said a tall gentleman with a distinguished upper class accent.

"Yes we are!" said the Ajahn.

"Oh wonderful. We used to live near there you know, moved here about five years ago, lovely to see you!" said the gentleman. "How is the Abbot there, what was his name?"

The Ajahn talked with him for a number of minutes as he passed on news of various friends they knew. The gentleman started to tell stories of his retreats at the monastery but the Ajahn wasn't looking all that interested. On several occasions, the monk lifted the lid of his alms bowl in a not so subtle way of pointing out that it was empty. The gentleman peered in and continued to ask questions.

"Oh, and I suppose you are here on Alms Round aren't you!" he said at last, pointing at the monk's alms bowl.

"Yes we are indeed!" said the Ajahn, clearly looking relieved.

"Oh well, good luck!" he said, and then turned and walked away.

He didn't return.

The preta or hungry ghost is a realm of existence where beings dwell tormented by insatiable desire. They are often depicted as having very small mouths and narrow necks with enormous bloated, forever empty stomachs. An obsessive greed for things that they may be able to take but cannot swallow. Often so confused and bewildered by addictive passions they are unaware that their senses are deceiving them, so they may feel cold in the sunshine and are burned by moonlight.

"Personally I am not interested
in family life anymore...

I am certainly not against it!

I loved living at home.

It is just that I now find a room
which is almost empty
more peaceful than one
which is almost full."

Sweet Temptation

After a few more days on the road, the monks were really getting into a stride. Suñño had a bronze complexion, blisters are turning into calluses and the bags are definitely feeling lighter. They had been through some fairly arduous nights; once sleeping underneath a broken down truck in an abandoned farmyard with a small stream flowing between them as it poured with rain. They started the night in the barn but they were driven out by biting insects and rats. At about midnight, they moved to the only other reasonably dry spot they could find, although the rusty old truck had enough holes to allow some drips to percolate through. They emerged in the morning, stiff and damp. The rain followed them to the town and drove most of the people off the street. That evening, they completed their full list of major challenges; cold, wet and hungry. Strangely enough, they faced up to it with great determination and a lot of laughter. Suñño loved a little expression his teacher often used. "Oh well, it could be worse... and then it was!"

Having just settled down to rest in a bus shelter on the next wet night, they were joined by a very drunk and unruly tramp who announced he had fallen in love with Suñño and insisted on kissing him. Fortunately he passed out quite soon after but stank the place out and snored loudly. The monks left at dawn, about 3:45am.

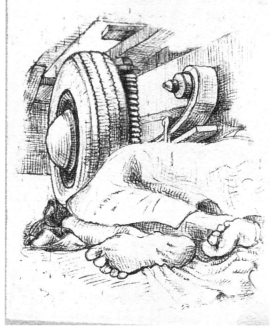

Sometimes the Ajahn would visit a vicarage in the evening especially if the weather was looking rough. He would explain to the vicar or priest that they were alms mendicant Buddhist monks on a walking pilgrimage. Then he would ask the vicar if he knew anyone in the village who might be sympathetic and who would be willing to offer shelter for one night. Often the vicar was intrigued and offered accommodation himself. This generally led to some late night inter-faith discussion, which was occasionally interesting for Suñño but hard work for the Ajahn. In present times, in southern England, many of the churches had little support. The vicarage was often sold off or rented out and one vicar may be responsible for several churches in different villages. The churches were still the natural sanctuary for our pilgrims but were regularly found to be locked and deserted. Still, they provided a peaceful focal point and generally attracted good people.

On another occasion, they were standing Alms Round in the rain when a stranger took pity on them. He provided a generous packed lunch and said that he was in a hurry to get to work otherwise he would like to speak to them more. He went away and then returned a few moments later. Visibly very concerned about the wellbeing of his new robed friends, he explained exactly where the monks could find his house, which was quite close by. Then he handed Suñño a small bunch of keys.

"Just let yourselves in," he said. "It is warm and dry. Make yourselves at home. There is hot water in the bathroom. I am working late so, if you don't want to stay long, just hide the keys under the doormat as you leave. Sorry I can't do more for you... Bye!"

This stranger's house was filled with many expensive and beautiful artefacts. The bookshelves packed with historical and philosophical books, almost all with a clear Christian emphasis. Suñño left an artistic arrangement of biscuits and fruit on his table. Together the monks composed a little note.

Those whose hearts resonate
with the needs of others
dwell in a beautiful world
surrounded by friends.

Bless you for your kindness
May you be free from suffering

One day, the Ajahn had missed his footing on the path and twisted his ankle. Nothing serious, he said. But Suñño noticed he was beginning to limp quite badly. As the evening drew in, the atmosphere between the monks was clearly becoming strained. Twice the young monk offered to carry his teacher's bag. Both times he was shrugged off quite firmly. Three times Suñño suggested stopping or calling in at a church and again he was dismissed or ignored. Several attempts at friendly conversation, even asking his teacher a question on Dhamma, usually guaranteed to get a response, failed. The Ajahn marched on. Slowly. They walked straight through a pretty little village. A boy ran to greet them and invited them to visit his home. The Ajahn would have always responded in a friendly way in similar situations before. This time he walked straight past like the boy didn't even exist. Suñño said a few friendly words to the lad but then had to rush off to catch up with his friend. The lane was an easier surface to walk on than the footpath, smooth black tarmac. Paths had been ignored for a long time. The map had remained in the Ajahn's bag all afternoon. He seemed determined to be going somewhere but said nothing.

The lane started making quite sharp curves as it climbed a hill. Hedgerows either side of the lane made it impossible to see approaching vehicles or, more importantly, it was difficult for motorists to see anyone walking along the road's edge. If two cars came in opposite directions, one car would need to steer two wheels off the road in order to allow the other to pass. Walkers need to be extra careful in places like this, which means they are often crossing the road to allow motorists space and time to manoeuvre. The Ajahn was a past master in this. Being a keen and rather fast motorist himself in his youth, the Ajahn was fully aware of the dangers. He would often correct Suñño as they negotiated the narrow lanes on foot, urging him to cross over. This time however, Ajahn seemed to be taking his life in his hands and crazily strolled up the middle of the road. Head down. A white pick-up truck came up the hill behind them. Suñño stepped to the side only to hear brakes being applied with a loud screech. The Ajahn walked on hogging the road. The truck driver called out but his words were not understood. The engine roared in first gear as it crept up behind the monk. More words came from the cab but neither of the monks could make them out. However the elder monk stepped to one side and the truck crept past on the right. Suñño could see the driver from behind who was trying to get the Ajahn's attention but the cab was too high and the left side window was closed. The vehicle passed slowly then stopped hard up against the left bank. The Ajahn almost walked into the tailgate without looking up, stood for a moment then continued to walk past the great white obstacle which seemed to be in his way. Both of the monks are halted as the driver opens the door and calls out again. Suñño is expecting a lot of verbal abuse but the old man looks friendly.

"Father!" cries the driver as he leans out of his driving seat. "God bless you father!" came a very strong Irish accent. He stepped out of the cab and gripped the elder monk by both shoulders. The monk looks up and both faces begin to smile. The Irishman claps his hands and exclaims, "Praise the Lord, I haven't seen monks in years!"
"We are a pretty unusual sight in these parts then?" said the Ajahn.
"Rare as rocking horse shit!" exclaimed the Irishman. The joke made both the monks laugh out loud.

The usual questions followed, where are you from, where are you going and so on. The monks explained but they kept their answers brief. This was a dangerous place to be standing for a long chat.

"Look I know a good family just a couple of miles away. Good Catholic family. I do work sometimes in their grounds. The old man is a priest, he doesn't live there but he is often there, you know. Nice folks, religious. They'll put you up for sure. Please Father let me take you there!" The Irishman begged them. Before the monks could answer, he was taking the monk's bag off his shoulder and placing it in the back with his chainsaws and tools. "We'll put these in the back then, it is a squeeze in the cab for three but it's not far." Then they were off. "Praise the lord!" again with a strong Irish accent. "Praise the lord!"

The monks' new friend told them that he was taught by monks in Ireland when he was a child. He loved them very much and was obviously delighted to be reminded of those times. Soon they were entering the gateway to a grand country estate. The driveway led to a large country manor house.

"It is very good of you to help us. Are you sure your friends will be happy to see us?" said the Ajahn.
"They are good people, I know they are!" replied the Irishman. "Tell me?" he inquired as they approached the house, "What kind of monks are ya again?"
"Buddhist monks. Theravada Buddhist monks" said the monk.
"Praise the lord. Praise the Lord!" then came an Irish pause... "Buddhist eh? Tell me Father... is that Catholic or Protestant?"

Suñño was losing control of himself trying not to laugh too much. He was uncomfortably squashed between these unlikely characters. Amused at their meeting and shaking as he straggled the gear stick. "Neither," he said, "Buddhism is different, it came from India."
"India eh? Oh praise the Lord!"

The monks waited in the cab for a few moments once the great white pick-up truck had drawn to a halt. A well-dressed gentleman in grey and his wife, wearing a long white dress in an almost Victorian style, approached looking apprehensive. The Irishman bowled over towards them with such a bold stride, his booming voice and huge muscular frame unnerved the couple who stepped back. Looking through the windscreen, the Ajahn observed the gentleman shaking his head. The Irishman continued talking undaunted, pointing at the monks. Children started running from the house as the Ajahn stepped out of the cab and walked slowly towards the couple, Suñño behind.

"We don't want to be any trouble for you," said the Ajahn. "Your friend brought us here."
"Oh no," said the gentleman. "You are welcome but I am afraid there will be no peace for you here." As he spoke more children came running and shouting from the house, two or three more adults are visible in doors or windows. "We are a large family, you will find no peace in this house!"
"We don't have any outbuildings which would be habitable either," adds his wife.

The Ajahn looks over to the garden where there is a small garden shed come summerhouse surrounded by bicycles and kids toys. They all look at the shed and then look back at each other.

"It's full of junk mostly, mowers and stuff but the kids camp out in it sometimes," said the gentleman. "I think there are even two bunk beds in there, under all the toys and stuff."
"Oh no, you can't possibly stay in there, can you? So small and not very clean at all, it would be so uncomfortable!" said his wife. "We must find you a place

better than the old summerhouse. What do you think about the Jenkins' place dear?" she turns to ask her husband.

"The summer house looks fine!" said the Ajahn.

Within a few moments, assuring the gentleman and pacifying the wife's concerns, it was settled. Before the discussion was over, the monks' bags were placed in the driveway and the Irishman was gone.

"Extraordinary fellow," said the gentleman, referring to the Irishman.

"Old friend?" said the Ajahn.

"I don't believe I have ever met him. I think he came to Mass at our church once, maybe my brother knows him."

"He told me he has been working here," said the monk.

"Yes well maybe my brother hired him, I don't know." The gentleman explained they were from a large extended family who jointly managed the estate. 'Or miss-managed it', he added laughing. One of his brothers was a high-ranking Catholic priest in the area who will be visiting in the morning. The family seemed enthusiastic that he should meet the Buddhists.

It took a while to clear enough space in the summerhouse. Inside it smelled strongly of petrol or 'gas oil', as Suñño called it, fertiliser and mouldy mattresses but certainly good enough. The monks were invited for tea in the kitchen, which reminded them of a communal monastery kitchen. The rooms they saw in the house were all very large, untidy and crowded with family oddments. Antiquated bathroom taps and toilet cisterns, engraved glass windows and brass door knobs which rattled. Toys scattered everywhere and lively, but beautifully behaved children, ran noisily across bare floorboards. A jovial tea session was punctuated regularly by new arrivals, family members of all ages, bringing smiles and interest in their shaven headed visitors. The Ajahn was visibly tired as he answered questions and told many old stories, by now all familiar to Suñño who sat there dreaming of breakfast. The monks retired utterly exhausted at 10:00pm. Their bunk beds, designed for younger bodies, swayed and creaked as did the whole building every time they moved.

"Bit like sleeping in a boat," said the Ajahn as they fell asleep.

* * *

The Ajahn woke up first. As he stretched, the bed moved further from the wall and he froze, afraid that the bed would collapse on top of his friend still sleeping beneath. His feet were icy cold and dangled in mid air. Lying perfectly still, he could hear the melodic voice of a woman singing. Gripping tightly to a shelf bracket screwed to the opposite wall, he gently lowered himself to the floor without moving the bed any further. As his weight pressed upon the floorboards, they creaked and sagged, bringing a set of steel shelves to lean a few degrees closer to his face. In the half light of the evening, this pretty looking summer house was very inviting. Now it was definitely time to leave.

Blistered Feet, Blissful Mind

There are fewer responsibilities out on the road for the elder monk but the physical challenge was really getting to him this time. He had been walking this way in Thailand, Sri Lanka and India, experiences which he knows changed his view of life completely. He certainly appreciates everything he had. Even so, he thought about the nice comfortable place he had in the monastery, his wood burning stove, electric lights and private bathroom. He remembers his attendant bringing his breakfast in the morning. And he really missed the superb food which comes to the monastery each day. The lively chatter of joyful Thai, Lao and Sri Lankan families as they come to offer support of all kinds.

As he stepped outside he noticed the woman, still wearing the Victorian dress she wore the evening before. She was hanging out children's clothes on a line to dry, singing gently to herself, about twenty yards away. Another woman beckoned her to the house as the monk emerged to sun himself for a moment behind the shed. The Ajahn rubbed his slightly swollen ankle and looked heavy. Maybe his aging body is getting beyond all this. The weary monk sat gazing over the grounds in front of the house. There was a makeshift fencing keeping a couple of fat little ponies in a small circle under an old oak tree. Their long faces amused the Ajahn. He started to attempt a secret and playful impersonation of them when he was startled by a sudden flash. The white dress jumped in front of him and a voice shattered the silence.

"Something dreadful has happened," she says, eyes wide open. "I am terribly sorry, what shall we do? It really is very bad. I am so sorry... you must come. Oh dear. We must put it right. Please come to the house, both of you."
"What's wrong?" asks the Ajahn.
"It was very wrong. Please come and I'll explain." She rushes back to the house.
Venerable Suñño steps out of the summerhouse and asks, "What was that all about?"
"Trouble," said the Ajahn.

The monks put on their robes properly, tidy their things and make their way to the house. The entire family, maybe twenty five of them are standing around the kitchen with some in the garden outside. There was a tangible air of upset among them all. The monks are led into the kitchen. A splendid meal is laid out on the table. Two chairs, which are facing away from the table and set in the middle of the room, are offered to the robed visitors. The monks sit in them. The family gathers around, most of them standing as there are few chairs. A small boy is ushered into the centre and the woman in white stands beside him.

"So, what do you have to say?" she says, looking firmly at the boy.
"Well?" prompted a man from behind, presumably the boy's father.
"I am sorry," said the boy looking at the floor. "It was wrong," he continued, then fell silent again.
"Explain," comes another older woman's voice from the doorway.
"I did a bad thing." The boy is close to tears now, speaking is difficult for him.

"What have you done?" asks the Ajahn. "Would you like to tell me about it?"

"I took some sweets from your bag," says the boy, twiddling the draw string at the hem of his coat. "I shouldn't have."

"Not mine," says the Ajahn.

"Must have been mine," says Suñño. He had kept some candies aside from the Alms Round the day before. These monks are allowed to keep sugar in the afternoons and can use it as a tonic. It is not considered as food.

"Sorry," adds the boy again, directing his attention to the younger monk.

"What shall we do with him?" adds the woman in white, presumably his mother. "He saw the bag of sweets in your bag and he stole them. I am so ashamed of him."

"Well I wouldn't be too ashamed," says the Ajahn and he offers his hand to the boy who flounders for a moment then steps forward. The monk gently holds the boy's hand. "Tell me young man, how did you feel after you had taken the sweets?"

"I ate them quickly, then I felt very bad," says the boy.

"Sick?" asks the monk.

"Sick in my heart. I was all shaky. I knew it was wrong and it was too late."

"Then what did you do?" asks the monk, squeezing his hand lightly.

"I couldn't sleep all night. I kept on thinking about it. Then I told Auntie Amy what I had done, in the morning."

"How did that feel? Telling your Auntie," asks the monk.

"It felt much better for a while but I knew she would tell mummy. And mummy will be cross." The boy swings round and sits on the monk's knee, his head lowered.

"Well young man I am very impressed!" said the Ajahn. "It takes enormous strength to do what you have done. I am very pleased to see you have such a good family who have shown you the way to live beautifully and honourably." The little boy looks straight into the monk's face.

"It was wrong," states the boy.

"Sure it was wrong but you needn't have said anything. You could have kept it quiet. In fact you did keep it to yourself for a while but keeping it secret was too painful wasn't it?" The boy nodded.

"You understand, if you do something wrong you'll go to hell," says a child's voice sharply.

"Exactly!" adds the Ajahn. "Now you know what hell is like. Don't you. You could not sleep all night, is that right?" The boy nods. "You were feeling really bad all night?" The boy nods again. "See, now you know what hell is like, you don't have to die first to know about hell. Now you see it for yourself?" The boy shakes then nods his head.

"It was hell alright," the boy looks grimly at the monks. Suñño smiles.

"The way to real peace and happiness is best supported by feeling good about yourself, eh? If you feel bad about yourself, the whole world feels bad doesn't it?" says the old monk as he puts an arm around the boy.

"Yes it does," says the boy.

"So you could see in your heart that you have made a mess and this morning you decided to try and clear it up. Is that right?" Ajahn smiles.

"That's right," smiles the boy.

"I say that is a very good and wise thing to do. It took strength and courage didn't it?" says the kindly elder monk who raises the boy's arm.

"Yes it did," agrees the boy who immediately stands up, still facing the monk.

"So if we see that we have done wrong and we want to put it right, we can begin to feel better about ourselves again, can't we?" the Ajahn gives a little chuckle which resonates through a silent room filled with anxious onlookers who just begin to relax. They can feel the pressure dropping.

"What shall we do with him?" asks the mother quietly.

"It seems to me that one night in hell is enough, don't you?" replies the Ajahn and laughs loudly! The family begin to make approving noises and a joyous mood pervades the kitchen. Except for the boy's father who is still a little perplexed.

"Well there will be no pocket money for you this week," says a nervous father.

"I would like to make a suggestion," interrupts the younger monk.

"Yes, they was his sweets," adds a childish voice.

"Would you do something for me?" says Suñño directing his attention to the boy's father. "Would you please give the boy his pocket money?" Then, turning to the boy, Suñño says, "And then I want you to spend all your money on candies. Then I want you to promise me that you will give away all the sweets, not keeping any for yourself."

"Excellent idea," comes a loud voice from the back. Everyone is happy again.

"Generosity is the best way of putting it right," adds the Ajahn. Then looking at the boy, "You reckon?"

"I reckon it is." The boy beams and throws his arms around the monk who whispers in his ear. Then the boy goes to hug his parents.

"These Buddhists would make excellent Catholics!" comes the loud voice again.

"Let us share breakfast together and welcome our guests properly!"

They gather around the table and the priest says, "Please, I would like to offer a prayer?" looking at the monks.

"Please do," says the monk.

They enjoyed their meal together. The priest had to go back to attend to his duties. The children went off to school and the grown-ups went to work. Once the monks were well fed, bathed and replenished they walked back down the driveway. A single solitary figure, wearing a white dress, standing in front of the house, waved energetically as the young monk glanced back.

"I never knew there were so many good people in the world... until now," sighed Suñño.

He noticed the Ajahn was still limping. They walked on for a while, in silence. Then taking a few brisk steps in front, Suñño made a little bow and once again offered to carry his friend's bag. The Ajahn stopped, looked up and smiled, lifted his load off his shoulder and slid it onto his friend's extended arm. He said, "It's really painful you know."

"The ankle?" enquires Suñño.

"No... pride," said the Ajahn.

Head Shaving

Some days pass like a dream. This one was looking perfect. A good cooked breakfast in the morning with very pleasant company, a light packed lunch for the road and a fairly easy walk over the hills and valleys in warm but not too sunny weather. The monks passed a Neolithic chambered tomb said to be of a great warrior who had died many years ago. Great stones balanced on top of each other, surrounded by an iron fence. It stood on a hillside in the battlefield where the hero was slain. Now it is a peaceful place with a commanding view of the town below. The monks spent a long time there in quiet contemplation, undisturbed although internally something was amiss. Suñño was unnerved at the uneasy silence which he felt had overcome his elder companion. The Ajahn was usually much more open and chatty. When their eyes met, it would normally lead into a few words of light conversation or at least a smile or a wink from his friend. But for the last couple of days, his glances had bounced off a face that looked elsewhere or gazed straight through him. Questions were given one or two word answers and sometimes were even ignored.

In the early evening they came across a few deserted farm buildings by the footpath. An open gate welcomed Suñño in to check out the place for the night's abiding. He had been walking ahead of the Ajahn for a while and he took this opportunity to scout out the way. He was amused to think that there was no way he would entertain walking into such a place in his own country. It was very likely he would get shot at! The friendliness and ancient beauty of southern England was dispelling so many fears and doubts. He was imagining himself as quite an adventurer by now, very much at ease.

An ancient red and rusty tractor came chugging into the farmyard as the young monk came out of the barn. The old farmer gave an angry shake of his head when he caught sight of the peculiar strangers. But Suñño confidently strode over to him, introduced himself and explained what he was doing there. In a few moments, the farmer was smiling and all was well. The tractor roared back into life and then rattled back out of the gate as the Ajahn came by. The farmer stopped and looked at the second monk and said,

"Do you smoke?"
"No," said the monk.
"That's all right then," said the farmer and then he drove off.
"It's perfect!" said Suñño. "Cosy and dry, a straw bed and even drinking water." He ushered the Ajahn into the barn. "He was just worried that we might burn the place down but now he trusts us."
"Good," replied the Ajahn as he went in and took a seat on a straw bale. He looked about and nodded. "Do you know what day it is?" he asked. Suñño shook his head;

"Now you have me... Wednesday?" replied Suñño

"Head-shaving day."

"Really? Already?" Suñño sighs. "Two weeks have gone so fast. Well we don't have a nice bathroom but we do have this hosepipe! Please Ajahn, let me shave your head before it gets too dark?"

The fortnightly practice of head-shaving comes before the observance days, which occur according to the lunar calendar. This was to be a full moon night. Which means that the monastic community will be spending the following night meditating and listening to talks on the Buddha's teaching. They also recite their training rules and take the opportunity to review any difficulties they may be having with their practice. A chance to open up, reveal and then make anew.

Suñño watched astonished as the Ajahn stripped down to a bathing cloth, which was wrapped around his waist, and hosed himself down after his head was shaved. The water was very cold and the elder monk chuckled to himself as he grappled with the intense physical feeling. He pulled a small bottle of liquid soap from his bag, rubbed it over himself and then opened the water pressure full power and blasted his body clean. Making all sorts of little squeaks and grunts as he went.

"Cor, that was horrible!" cried the Ajahn as he jumped up and down shaking off some of the water. Taking a fresh under-robe, he towelled himself dry. 'For the first time in what felt like ages, the Ajahn had smiled,' thought Suñño. Then the younger monk decided to take up the challenge and followed suit. He took the hosepipe in one hand and the tap in the other. Standing in a puddle of rather muddy water, he hesitated for a while.

"I don't recommend it!" cried the Ajahn as Suñño opened up. Water sprayed everywhere and laughter pealed out of the farmyard as dusk arrived.

The monks sat cross-legged in meditation on straw bales, wrapped in their robes for two or three hours after the bathing entertainment was over. It was shortly after midnight when the moon was really bright that they started talking again.

"Is everything ok, Ajahn?"

"Sure."

"It is just that you have not been your usual friendly and chatty self lately. I am sorry if I have done anything to offend you but I am a bit concerned." There followed a long and awkward silence as Suñño hoped for a reply.

The Ajahn stood up and walked over to the barn door. He stood silhouetted in the silver moonlight that streamed in. Stretching his arms, shoulders and lower back, he gazed outside. Suñño climbed down off his seat, stumbled a little in the dark before slowly approaching his friend who had stepped into the farmyard. They stood looking at each other for a moment. The elder turned away and went towards the gate.

"Ajahn?" pleaded Suñño.

The Ajahn signalled to his friend to follow and they walked a few yards to the edge of a field. Many years of ploughing had carved a bank at the base of an old and crumbling stonewall. The bank provided a comfortable looking seat with a view across an expanse of tall wheat which shone in the moonlight. Some hidden brambles meant that it took a few moments for the two monks to find a good spot without being pricked by sharp thorns. They sat together for a little while more in silence, wrapped in all their robes with woolly hats on their heads.

"You haven't upset me at all. You have been good company," said the Ajahn. "It is just that I have had a few things on my mind. Nothing to do with you."
"Do you want to talk about it?" asked his friend. "Are you feeling tired; maybe we should start making our way back to the monastery? I don't mind cutting our expedition short if you need to go back." The Ajahn sighed and stared at the moon saying nothing. "Maybe you don't want to go back so soon. We could just keep on going. I am into it. They would never find us!" Suñño joked and the Ajahn smiled.
"That's about it," said the Ajahn. "I have to be back by the 25th or there would be trouble! The next day it is ordination's time then the following day our driver will take me off to the airport and I have to go to teach a 10 day retreat in America. Then I am back for two days then off to an elder's meeting in the North. Then and I'm back in time for the beginning of the monastic retreat, which is generally quite a lot of work for me."
"The Ajahn's lot is a heavy one eh?"
"Sometimes."
"I really appreciate you taking the time to bring me on this tudong. I am learning so much! It has been truly wonderful. Thank you."
"I am happy to have you along too. My last tudong was two years ago with Tan Pañña. It turned out to be something of a battle."
"I heard you went with him. Why Tan Pañña? He would try the patience of a saint. I heard he disrobed in Thailand after getting into a fight with another monk?"
"Tan Pañña had a soft side which I really liked. He was very kind and strong but he couldn't let go into the mendicant life. He would always be complaining and making demands. Everything had to be on his terms. A very unhappy monk!"
"We seem to be getting on OK though?" enquired Suñño.
"Absolutely fine!" smiled the Ajahn. "We haven't had so much time together before and it has been good getting to know you better. You see, I don't really get that much time to spend with anyone in particular. The community is always changing and I am often drawn away to support the wider community in other monasteries and to teach elsewhere. I am often subject to almost constant contact and interruptions from strangers for weeks or months on end. Not like my earlier days in the robe when I used to have a lot of time on my own, or with close friends, sitting quietly while the Ajahn spoke!"
"I see. I hadn't really understood before."
"I love the opportunity to go on tudong too. But I really have to etch it out in my calendar! Our friends are very persuasive and needy. It is difficult for me to turn them down but I really do have my limits. There comes a time when I have to say

no to their invitations and look after myself, which I don't find easy. Once I am away from it all, the mind naturally becomes more introspective and peaceful. I am sorry if I have seemed a bit distant for the past few days but it's true, I have been a little distant! Nothing personal." He laughed.

"Oh, now I am sorry if I have been bothering you with all my questions!" said Suñño.

"No bother at all." The Ajahn gazes kindly at his friend. "What does sometimes bother me though, is that it often seems necessary for me to develop a kind of blinkered protection in monastic life. There seems to be a need to cut people off otherwise I feel I become swamped. Many of our friends and followers seem to require more of me than I can realistically give them. They seem to want me to be a father or take some kind of parental role; to be completely up to date with all their problems and situations, which I don't feel able to do."

"Too many people."

"Yes… If I give a lot of special attention to one person because they really need it, they then feel upset and abandoned when I choose to turn my attention to someone else. I love to help people whenever I can but I am increasingly aware of my limits."

"And you feel hurt when they criticise you?"

"I do!" The Ajahn begins to laugh again. "Still caught up in praise and blame. Let's face it. People used to criticise the Buddha. So what chance do we stand."

"It sounds like you needed a break Ajahn."

"There is nothing like a good back breaking tudong for calming the mind, don't you think?" said the Ajahn in a joyful, teasing tone.

"Unrelenting pain and suffering punctuated by miracles and angels!" laughed Suñño. A tawny owl cries out and the two monks fall silent instantly. After a short pause, Suñño asks, "Please talk some more about the 'worldly winds' of praise and blame. We shouldn't get caught up in them, but how?"

"Well, it is helpful to consider this word 'should' or 'shouldn't'. This infers a judgement which is divisive and therefore leads to problems. The Buddha points to Dhamma, the natural law, the way it is. Not to how it should be. Praise and blame are worldly conditions. They are impermanent, unsatisfactory and not self. The message is clear. If we are to attach to these things, it will invariably lead to suffering. There is nothing intrinsically wrong with them. In the same way, there is nothing really wrong with being young or old. They just are the way they are. The problem arises when we attach to them. It is as if I put my finger into a flame; it burns and it is painful. There is no right or wrong. The fire burns because it does. If I don't put my finger into the flame, it doesn't trouble me. The same happens with praise and blame. If we don't get caught in it, we won't get hurt. There is no lasting satisfaction or refuge there."

"All my life I have been taught to give a great deal of importance to praise and blame," adds Suñño. "No wonder I have been so miserable!"

"We are taught to be critical and judgemental, right from schooldays. We also direct this inwards and this turns our lives into a hell realm. It is a hard habit to change but the more we meditate and examine what goes on in our hearts and minds, we begin to see that so much of what we hold onto actually hurts us. Then letting go of it becomes natural because we have wised up!"

"So it is more about letting go than getting rid of?" said Suñño.

"Exactly!" The Ajahn laughed. "The habit is that we hold on. Just like I have been holding onto a load of old baggage the past few days. Thanks to your questions, light has been shone into another little dark hole in the mind and I can put the baggage down again!"

"Thanks to me?"

"Knowing the answer is one thing. Practice is another! Thank you venerable brother, you have helped me a lot," said the Ajahn as he reached forward and held his friend's shoulder.

"It seems to me that you have talked your own way out of a hole!" said Suñño.

"I get by with a little help from my friends," sang the Ajahn as he stood up and made his way back to the barn.

*"A pure life
having no regrets,
like travelling with no luggage,
very light!"*

"So what is this for?"

"Please," said the Ajahn in a quiet and calm tone, "please let the dog go."

"We train ourselves to be content with whatever we are offered."

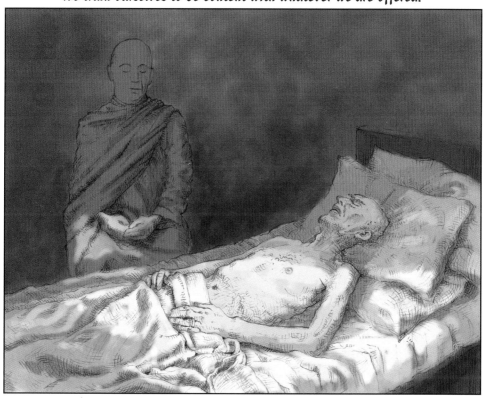

"Seeing the end so clearly really helps us to appreciate the wonder of life."

*"She was good to the kids.... Pretty firm but fair....
She wanted a fight for sure."*

Venerable Suñño had realised after waiting at the 'T' junction for a while that he must have wandered off the Pilgrims' Way.

Real Power

Venerable Suñño was amusing himself as they walked in silence. The Ajahn had referred to him as the 'vulnerable Suñño' as they took leave of their friend that morning. In choosing the monk's discipline, they deliberately put themselves in a vulnerable position. The young monk reflected that his chosen lifestyle often leaves him with a profound sense of vulnerability, his heart and mind suddenly dropping into a scary dark hole in a split second when, just before, everything was feeling wonderful, sweet and friendly. Events the previous afternoon had shaken him very deeply. Taken him pretty close to the edge of his personal safety zone. It seems that when the mind becomes calm, it also becomes quite sensitive. A steady confidence grows which occasionally leaves us open to influences which were previously obscured by confusion. Much of our behaviour is steered by memories or earlier conditionings which have become subtly hidden. Our past affecting our present. It may perhaps feel as if we are haunted by something. Our reactions seem out of proportion to the situation and we feel out of control. There were moments yesterday afternoon when Venerable Suñño was feeling out of control. But those were only feelings. He was able to put the teaching into practice. In reality he now sees he stayed in good control, being the observer. Aware of the panic but not completely blown away. But it was a rough ride.

The monks had spent the night with an old friend of the Ajahn, someone he used to work with. Suñño spent the evening on his own, pondering on his process that afternoon. Late that night he shared the whole story with the Ajahn. Talking about it had been a great help. This morning he is as light as a feather. Once again he is happy to have so many preconceptions blown out of the water. From an outsider's point of view, nothing really happened that afternoon but for a certain young monk, it was one hell of a workout.

* * *

Venerable Suñño had fallen a little behind the Ajahn as the path they followed met the edge of a lake. There were swans and ducks; some beautiful flowers; vivid greens and bright colours. The path was soft and earthy. It weaved through long grass and weeping willows. Many trees were covered in climbing ivy and unfamiliar creepers. It was shady yet very bright. Sparkling light reflected off ripples on the lake with just the sounds of the water gently lapping against a stony bank and lively quacks from distant ducks. Dawdling along and gently reminiscing, he became lost in memories of his youth. He saw beaches by the Pacific ocean, vast landscape memories. Sand dollars, lonely seals and great whales were breaking the cold water's surface. He recalled running on firm wet sand with a surfboard under one arm, surrounded by college friends, shouting and fooling about, really trying to be someone special, needing to be someone special for someone. Then Debbie appeared in his mind again.

Suddenly a chill ran through his body, then an empty feeling in the pit of his stomach. 'Oh hell. Will I ever forget about Debbie?' he thought aloud.

Standing still and staring at the water he became lost in memories. Her short spiky hair, skinny legs and fancy Russian cigarettes. Their first date at the Red Spider Cafe. Gazing at a multi-coloured ocean sunset, snuggling under a blanket on a cool January evening. Her gentle Irish accent and her crazy laugh! Venerable Suñño's guts began to twist as the images changed. The voices bringing doubts, snide comments and ridicule all returned too. The huge frame of Brock Steinmann running into the surf with Debbie struggling helpless

under his arm. Their endless laughter together, the way they would always embrace each other in front of him. Then the night they smashed his heart; mocking then urinating over him as he laid, blind drunk in the bathroom, stinking in his own vomit. 'I could not move,' whispered Suñño to the ducks. 'If I could I would have killed him... for sure'.

He turned back to the path, his attention drifting about. Then, as he turned a corner he became more aware of a different sound. Music, distant and distorted. Then shouts and cries from people, not children's voices, certainly not restrained, excited and wild. His heart was pounding as he came closer. The bright colours and vibrant

designs of beer cans, bottles of spirits, cigarette packs and food wrappers grab his attention in the long grass. A few steps further, he sees the grass is trampled flat. Blankets, half eaten food, bottles and various items of clothing are spread about. A wild menacing voice screamed a frenzied song and mechanical jangle music rattled out from a small black plastic box which hung from a tree. The image was instantly replaced by a picture of a crazy little Mexican kid who hanged himself in grade 7, his body swinging from a tree by the creek. Suñño's mind was beginning to lose it. Voices were heard. They were English voices; loud, rough and very close but not yet distinguishable for an American ear. They were still not visible either. A thick bush separated them as they splashed in the shallows. The monk's disjointed mind began to hear the violent voices from his college mob days. A creeping terror was beginning to overwhelm him.

Suddenly, two men appeared wrestling each other out into the water, swearing and cussing. Big white bodies, tattooed and almost naked. For a moment they were unaware of the monk who was standing quite frozen, a few metres away. Suñño decided in a flash it was time to move on and quickly. As he passed the bush, more white skinned bodies appear in the corner of his eye. There are women there too and he noticed they seem to be naked or topless at least. A woman screamed and real madness seemed to spiral out into the air. More shouting and cries of;

"Look at him!"
"Pervert!"
"Get him!"
"No, leave him alone!" came a woman's voice.
The young monk quickened his pace, walking really fast, head down, running for the shadows. The soft earthy path surface and its windy route was all the monk had his eyes fixed upon. Part of his mind was still wearing jeans, running for his life. Brock's voice still bellowing, "You are gonna die you little snitch!"

In his panic he dropped his robe, which he had slung over one shoulder. He stopped for a second to pick it up, glancing back. No one in sight and it was quiet. He paused for a moment to catch his breath but not for long. More shouts rang out clear, as they bore down the track towards him;

"Skin heads!"

Turning quickly he moved his attention to the path ahead. Looking briefly upwards, he could see the familiar brown robed figure of a monk by the water's edge some distance away. The path was leading him straight to his friend who was standing there motionless. Travelling the next few metres was something like an acid trip for Suñño. It all seemed to happen very slowly, although in reality the distance moved and the period of their meeting could only have taken a few seconds. The young monk's mind was still very fragmented. The robe ahead now adorned a wonderful old monk he met in San Francisco a few years ago. His preceptor and teacher Ajahn Suvïro was saying, in his very distinctive deep voice;

"Simply knowing it, as it is right now. Don't get caught up in the story, Suñño. Just be present with what you know... right now."

He approached the Ajahn who had turned back, walking quite slowly to meet him. At the same time, two large and puffed out hooligans loomed up towards them. They had both pulled on pairs of baggy shorts, one had palm tree designs printed on, the other football shorts. Both hooligans were bare foot. These four men stood in a clearing at a point where the path widened and where it touched the water's stony edge. They stood equally spaced apart for a few seconds, which felt like minutes. Suñño studied the lads, taking rapid mental snapshots as their glances ricochet about, still unsure of eye contact. The lads kept moving about, swaying a little, facial expressions flickering, always changing. Both men were well tattooed. One had an impressive looking dragon on his right arm and shoulder. The other wore a naked woman on his shoulder. Both had numerous small designs, names and scars covering their bodies. One had the word 'left' tattooed on his right foot and 'right' on his left and 'LOST?' written upside down across his large sagging belly. Both had very short, cropped hair on top and shaved sides. Suñño's mad mind tried to see them lash out with knives, kicks and punches but the picture wouldn't fit. The more he stayed with what he saw, the less the mind drifted off. They all turned to look at the Ajahn who was perfectly still, smiling gently, who then said;

"Good afternoon gentleman."

The lads just sniggered. They swayed about more heartily, reaching out to take each other's shoulder. Their eyes moving deftly around, trying to stare out the monks but retreating again with uneasy smiles. Their feet shuffling. One stood on the others foot and pushed his mate playfully who returned a friendly head-butt.

"Ow!... Dickhead," said Lost Belly. They grinned at each other, then at the monks.
"Are you real?" slurred Dragon Shoulder.
"Are you?" said the monk. Another pause. The warriors wobble some more.
"Are you Buddhist monks?" asks Dragon Shoulder.
"Yes," replied the monk.

Then Lost Belly crouched down, bracing himself in a kind of Kung Fu martial arts pose, one hand in front, fingers beckoning Suñño for a fight, the other hand held over his head.

"Orr..!" cries Lost Belly and immediately received a heavy punch on the head from Dragon Shoulder, which floored his mate with another "Ow!"
"Don't mind him, he's pissed!" said Dragon Shoulder.

Then another likely lad came running towards them, much younger than the first two.

"Yeh, Buddhist monks!" calls Dragon Shoulder. He lifted his mate onto his feet and they swayed about for a moment.

Then with a wide eyed smile, Dragon Shoulder vigorously extended a clenched fist towards Suñño's face, then popped up a thumb and said,

"Well good on ya!" and they all turned around and ran off.

Suñño stood transfixed, watching them move out of sight. He was trembling, pale and sweating. His breathing was rapid and he started to walk on the spot.

"Are you ok?" asked the Ajahn.
"Don't know," replied Suñño.
"You don't look too good. Did they frighten you?"
"Like hell!" he said pacing up and down.
"Let's walk it off for a while. You look like you are about to run off anyhow. Are you feeling like it?" asks the Ajahn.

Suñño just nodded and without a word they strode off down the path. After an hour, they came to a church with a picnic table and two benches in the yard. They instinctively sat at the bench and took out their water bottles.

"You've been through quite a turn, eh?" asked the Ajahn.

No reply. His young friend sat fiddling with the cap of his water bottle. Still without a word the two monks sat together for a while, cross-legged, facing each other across the table. Eyes closed, meditating or contemplating the situation, just aware of the sounds of birdsong. This was a peaceful spot, way off the main road. A child sped past down the lane on a bicycle and rang the little bell on her handlebars when she saw the monks sitting there. They both opened their eyes and looked at each other.

"Are you real?" said Suñño with a smile.
"How about those guys?" said the Ajahn.
"They were real enough!"
"Did they freak you out a bit?"
"Some of my past history is pretty messy," Suñño sighed. "Some of it was very violent. Some kids at school behaved like animals. They were great kids really, just confused. Two of them, one a girl who I loved, ended up dead. In true American Hollywood tradition!"
"I am sorry. Do you want to talk about it?"
"Not now. I'll tell you later."

They walked on for another hour, a steep hill climb. The Ajahn was reading the map as if he had a clear plan ahead which was unusual because for the past two days they seemed to be wandering fairly aimlessly. The young monk was happily lost at this point, pretty much carefree.

"You know what?" said Suñño.
"What?"
"I just stood there and watched two guys change from being hardened thugs into a couple of stupid looking school kids. Right before my eyes!"
"You did, eh?" Ajahn was grinning. "And what do you think they are now?"
"Don't know," said Suñño with a frown.
"Memories?" came a gentle reply.

For a moment Suñño's mind stopped, cleared and bright once more.

"Yeah, memories."

* * *

Most of us go through life doing our best to avoid things which are unpleasant and put most of our attention into seeking pleasure. It seems natural enough and the world which surrounds us continually confirms this. It is the promise of every marketplace. After all, it keeps the cash tills ringing, the families growing and the urge for becoming someone, going somewhere flows on through a myriad of outlets. Invariably we come across problems in our search for happiness. We experience disappointments. Sometimes shocks or unpleasant experiences which leave us with a clear signal 'Don't go there again!' So we develop personal 'no-go' areas. For example, if we had been bitten by a dog when we were young, it would be natural that we would choose to stay away from dogs, especially if we had been bitten by the first dog we had come close to. Having had no experience of friendly dogs, we would probably see them all as potentially painful on close encounter and would shy away. Very often, however, our minds do not make such an obvious link. According to the scriptures, the Lord Buddha told many stories and similes to illustrate the way we can become confused and thereby suffer needlessly as a result.

There is a story of someone who was afraid to enter their garden because they had seen a large snake, coiled up in the grass. Having been attacked by a snake before, it seemed only natural to be cautious. Several days went past and the garden remained a no-go zone until the gardener returned to discover he had left a coil of rope in the grass. This was mistaken for a snake and had caused a lot of trouble! But where was the trouble? Was it the gardener's fault? Was the gardener ever the problem? Where is the snake now? Or was it always only in the mind. We often make lightning decisions or judgments like this, on just a suggestion of evidence. Then instantly, the rope becomes a snake!

When we understand that the mind tends to jump to conclusions, we are careful not to jump with it. We practice mindfulness. Being mindful, we develop wisdom. This way, mind becomes a trusted servant and not a nagging dictator. There is real power in a well-trained mind.

Empty

The Ajahn's prediction was becoming painfully true. The small wealthy towns have proven to be the least likely to produce generous offerings. Venerable Suñño was fighting an inward battle. A growing sense of panic and dismay was gnawing through his empty stomach, his aching back sending painful twinges down both legs as he shuffled his burning feet on the pavement. He noticed that his inner struggle with judgemental and critical thoughts were again in danger of poisoning his mind. Growing wary of this poison, he tried to view the same picture from a more compassionate position.

The bakery was doing a good trade providing cakes, rolls, sandwiches and pies for young students who stood in the street stuffing their mouths as they watched the shaven headed freaky visitors from a safe distance. They grinned, nodded and sometimes pointed at the monks but did not approach them.

"So many overweight and sickly looking youngsters," whispered the Ajahn.
"They're not that fat. It's much worse in the States," replied Suñño smiling. "Most kids in the mid-west can't even see their feet or sit on the floor without rolling over. But they all have beautiful shiny white teeth!" His smile was picked up by a spotty teenage boy on the other side of the street whose facial expression momentarily lit up in appreciation. A moment's friendly connection was quickly ambushed by a jeering friend, then it changed into an embarrassed glance before it turned away. "It is a blessing there's no 'Big Macs' or 'KFCs' in this town or they'd turn into hippos too!"

Suñño was a little amused with himself as he noticed that most of his own attention was focused on the food that the schoolboys were scoffing yet the kids themselves seemed radically unaware of what they were doing; standing, lolling about, prodding, sometimes kicking out at each other in playful mock combat. Potato chips, chocolate bars and cakes were shoved in between teeth, in between words, chewed between words and sometimes bits falling out between syllables. They were totally preoccupied with each other. Food was unconsciously consumed as if they were breathing it.

A group of girls came by and joined them. They went foraging in the bakery too and came out in the street to stand and gaze at the monks, munching as they did so. The gaze turned to furtive glances as the teenage school children turned into a huddle, grouped into a tight formation as if plotting something. Then two of them, a boy and a girl, walked over the street making a beeline for the monks.

"Hello," said the girl. "Who are you and what are you doing here?"
"We are Buddhist monks and we are here on our daily Alms Round," replied Suñño.

"What's that?" asked the boy.

"This is the way we live. We are collecting food for our meal of the day," explained Suñño.

"Why don't you get it for yourself?" asked the girl.

"Because we don't have any money. We rely on the offerings of others," added Suñño.

"Weird," said the girl. "Can we take a picture?" A small silver gadget is pulled out of her shoulder bag.

"I am not an exhibit," said Venerable Suñño, a little gruffly.

"You look really cool!" she said as the camera flashed in his face.

"Good luck," said the boy.

"I reckon that I'm gonna need it," mumbled the young monk. "Mostly... patience I guess."

The youngsters regrouped for a few seconds and moved away leaving empty crisp packets and greasy paper bags to blow away down the street. A moment later, a solitary young lad called out to the monks as he passed on the other side.

"What are you meant to be?!" he shouted. The young monk grunted and the Ajahn began to laugh. The boy walked on without another word.

"I like it!" said the elder monk who was clearly amused. "What are you meant to be?" He directed his attention to Suñño.

"Don't you start!" he grumbled, his sense of humour was running very thin.

"What are you meant to be!" the Ajahn repeated. "What a great question!"

"A bloody saint," growled Suñño.

The Ajahn looked a little shocked at his friend's reply and studied him for a few moments. His attention was completely ignored, almost avoided as Suñño turned away.

"And what are you meant to be!" the Ajahn went on, still laughing. "It's the quote of the day... yep, really profound don't you think?"

"Oh do shut up!" barked Suñño. The Ajahn paused and with a gentle and kindly smile, he dropped the subject.

A very dark cloud was hovering over the young monk. Their bowls were empty and time was running out. If they received something now, they would have little time to consume it.

"Are you Buddhist?" asked a tall gentleman pushing a large trolley with bulging black sacks, half full of leaves and litter, a simple metal frame supporting brooms and other street cleaning gear. Huge gloved hands rested motionless on a rail, his overalls were spotless and his face expressionless. He approached quietly and stood slightly to one side. His voice was gentle, his gaze never leaving the pavement but his attention clearly fixed on the monks.

"Yes," said the Ajahn.

"You don't believe in God do you?" asked the gentle street cleaner.

"Well... You see, we try to look at things in terms of what we know, rather than what we believe in," replied the Ajahn. The cleaner remained silent but obviously curious. "Right now you may believe your home is just exactly the way you left it but you don't know, do you? But you do know that standing here and talking to me feels like this, now don't you?"

"I guess so, but... so what?" He shrugged his shoulders. Suñño perks up with a huff.

"Do you know how to find inner contentment? Peace of mind regardless of whether you get what you want or not, or get free from what you don't want or not. If you understand the real cause for all your suffering, then you will know how to be free. You won't need to believe in anything else or in anything anyone else will tell you. You will be knowing it for yourself," Ajahn replied.

"Knowing what?" the cleaner frowned.

"That real pleasure comes from serving others, from giving our attention to that which is wholesome, from kindness, compassion and generosity. Knowing that the street is never really cleaned and yet doing it feels good. We are rewarded in knowing that it helps to make a better place for everyone to live in. Regardless of whether anyone really notices it or is in anyway grateful!"

"It's all in God's work," said the cleaner looking up and nodding.

"Yes, maybe it is. Whatever that means!" smiled the Ajahn as the cleaner moved on.

Without another word, the monks left the street and found their usual refuge in the church cemetery. There was no need to clean things or sort out any mess that day. Their belongings were silently re-packed into their alms bowls and bags and they were quickly ready to move on themselves. The Ajahn pulled out a small plastic box with a few mint candies which rattled inside.

"The last of the little girl's offerings," he said, holding them up to his forehead. He carefully tipped half of them into Suñño's hand.

As they walked off in search of the footpath heading east, Venerable Suñño felt a sudden and unexpected burst of energy. Now more than ready for a good long day's walk, his heart was feeling much lighter again. Alms Round was over until the next morning. Now he could let go. Free from further concerns, he decided to take one peppermint per hour. This would last until teatime. Only there probably won't be any tea but the idea was entertaining enough! They walked on for a few hours in silence. Suñño was beginning to really glow with delight. His friend could see it and rejoiced in his presence. They stopped for a moment on a hilltop and it started to rain.

"Bliss!" whispered Suñño.

Bowing To Conventions

Plucked off the street, it is time to relish luxury. Tables laid with pink and silky cloth, silver cutlery and crystal glasses. Beautifully carved upright dining chairs, ferns, orchids and delicious smells. This is as close as it gets to paradise, Thai style. Suñño knows that he is living the life of a Buddhist monk springing from the Thai forest tradition but he has never been to Thailand. He speaks no Thai and feels very insecure in these situations. He thinks that he would prefer to be outside in the street at this time, feeling more confident out there. He looked out of the window, alienated and nervous. This coastal town was busy enough and the alms round seemed to be an easy prospect. But after half an hour of standing in the crowded street, nobody had even come close. The monks had just walked round a corner looking for another place to stand when they found themselves outside the bright blue and sparkling River Kwai restaurant. Within a few seconds, a charming little Thai woman appears in a tight blue traditional dress and they are invited inside.

The Ajahn can speak a few words of Thai, but he feels he has to be careful not to give the impression he understands the language very well at all. There have been occasions when he has made mistakes with pronouncing a word using the wrong tone or mixing it up in some way and landed himself in a mess. This usually resulted in great guffaws of laughter and giggles from the Thai people, which appears to be their usual response to being very embarrassed or confused. But the delightful thing he has noticed, and dearly loves about these people, is their ability to make light of almost anything. And their legendary generosity.

The monks were offered seats at a table close to the window. Immediately each of them is offered a pot of hot green tea, a bottle of posh mineral water and a coke. They were beautifully placed on a special cloth which the Ajahn had placed on the table, following the Thai tradition. Pleasant conversation continued between the Ajahn and the women who surrounded him. They were all sitting on the floor and gazed up at their prize guests with an air of excited anticipation and puzzlement. Western monks are a rare sight for them. The eldest of them, there were four in all, was very animated and seemed to rattle away in very fast Thai. The Ajahn was finding it difficult to keep up. Laughter and beaming smiles prevailed.

Suddenly, the atmosphere changed and the ladies sprang into action, disappearing into the back of the restaurant with more excited chatter. A moment later, the older woman whose complexion was much darker than the others, returned with a familiar Thai expression.

"Nimon Ka," she said, inviting and beckoning the monks to move into the back of the restaurant, partly obscured from the window by a bar and several well placed tall and luscious plants. Furniture was already re-arranged, tables set to one side and special seats prepared for the monks.

"It seems we are to perform a restaurant blessing," said the Ajahn with a grin. "Yorm Lek is from Ubon. Her mother used to take her to see Ajahn Chah when she was a child. And she's seen Luang Por in Bangkok."

Lek bowed her head sweetly, her palms held together.

"I am so happy you come!" she smiles at Suñño. "You like Thai food?" Suñño nods and smiles back. "We make special for you... you like sticky rice?" More smiles. "Isaan[5] – food special for you." As she turns, Suñño noticed she was struggling to hold back tears, her lip quivering. Then she cries out, "Ooii!" and rushes into the kitchen waving her hands in the air.

Sounds emanating from the kitchen remind the young monk of an avant-garde steel band playing at a music festival in Palo Alto some years ago. The red hot wok band. Shrieks of excited laughter bubbled over the chopping, metal scraping and sloshing noises. Meanwhile these chirpy cooks were taking turns to slip out of the mêlée to call their friends and family from a phone at the bar, mostly Thai talk but some in English.

"Oh please come! You must. Very good. You can talk!"
"It looks like we are going to have more company," said the Ajahn.

Just then a scruffy young Thai lad came rolling in through the side door, looking like he had just climbed out of bed. He immediately prostrates himself in front of the monks then promptly disappeared into the kitchen, receiving clear pointed instructions from whom we assume to be his mother. Half an hour passes and the small space at the back of the River Kwai was filling up. Most of the tables on one side were decked out with beautifully presented dishes piled with food. And they kept on coming! Gradually more children, three more Thai ladies, one Thai gentleman (all bearing gifts) and three very awkward looking English husbands join the party. Meanwhile the Ajahn received them all with joyful appreciation. Two of the young Thai women are keen to get their husbands to talk with the monks but the occasion doesn't permit them. They seem embarrassed by their partner's harassing and prodding. "Talk! Go on, you can talk."

Then a very upper class and elderly English couple arrived. One of the ladies introduced them as Jay and Robern.

"Dey want to hear about Buddha," she said. "Please tell dem Ajahn!"
"Robert and Jane Ellington. Pleased to meet you," said the gentleman who was wearing a grey flannel suit and bright red tie with white spots. He reached out to shake the monk's hand and was startled as their Thai lady friend interjected, grasping Robert's wrist and pulling it aside.
"Not to shake hands with Ajahn!" she said sternly.
"Thai custom," adds the Ajahn, standing up to receive his fellow countryman.

[5] *Isaan - North Eastern part of Thailand*

Their friend ushered the elderly couple to chairs set to one side.
"They are lovely people," said a very tall shaky and curly white-haired Jane in a frail voice. She is embraced by her little, dark-haired Thai friend who guides her bottom to the seat. "Oh, you're so kind."

Roger Hemsley

Everyone else was directed to sit on the floor but one large western fellow seemed agitated and refused to. He pulled up a chair and sat close to the monks. Lek glared at him for a moment, then sweetly invited him down. He still refused.

"My husband does not understand about Buddha, about monks," explains Lek. She turns to her husband and pleads, "Darling!" She is clearly agitated. The couple steal stern glances between each other. For Thai culture, it is considered disrespectful to sit at the same or higher level than a monk, especially during such a ceremony.

"It's ok, please sit where you feel comfortable," said the Ajahn directing his attention to Lek's husband who nods in agreement.
"Well, I do own this place," he explained loudly.

Lek then exchanged a few words in Thai with the Ajahn. Then she turned to talk with her friends. Ajahn explains in English.

"We will leave the special chanting and blessing ceremony until after we have eaten," Ajahn explained and he gave Lek a nod. With detailed Thai instructions from behind, the young Thai lad was ushered forward to light the candles and incense on the little makeshift Buddha shrine set up next to the monks. They all looked to each other for a second then a man's voice from the back said.

"Graap," and the Thais all bow together three times in unison. Western husbands are given some coaching; they are struggling to get down on the floor. Lek's husband looks sternly at the monks, unmoving. A few lines of chanting ring out from high-pitched voices, almost in unison, then they all bow again. The women sitting very low with their feet tucked behind, move very gracefully forward and touch their hands and forehead to the floor in front of them. Their husbands clutching their knees to their chests strain their necks to nod forward, their bodies are nowhere near as flexible as their Asian partner's. They both had pained expressions on their faces. Lek picks up a small tray carefully balancing a bottle of soy sauce and other condiments and decorated with a few flowers. She shuffles forwards on her knees to offer it to the monks.

"For goodness sake, stand up woman!" barks her husband.

Lek completely ignores him but her body language said a lot. With a firm, steady resolve, she carefully placed the tray on the monk's receiving cloth spread on the table, reaching up as she did so. Her husband huffed loudly. The first of the platters of food were passed forward from the tables at the side. Each dish was carefully lifted and carried over heads while their bodies remained seated.
"Too much!" said Lek's husband. "Why so much? They won't eat all that." As the basket of sticky rice reached Lek, her husband reached forward and grabbed it from her. "Stand up. Here let me do it." He stood over the monk and pushed the rice basket into the monk's open hands. Lek pulled at her husband's belt and he swings a hand towards her face. She deftly avoided a slap. Everything stops. The atmosphere freezes.

"It is only right that the restaurant owner should offer the first dish," said the Ajahn, in a masterful attempt to restore peace. Suñño raised shaved eyebrows, nods and smiled at his friend. The Ajahn fixes all his attention on Lek's husband. "I am sorry I don't know your name?"
"Roger... Roger Hemsley," he said.
"Well Roger, I am very happy to have been invited into your place. This is a big surprise for all of us. Now let's give all our friends a chance to join in with the occasion. Please sit down and relax." Ajahn, now standing, offers an open palm and reaches out towards the empty chair. "Thank you, Roger, now please take a seat."
"I don't go for all this grovelling stuff," Roger grumbles as he takes his seat whilst glaring at the monks and avoiding worried, fleeting looks from Lek.

The young lad in the front introduced himself as Gop and took a kneeling position in front of the monks, serving them attentively as the dishes were passed forward. The older Thai gentleman, named Som, took the dishes away from Venerable Suñño and they were taken into the front of the restaurant. The monks were aware of more people arriving through the front door but only glanced up to see them. However, the Ajahn had most of his attention on Roger who was quietly jabbing pointed remarks into the space immediately around him.

"Roger, are you a Kentish man or a man of Kent?" asked the Ajahn.
"A man of Kent!" said Roger with a smile, amused that the monk should be asking such a thing. A Man of Kent comes from the area to the east of the River Medway and a Kentish Man comes from the west of the river.
"Same as me," the Ajahn replies. "Isn't it interesting that we all have such a mixture of cultures and backgrounds and yet we find ourselves meeting here. Did you meet your wife in Thailand?"
"Yes, I was on holiday. My first marriage had broken up. Lek has been with me seven years now," said Roger.
"And Yom Lek must be surprised to see monks, especially 'pra farang' (western monks) on Alms Round right outside your place."
"Never seen before I leave Thailand!" added Lek. "No, since I leave," she

corrected herself.

"I guess you would invite any monk, Thai or English into your place if you could, wouldn't you?" asked the Ajahn.

"Ka," (yes) said Lek.

"What brings one English and one American and this group of Thai people together is a shared love and respect for Buddhism. For wisdom, truth and virtue." He turns his attention back to Roger. "When your wife sees me, she sees a monk wearing a robe which means a lot to her and to her friends here. When she is bowing to me, she is bowing to this robe. I don't take any of this personally. I am sure she would be just as respectful to any monk she meets. What she and her friends see here is something very special. It reminds them of their roots and it gives them an opportunity to reconnect with a cultural tradition which goes back some 2,500 years."

"I see," said Roger.

"It is the privileged life of a Buddhist monk which has enabled me to meet with some great teachers and receive generous support whilst living in Thailand for a few years. I am very lucky to have had this chance. Our Buddhist community here, Thai and Western, has continued in this way with the lay people supporting the Sangha. Then the Sangha do what they can to support the lay community. We look after each other. Now it brings us to this point." The monks had now taken the food they needed, so the Ajahn then spoke a few words in Thai to the gathering. He put his hands together and said, "Now the chanting for the food offering. We'll continue with the restaurant blessing and talk some more after the meal."

After a few minutes of chanting in the Päli language with everyone paying silent and respectful attention, the monks begin to eat and the rest of the group move to the front of the restaurant with excited and babbling party spirit. Plates are handed out and everyone is invited to eat. Roger was upset that some potential customers had appeared to gatecrash their party but the Thai's in their usual hospitable way welcomed them saying it was their good luck to come that morning for lunch. This meal was on the house.

"We were hoping to make a quick getaway after pindapat today," Suñño reminded the Ajahn as they finished eating. "We have a big city to clear before evening, a fair distance to walk."

"Well, we will see," reaching for the coffee. "Now they want me to give a Dhamma talk, chant paritta[6] and sprinkle holy water. See if you can get the bowls sorted out and pack our stuff ready to move on."

The Ajahn turned to receive a growing crowd of interested visitors. He was looking very tired. They had been walking since first light, then they had changed direction twice. This was to be a short cut, an easy looking Alms Round. They planned to spend that night on or near the unpopulated beach on the other side of the city. It was a long way off. Venerable Suñño needed to fight as hard as he could to stay awake as the Ajahn's talk and questions went on. The rich food weighed him down and the room was hot and stuffy. At one point, he was

---

[6] *Paritta - chanting of blessings in Päli Language*

physically spurred into life when the Ajahn prodded him in the ribs after he almost fell asleep and collapsed on his teacher's shoulder. The Thais giggled and the young monk glowed red with embarrassment.

At last the ceremony was coming to an end. Roger seemed to be getting on well with the Ajahn and one of the gatecrashers. Roger said that his loving wife had adopted the entire Thai population from the area. They were always congregating around his restaurant and he was thinking that they were eating all his profits. But he was gladdened to hear that the visitors all felt it was the best and happiest place to eat in town. They would all be bringing their friends to dine there soon. This group of newcomers gathered around the monks as they started to leave; some local ladies had blocked the doorway.

"Can we take a picture of you please?" asked one.
"Why?" said Suñño. The lady looked a little embarrassed.
"What would you like to use the photo for?" prompted the Ajahn in a kindly tone.
"Because I'd like to remember meeting you both and to remind me of the nice things you have told us," replied the lady.
"That's a good reason," smiled the elder monk and sidled up to his friend who looked at the floor.

A couple of flashes later and then they were free. The monks emerged from the darkness like hamsters being pushed out of their nest in the middle of the day, squinting in the bright sun of the afternoon. They spent a few moments getting their bearings and decided to aim for the coastal road. They had only walked a few paces when a large four-wheel drive machine pulled up beside them and Roger jumped out.

"Let me drop you off at the edge of town!" he said. "You don't want to walk through all that traffic. Let me drive you, let's face it, I reckon you've earned it!" The monks climbed in without a word. "I can take you to a nice little campsite at the edge of the cliffs."
"Perfect," said Suñño. They drove on slowly through the traffic. The Ajahn fell asleep almost immediately but Suñño was perking up.
"I was a real plonker back there, wasn't I?" said Roger.
"What do you mean?" asked Suñño.
"I behaved like a real jerk, didn't I," adds Roger shaking his head. "I am sorry... it is just that the really formal Thai thing really gets on my tits sometimes!"
"Not very British!" said Suñño trying to do an English accent. Roger laughed out loud. "Not exactly Californian style either," added the monk.
"How do you feel about it all then? Do you have to go through all that every day?"
"Thankfully no! I found it hard at first although now I am beginning to appreciate it much more. All the ceremonial and formal things brings people together very nicely and it reduces a lot of complicated unknowns. They know it is an artificial form and they seem happy to treat it as such. The odd thing is I have noticed that

Thai people really know how to relax within it. They use a discipline to enable some real relaxation together. Sure we don't like the discipline but we aren't much good at enjoying ourselves either, are we! Only the Thais can really tam sabaai[7]!"

"Very true!" agreed Roger. "I thought it was great what your friend said about giving. Especially the bit about letting go! My wife tries to explain Buddhism but it all seems very complicated. Her English still isn't that good. We will come to your monastery sometime soon I am sure!"

"You'd be very welcome," said Suñño.

They drove into a kind of holiday park. The man at the gate waved them through with a smile. Roger took them straight to the beach. Remarkably, it was almost deserted. There was no sand, mostly rocks and pebbles. A giant cliff rose up in front of them, a great white wall facing the crashing waves and the tide was high so just this little cove gave them access to the water's edge.

"Rest here a moment, I'll be back," said Roger and he drove off. The senior monk lay down on a smooth rock and groaned.

"Oh dear, I've blown it. Eaten too much. This morning I was striding along like a young gazelle, now I feel like a beached whale!" said the Ajahn.

"A young gazelle, eh?" amused Suñño.

"Well ok, more like a middle aged mule with a carrot fantasy!"

"What was wrong with us this morning? Everything was turning into an argument," asks Suñño.

"What do you mean? You started it!" said the Ajahn and roared with laughter.

"Are you sure they didn't put sherry in the trifle!"

"Definitely, yes definitely not...erm... not sure!" The monks continued to pass the time fooling about while watching the occasional cloud pass by. Then Roger walked up to them looking a little bemused at their tomfoolery.

"I have something to show you," he said. The two monks stood up and tidied their robes. "Come, follow me."

They followed a winding trail a little way through some stunted trees and up a short rocky rise. Hidden in a very private spot was a small cabin. On the deck at the front of this brightly coloured yellow and green hut were the monks two bags. Roger held up a key tied to a wooden tag.

"It's yours for the night, if you want it that is!"

"Well it looks... absolutely perfect!" said the monk.

"It is a little hide out I use from time to time. We are lucky it is free! It is all paid for. The showers are just by the yellow post over there. I must go now." He handed them the key, and started to walk off. Then he turned around, knelt down and bowed three times.

"How does it feel?" asked Suñño.

"Great, it has been a pleasure. Thank you," said Roger.

[7] *Tam Sabaai - to relax, make yourself comfortable.*

"As alms mendicants,
we choose to rely on others.

We rely on the fact they respect what we do.

They see the value in what we do, how we live.

They witness for themselves
the beautiful fruits this practice can bring
and they support us.

If they couldn't see the value,
they wouldn't offer us what we need.

Fortunately there are plenty of people who do.

In this way,
we look after each other."

Fiery Beast

There is a remarkable thing about walking in England, which the Ajahn appreciated more than ever, especially as he had not yet seen anything to match it in any other part of the world he had visited. That was the network of footpaths. Before they set off on their journey, they had prepared themselves with a collection of Ordinance Survey maps covering the area they planned to explore. They also took a few large, pre-addressed and stamped envelopes enabling them to mail the maps back to the monastery as they finished with them. The other invaluable item to aid navigation was their compass. The Ajahn had a tiny key ring fob with a compass and thermometer, which he had kept for years. For the first part of the trip, this handy device had gone missing and had led to some conflict one night when they were lost in a dark forest, each monk blaming the other for losing it. Then one day it miraculously appeared hooked onto the back of the Ajahn's tee shirt.

Suñño was learning the art of map reading. He often stopped, re-folded and rotated the map whilst balancing and turning the compass in his hands.

"We must be here!" he said pointing at a spot on the map. "The sign on the stile is pointing east so I guess we cross the field here and cross a dismantled railway line running north to south, which must be that bank over there," said Suñño pointing with his chin. "Yes, the map shows the embankment too and I can see the top of the church. Wow, these maps are amazing!"

Cattle had carved deep scoops in the edge of the marshy field when it was wet. However, there had been a long dry spell and the ground was now baked dry. The Ajahn had stumbled into a hoof-print hole and scraped a toenail hard against the edge. The nail jutted upwards and blood trickled from underneath. He grunted a muffled curse and tried to walk on as if nothing had happened. He limped a few more paces to the stile set in a barbed wire fence. Placing his injured foot up onto the first step, the monks took a moment to assess the damage.

"Messy! And I've no water to wash it with," said the Ajahn.
"I'm fresh out too. Maybe we'll see something in the village - it's not far," said Suñño.

There were well-cut steps, shored up with wooden risers and each filled with gravel. The steps climbed steeply up the embankment. Being careful not to put too much weight on his hot and bothered toe, the Ajahn side-stepped upwards. His attention was so fixed on his foot that his face was only a few inches from a brightly painted sign before he noticed it. In large raised letters it read, 'BEWARE OF TRAINS'. A beautifully preserved notice in cast iron, bolted to an oak post.

"Wow, that's in good nick!" said the Ajahn, "I am surprised nobody has run off with that." When they reached the top of the steps, they both stood for a moment amused by what they saw. Two shiny steel rails on wooden sleepers all spotted with oil. "Doesn't look like a dismantled railway to me. Let me see the map."

Standing on the rails, the monks examined the map. If they were in the right place, this railway line wasn't going anywhere. There were no towns, stations or places it would go to. They must have made a mistake? Staring down the track and squinting into the sun, the Ajahn said he thought he could make out a building on the bank. Well, it looked like a building only it appeared to be getting bigger. Then they heard a whistling sound.

"Hell! I think it's a train!" shouted Suñño but neither of them moved.
"No, really!?" replied the Ajahn.

Suñño grabbed his friend's arm and pulled him out of the way as the whistle pierced the air and a great black engine bore down upon them, steam and smoke belching out in rhythmic white wheezy puffs. As the black and red iron monster swept past, a single oil and soot smudged face with a white collar and oily overalls leaned out, swinging from a gloved hand holding a polished brass handle. This local church vicar stared in open mouthed disbelief at the two robed figures who stared back mirroring his expression in unison. Then the train was gone.

"Pinch me!" said the Ajahn. "Were we nearly killed by a vicar driving a steam train?!"
"Was that a ghost train?!" laughed Suñño, "or did they put acid in our cornflakes this morning?" They hobbled across the line and down the steps on the other side, then rested for a while sitting on the style.
"The archetypical up-county vicar!" amused the Ajahn. "I've several memories in my youth of vicars driving steam engines. The county show would always have a steam traction engine rally manned by men of the cloth!"

The map indicated a local railway museum some five miles north. Further investigation showed the map was nearly ten years old. It seemed the museum had extended and restored the old line.

The village seemed deserted except for a couple of ladies who were arranging floral decorations in the churchyard. Suñño asked them if they would have any water with which they could bathe the Ajahn's injured foot. Without a word, one of the ladies went into the church to fill the monk's plastic water bottle whilst the other lady started polite conversation, beginning, as is the tradition, with the weather. After a few minutes the first lady, wearing a wide brimmed hat with artificial fruit around the brim, returned with the bottle. By this time Venerable Suñño was well into the familiar explanation of their pilgrimage. All the Ajahn could hear of the conversation, as he was some distance away on a bench in the church porch, was a loud voice saying;

"Oh really?" repeated again and again in variable rich upper class tones. This large lady was wearing a bright yellow floral dress and stood very stiffly listening to the monk. "Really?" she went on.

Suñño returned to rinse the mud from the Ajahn's bleeding foot and then used their last plaster to secure a piece of tissue paper and the corner of a plastic bag to protect the wound. The ladies came to see what the monks were up to as they left the churchyard. They both peered at the robed figures as if looking at specimens in a cage.

"Tell me," said one of the ladies. "What do Buddhist monks do to help society? I mean what do you do for the world?"
"Well... We have our own way of taming the fiery beast," said the Ajahn in an absurdly serious tone.
"Oh really," came the reply as Suñño buried his face in his robe, fighting to suppress his laughter.
"So you do work?" she said.
"Oh yes, we all have to work at it, don't we?" said the Ajahn with a broad grin.
"God's work of course. I suppose we all serve the Lord in our own little way, now don't we?"
"We do indeed," said the monk and then broke into laughter.
"Frightfully jolly sort of fellows," said one lady to the other as they walked away.

*"Another majestic old country estate,
sensitively restored, protected and cared for
with extraordinary attention to detail.*

This is the suffering of the rich."

Hunting Opportunities

"They're monks," said the elderly lady as she walked on a collision course towards the shoppers, pointing at two strange, robed men standing outside the shopping mall. "They're real monks and they want food. They don't want money, only something to eat... real monks!"

"It seems like we have ourselves a promotions manager," whispered Suñño.

"They've walked here, for miles... They're just collecting food to eat... They are real monks... They won't take money." And on she went weaving among the crowd as they passed by, trying her best to catch everyone. She needed to let everyone know whilst pulling her wheelie basket behind her. Those who weaved past were instructed from behind. Her voice was rapidly becoming weaker but she continued her mission, undaunted. Then she suddenly vanished.

This was a small town built around a crossroads. It was easy to find where the shoppers were heading as all business was conducted in a small area next to the traffic lights. Most of the houses were fairly old and traditionally designed but the shopping mall was modern. Everything was there; supermarket, bank, post office, newsagent, video store, hairdresser and a hardware store. All were linked within a semi-covered series of alleys and small squares. All were built in flat yellow brick with flat roofs, flat concrete street furniture set in crisp right angled lines and in complete contrast to the old town surrounding them.

Their 'promotions manager' had appeared shortly after the monks had positioned themselves for the morning Alms Round. She had made a beeline for the brown robed strangers and ascertained their situation very quickly. All the time she spoke to the Ajahn, she took hold of his forearm, tugged at his robe and looked up directly into his eyes, her head just reaching above his bowl. The long handle of her little red wheelie basket, battered and sagging empty, was always clutched in her other hand. Using it to lean on when standing still, its plastic wheels wobbled and the rubber stops which supported its two legs were worn down to the metal frame. A long grey coat covered her from neck to shins, revealing just the hem of a lighter grey skirt. On her feet, which were always spread apart at 'ten to two', were sporty looking trainers with red go-faster stripes. It must have been these shoes which gave her such youthful vitality, amused the Ajahn to himself.

With a brick wall in front and another behind, after a short exploration the monks chose to stand in a passageway which was feeling more like a tunnel. Pouring in at one end were traffic sounds and fumes from the crossroads. From the other end, they had the familiar plastic perfume of mixed fruit, bread and vegetable aroma of a supermarket and the droll melodies from a guitar and flute duet where two young buskers were performing just out of sight. These quite talented musicians had set up a base on the other side of the supermarket, in a small square. They had two small children and a dog tied to a pram. A young family of matted-hair travellers, noses and lips pierced with silver metal trinkets, hipster jeans displaying a tattooed abdomen and plastic sandals. A large red floppy hat lay expectantly on the pavement with a few coins thrown in. Alms mendicants of a different kind.

A little boy came out, pacing confidently across the small square, and stood directly in front of Venerable Suñño, saying "Ain't you got no arms?" The monk smiled and raised his arms, which were hidden inside his robe. Satisfied, the boy went away again, nothing more to be said.

There followed a short pause in the stream of passers-by. The music stopped and the guitarist made a purposeful stride from just around the corner, over towards the monks. Standing a few metres away, he finished rolling a cigarette, then taking an old fashioned petrol lighter from his pocket and cupping one hand to shield off the breeze, he squinted at the monks as he lit up. Two long and deep lungfull's were needed before he could come close, face to face with the older monk.

"Look, this is our regular place," said the matted-hair traveller. "Besides, we was 'ere first." He shuffled about. "And there 'ain't the space is there... you know, for all us."
"I see," said the monk. "So you are afraid we are encroaching on your patch eh?"
"Well yeah. You know I don't want to get heavy or anything like that but you know, we was 'ere first."
"I don't want to get heavy either!" smiled the monk. "Would it be OK if we aren't taking any money? I mean, if someone insists on offering us money, I could ask them to give it to you instead. Would that be OK with you?" The young fellow is flabbergasted, his cigarette hand fails to find his mouth for a second and he singes his hair.
"Oh right... ok... well yeah.. sure." He was completely lost. "That's fine!" He turns to walk to his spot, then turns back. "Yeah, you're welcome man!" he added.

Just then a young girl walked up to the younger monk with a loaf of bread and popped it into his bowl. The traveller stalled for a moment more, blinking with smoke in his eyes and stared. This was a new act, radical and daring. He went back to his guitar but moved out slightly so to keep those robes in his sight, suspicious and yet fascinated he ignored pleas from his wife and children and played on.

"This is all I can do, I am so sorry but my pension is all gone for this week." The bright old face was back and her hand was tugging on the Ajahn's robe again. The little old lady had brought two sandwiches and two pots of yoghurt. She parked the old red basket between the monks, lifted out her offerings and placed them into waiting bowls. "They are collecting food. They are monks who don't want any money. We must give them food," she announced loudly, looking around trying to get as much attention as she could.

"Bless you," said the Ajahn.

"Oh God bless you too," she said.

"You've been a great friend for us," said Suñño to the lady as another donation came his way from a young man in a smart suit.

"That's it! They must eat!" she went on. Then she took a few paces backwards to look gladly at the two monks she was proud to have adopted. A strange shadow seemed to come over her. Her brilliance dulled and a quiver flickered in her lower lip. Returning close again. "Can you help me?" Her hand pulled at the Ajahn's arm.

"What's your problem?" asked the Ajahn.

"You see I think I am going mad. Well... I am doing silly things. Do you think it is silly?" She was becoming tearful.

"Tell me more," asks the monk.

"It's my hubby you see. I lost him almost a year ago now... He died in his sleep." She lowered her head and covered her eyes with one hand. "We were together 52 years... Married 52 years and I don't know what to do without him. I am thinking about him all the time. I miss him so much!"

"I am very sorry," said the Ajahn.

"So am I!" she replied, looking straight at the monk. "You see I sit on the sofa, in the evening and I put his old sweater next to me. Then I put the arm across my shoulder, like he was still there, you know. Like... am I being silly or what? I don't know what to do anymore."

"Well, grieving is a natural thing.." said the Ajahn

"Bah!" she interrupted and slapped the monk on the back of his hand.

"Oh, don't give me all that old rubbish!" she said. "They all say that. 'It'll pass' they say... But it doesn't, it doesn't give up! Not at all. Now I don't know what to do anymore! Please help me."

There was a short silence, both looking at the ground in front of them.

"You still love him so much, you want to express it. You need to, only he's not here to receive it anymore?" said the monk.

"That's it! I am completely lost."

"Now you have a big hole in your life and you don't see any way of filling it." The monk shook his head.

"A big hole, that's right!"

"Yes I have been there myself," adds the monk, "when I lost my dad."

"Am I going mad?"

The doubts and confusion on her face were making her tiny body shrink, just her face remained for the Ajahn, wide eyed like the Cheshire cat and floating above his bowl lid. The food offerings were all going to the younger monk. It was very hectic just three yards away. But the other monk and the old lady had drifted into a different space together, in a quiet and private little bubble, intimate and extraordinarily alive.

"There is something you can do. In fact, you are already doing it only you aren't quite getting the point!"

"What do you mean? Tell me." Her attention was rapt.

"It is often called dedicating merit or sharing merit. It is an ancient practice but often misunderstood."

"I want to understand. Tell me about it."

"Many people come to the monastery, mostly Asians, to make merit for their departed loved ones. They understand that bringing offerings to the monks and nuns is a very meritorious deed and they ask us to dedicate our chanting to their lost loved ones. Many understand that these rituals attract... err... angels, we call them devatas, who love to gather around such lovely occasions, attracted by the good vibes!" He smiles and she begins to brighten up.

"So?"

"Well, a Sri Lankan monk told me this. The idea is that these angelic beings understand where the departed friend or relative has been re-born and can go and support or offer protection to them in their present life. So if they feel that their lost one would appreciate or can use some good karma (we all can!) or maybe they are afraid that they are indebted to their friend, they can sort of 'top up their heavenly bank account' for them. In a manner of speaking!" The Ajahn laughed, which brings a toothless grin from the sweet little lady but she is obviously quite confused.

"All this comes from a different culture from ours, I know. We have to understand a whole load of traditional Buddhist cosmology before it makes sense. But we don't need to go that far. It works quite logically actually, almost scientifically. It means you have to do things in a particular way and then the miserable hole you are often falling into, gradually gets filled. Naturally, it works every time. You must not simply believe in what I suggest you do but you must put the instructions to the test."

"Ok, I'll try."

"Like a medicine, if the doctor gives you a tablet and you just put it in your pocket or you think it is a really magical medicine and you put it in a special place on a shrine or something and worship it. It isn't going to make you better is it?"

"No, I understand."

"Ok. Now you have to go hunting!" said the Ajahn with a chuckle. "I know you are already very good at this but you need to add some extra purpose."

"Hunting for what?" asks the lady. She is enjoying this.

"Opportunities!" says the Ajahn, lowering his head towards hers, wide-eyed and playful.

"Opportunities?" her forehead puckers a little.

"Opportunities to make somebody happy. Anybody. To do something to brighten their day. Just a smile will do." He nods his head, then raises his chin with a foolish grin. "You won't find it too difficult!" he laughs. "Maybe a bit hard at first. It gets easier as you practice it!"

"Ok but..?"

"Now the important thing is this. It's in the timing. What was your husband's name? What did you call him?" asks the monk.

"Harry. I always called him Harry," she replies.

"So the very moment you get the smile you were looking for, you say to yourself, 'that's for you Harry'!" He points a finger at her. All the wrinkles on her well lived-in face come to life. Like the soft petals of a flower as it blooms.
"Wow!"
"Every time you look for an opening. Maybe you can think of something that Harry would love to do?"
"Animals, he loved animals."
"So find a way of helping animals, any one will do. The moment you see the goodness taking effect, live action probably works better than sending it in the post, that second you take a mental snap-shot and say, 'that's for you Harry'. You can say it a little later if you want but it won't be so effective. Just say it to yourself, you dedicate the merit there and then."

"I love the sound of it!" she cries.
"What happens is that gradually, when the memory of Harry comes to mind, instead of feeling awful you will then remember all the lovely and beautiful things which were part of your relationship with him. The love which is always part of you, which you have already received from him, that you are, and can never be separated from."
"I will?"
"We are healing a wound. You are putting lots of goodness into a gaping wound, replacing the unhappy association with a beautiful one. Like applying a medicine. The painful place is filled with loveliness. You can treat it like a game if you like. A special get well game. Especially when the feelings are really heavy, you must go out hunting, straightaway. Find the opportunity, set it up, direct the action and hit the target! Spot on 'that was for you Harry'. You have to hit it precisely!" the Ajahn swings his arm as if playing some kind of sport. "Pop one in there, straight into that hole!" he laughs again. "Just keep on doing this." The old lady raised her hands and clapped a few times, then keeping her hands together she called out "Splendid!"
"You have already been making lots of merit this morning, haven't you?" said the Ajahn.
"I have?"
"Absolutely! In a little while we will go off and take our meal for the day. We will be chanting the blessings. Today we can share the blessings and dedicate the merit for Harry. We can make it special, can't we." He holds his palms together. They exchange long looks which turn to tears for both of them. They both know how painful it is to grieve and how painful it can be to love someone so much.
"That is the most beautiful thing I have ever heard... ever!" she says. She steps backwards and stands motionless for a while.

"You are doing fine," says the Ajahn.

She goes further away and takes a concrete seat near the musicians, her gaze barely leaves the monks for a second.

"Have you any books?" came a young man's voice from beside the Ajahn. "That was really good stuff. Common sense, pure and simple."

Coming out of his bubble the monk looked at the lad.

"That is the Dhamma. That is what it means. Natural common sense." The Ajahn put his hand on the lads shoulder. "This is what the Buddha is pointing to, so we can see it for ourselves."
"How do I learn some more?" said the lad.
"By asking questions... And looking... You'll find the way, now that you know what you are looking for."

The little boy, who was worried about Venerable Suñño's arms, returned with a friend who could almost be a twin;
"Do you fight?" he said.
"Me?" said Suñño. "No we're 'armless!"

Floating Free

The meal that day had been really heavy, fish and chips, cheese, egg and cake. Both monks had been careful not to consume very much but the substance itself took a lot of digesting, consequently their bodies felt heavy and their minds were very sluggish so walking was not a good prospect for a while. They found a quiet spot in long grass, just off the footpath on a steep slope, which led out of the town, and collapsed there. Venerable Suñño went straight to sleep, which was understandable because the previous night was pretty uncomfortable and neither of them had had much rest.

Bug Lunch

The Ajahn sat up for an hour or two, feeling distinctly unwell. He remembers beginning the day with a significant lack of energy, then when it came to the time to eat, his desire for food had almost gone. Past experience had taught him not to eat without an appetite, which was a sure way of making himself sick, so he hardly touched his meal but he still felt as if he had totally gorged himself. Once the nausea passed, he laid down and drifted off into a foggy half dream state.

He remembered his time living in Thailand. On many occasions there, he witnessed his appetite vanish in a second as he had to face rich food dressed with a pickled fish sauce which smelt rotten to his senses and he could not bring himself to eat it. In some areas, he was served silk worms, basically a blue maggot curry, or grilled locusts and often found large red ants which were boiled up in his greens. His conditioning was to keep insects out of his food so it was a challenge to put these things into his mouth and chew them. He suffered diarrhoea almost every day for three years and he became very thin.

Some of the other monks would scold him for being choosy about his food - 'a good monk should just accept whatever he is given'. Then he remembered the Thai monasteries, which he had visited abroad, where they would not touch anything else but Thai food. He met some very poor villagers in India who were impressed at first at seeing the Thai monks going on Alms Round and gave them food to eat. Their faith was later completely shattered when they discovered the monks threw their food offerings to the wild dogs. The monks would only eat Thai cuisine especially prepared in their own kitchen by Thai cooks. They did not want the local food because it had no meat and it was not spicy enough!

He remembered the Thai temples in India, acting like hotels, predominately obsessed with making money and showing off their wealth. Their monks would travel in style, staying in five star hotels, waving expensive cameras and shopping with fat wallets. Mostly thanks to them a Buddhist monk in the Buddhist holy sites of India is seen as a wealthy tourist and is treated as such. The Ajahn was very grateful to a friend, another monk, who took him for a walk into the Indian countryside a few hours from a Buddhist tourist site. There, the local people recognised the sämaòòa[8] and they started to make offerings of support. There, the people were open to listen to the monk or at least they would try to communicate with friendship and out of respect for the discipline that they saw he clearly kept. Some children had approached them and offered a mango. The Ajahn's friend, a Sri Lankan monk, said to him;

"If you stay in India long enough you will see this is the wealthiest country in the whole world." After wandering alone for a little while in the countryside, the Ajahn was inclined to agree, certainly spiritually the wealthiest. He received food and medical help from Muslims and Hindus, not just Buddhists who are pretty rare in India.

The Ajahn looked across at his venerable travelling companion, fast asleep, with fatherly love and admiration. He realised that this experience was not easy for him and he was rising up to the test with great courage and enthusiasm. Suñño was always interested to hear stories of the great masters in Thailand and other exotic sounding places and the Ajahn liked to dwell upon them. Although the reality being, as the elder monk had seen for himself, there are very few monks in the world who are in anyway interested in following the training as it has been given in the scriptures. They wear the robe but don't live the life as The Lord Buddha advised. They squander the greatest opportunity they could ever have had and instead, they pollute the Sangha with foolish conceit and greed. Certainly, it seems it is much harder to practice a simple life of renunciation and practice a pure holy life in a place where the monasteries are wealthy and so become powerful and influential in worldly terms. The Ajahn recognised he had been deliberately trying to protect this young monk from seeing any of this corruption until he had tasted the sweet fruits of good, well-directed practice for himself. Although Suñño was actually well travelled and had already recognised these signs, as a result he was led to this austere way of life, he was a lot wiser and more experienced than his elder knew. So far, that is.

It was late that afternoon before the monks started to gather themselves after their extended rest. Suñño groaned at every movement. The map came out of his bag and they poked at it with little enthusiasm. The next town was a long way off no matter what direction they went and neither of them felt like going anywhere. The Ajahn recognised a name on the map, due north of them, in the

[8] *sämaòòa - an alms mendicant monk*

direction of the biggest town.

"I know of this place," said the Ajahn. "It is a kind of hippy community. One of our monks used to stay there from time to time, years ago, before he disrobed!" and he laughed. "I've not been there before." He handed Suñño the map. "I guess they might be willing to feed us if we reached there in good time tomorrow morning. It's probably a better chance than the village here or here," pointing at the map, "and if not, we may make the town here by 11:00 in the morning."
"So now we look for a place to stay the night... where?" added Suñño pointing at the map. "There's no church, farm or anything much before... Oh well another night sleeping rough. At least it doesn't look like it is going to rain but I reckon it'll be cold." A crisp north easterly wind had arrived.
"We'll head for the hippy place then. It's almost a straight run on paths and small lanes. If we get halfway there, we are in with a chance tomorrow," said Ajahn. They picked up their bags and moved off.
"A spaced out, magic mushroom, free love, hippy community?" quips Suñño.
"I think it's more pure organic, wholesome and alternative with a little crystal healing added for seasoning!" the Ajahn raised two fingers in a peace gesture and Suñño returned it.

As soon as they set off, the prospect of going very far looked bleak. The Ajahn began to limp and Suñño complained of back pain. They left the fields and came to a main road. It seemed they had to follow the main road for a couple of miles before heading north. Traffic fumes and noise pressed heavily on the monks, as well as the constant care and attention needed in avoiding an accident, as there were few places to walk away from the perilous tarmac. After a couple of 'near death experiences' as Suñño loved to call them and several long and intense horn soundings and screaming motorists, the Ajahn suddenly started to thumb a lift. Surprised, Suñño asked why and where he was intending to go.

"Anywhere out of here!" shouted his elder. They stood together for a while hoping to attract the sympathetic attention of a passing motorist but the two monk's grim and desperate countenance probably frightened off any possible rescuer. They gave up standing as it was more painful than walking and continued on to the lane heading north, those two miles taking a couple of hours. Once they were on the quiet and narrow lane they stopped again, took off their bags and drank some water. Nothing was said. They looked ahead and rubbed sore legs, backs and shoulders. It was getting cool so the Ajahn put on his woolly hat. Venerable Suñño swiftly lifted his bag from the ground, swinging it onto his shoulder, he let out a very definite and powerful;

"Right then, I'm off!" and started striding down the lane, which began with a gentle down hill slope. Slightly startled, the Ajahn grabbed his bag and followed.
"Hell it hurts!" added Suñño. He was very slowly increasing the pace, glancing back to see if his companion was with him, which he was. But only just.
"Oh suffering!" shouted Suñño again as he pushed on, his elder was struggling to keep up but at the same time he was also rising to his new challenge.

Blistered Feet, Blissful Mind

This was becoming a walking meditation exercise with a special edge with the mind steadily focused on the feelings and sensations, being completely present, maintaining a broad sense of pure awareness, just simply being with what is. For a while, Suñño's whole body felt a cutting jar every time each foot hit the road. The sheer shock would resonate through every fibre of his tall and skinny frame. His teeth picked up the final shock wave with a tiny, audible and internal 'clack' on each step. The pulsing headache from stuffed sinuses, caused by constant hay fever, was rhythmically stretched as heavy sacks which hung from beneath his eyeballs bounced up and down. His hot feet would slide a little, strapped into sandals which allowed a slight movement, giving the impression a warm thick liquid flowing between sole of foot and sole of sandal. He imagined walking on sticky coagulating blood which lubricated his stride.

"Pain!" shouted Suñño and continued to walk faster. Then he started to growl like a dog. The Ajahn began to laugh, which was barely possible because he was quite short of breath. A few minutes later both the monks had taken to regular growling. They had reached maximum velocity and glanced at each other as the first steep hill climb approached. Both knew that slowing down for the incline was out of the question. They growled again and went for it, piling on the pressure they made it. Then they made the next one, then the next. The Ajahn had pulled off his hat. Both monks were developing a good sweat. Both aware that the evening was drawing in, the light was failing and it was getting quite cold. Unaffected for now, they were beginning to fly.

Trees and hedges were sweeping by. Buildings close to the lane just danced, walls and windows twisted themselves around and disappeared behind the young monk as he entered overdrive. His head was perfectly clear, every smell a heavenly scent. Cow dung, fresh mowed grass, wild garlic and even the breath of a singing goat as it poked its head through the fence. Every pore of his skin opened to the air, the sounds, and the light was strangely luminous and peculiarly metallic. His heavy bag, his body and his empty mind had become one, like a cloud floating free.

"I am afraid he's stuck lower than that," said the Ajahn.
"A hungry ghost that fellow."

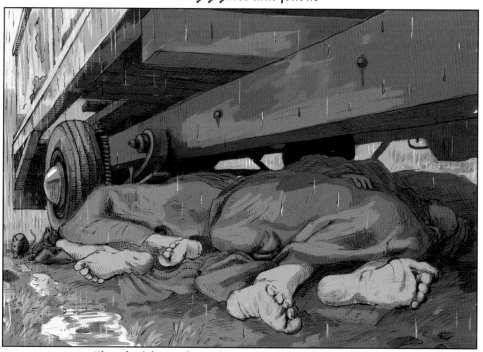

They had been through some fairly arduous nights;
once sleeping underneath a broken down truck.

"I really appreciate you taking the time to bring me on this tudong."

"Oh hell. Will I ever forget about Debbie?" he thought aloud.

There was no need to clean things or sort out any mess that day.

A few lines of chanting ring out from high-pitched voices, mostly in unison,
then they all bow again.

Suñño grabbed his friend's arm and pulled him out of the way as the whistle pierced the air and a great black engine bore down upon them.

"The moment you see the goodness taking effect... take a mental snapshot and say 'That's for you Harry'."

Silvery light and a very dark blue sky almost merged as the silhouette of a great house appeared before them, barely distinguishable from the massive trees which surrounded it. A sign by a gate read clearly 'Friarsfields'. As if by magic, the hippies' place had happened upon them. The monks stopped astounded. They looked at each other for a while, sparkling and radiant, still speechless. Neither was out of breath or in any way tired, just very much awake. Extraordinarily so.

"Shall we enter?" whispered the Ajahn.
"Absolutely," came the reply. "This night vision might not last!"

The house was completely dark but they could see a light from another building to the side. The monks opened the gate and entered slowly. As they did so, a dog began to bark. The barking continued as they approached the light which came from an upper story. An orange lamp glowed from a large window, looming above what looked like a garage in the gloom. The orange face of a young woman with long dark hair appeared, looking a little dazed. She was almost naked and seemed to be tucking an orange sheet under her armpit which barely covered her large orange breasts.

"Who is it?" she cried. The window slid to one side as the woman crawled about the floor of a small room above a low garage. The thin alloy window frame extended to the floor which meant someone would have a mouse eye view inside the room if they walked up to it from the driveway. Unaware of the exposed position the woman was in, Suñño had walked quite close before his eyes became accustomed to the relatively bright light. Before the monk registered eyesight, rather unusually his first sense impression was of the odour which almost billowed out from this stuffy little room. Old and stale ash tray and alcohol fumes were quite strong. Then behind that was a sweaty body aroma and the stench of something else which sent him reeling backwards. A baby started to cry and then he recognised what it was, dirty nappies. Suñño immediately diverted his gaze as soon as he realised the young woman was sitting up in her bed, which was a mattress on the floor. Clothes, books, bottles, cups and plates were also strewn about the carpet.

"Who are you?" she said in a cute and seductive voice which astonished Suñño.
"I am sorry if we have disturbed you," said the Ajahn, "we are wondering if the community may have a place here where we could shelter for the night. I am a friend of Ajahn Hitessi who I believe used to stay here before."
"Who are you?" repeated the woman a little more firmly this time.
"Oh yes, I am sorry. We are Buddhist monks from Hartwood," said the Ajahn.
"Nice... well you can sleep with me if you like?" she said, leering at Suñño.
"No shit!" sneered Suñño as he turned away to face his friend.
"I think you'd like it!" she went on in a girly voice. "I've never had a monk before."

Without another word the monks both turned back towards the gate, the woman's enticing voice was instantly covered by a dog's piercing bark as they moved away. A light flashed on in the main house and a large oak door opened. A rotund and jolly looking man with greying hair tied back in a pigtail came out and greeted the monks with a polite salute, palms held together.

"Oh Bhante! What a delightful surprise, where are you from?"
"We're from Hartwood," replied the Ajahn. "I hope we aren't intruding?"
"No, no! What an honour," said the man and the conversation drifted on in the half light of the open door. The dog seemed to be tied up behind the house and continued its excited yapping as the attention of Venerable Suñño wandered back to the little square of orange light behind them.
'She certainly has a pretty face,' he thought to himself.

His mind followed a sexual fantasy for a few moments and then veered off into repulsion at the idea of living in such a ghastly mess. A few minutes of passionate embrace followed by a virtual nightmare of chaotic possibilities. Memories of a time in his own life when he was obsessed with seeking sensual pleasures. Everything he did was committed to getting any kind of quick hit or short thrill with little regard of the consequences. He had started to wise up to the potential disasters he was causing for himself and for others when he was still quite young. He can see this now but many of his old friends did not. Feeling like he'd just escaped from a dense and thorny jungle he breathed a deep of sigh relief. Then to his surprise, a clear image of the pretty young woman's face bathed in an orange light appeared in his mind. Slowly it began to change, ageing very quickly, putting on a lot of weight, her expression turning into a frustrated and bitter hatred, then very sad and dejected. For another few seconds, he fantasised himself as a great saviour, sweeping into her life, instructing and inspiring her in the beautiful rewards of true unconditional love and compassion. But quickly woke up to the clear realisation he wasn't up to it. 'Like the blind leading the blind!' he chuckled to himself.

It was the image of her sadness that stayed with him. What had happened to the child's father? He decided not to consider what might happen to himself if he became involved. Getting any closer was definitely out of the question. Like putting a hand into fire, he'd expect it to be painful. He snapped back into his senses. 'Imagine disrobing for her?' he said to himself.

"Venerable!" called the Ajahn. He was standing, waving in the doorway, inviting his friend in. Suñño swept round and joined him.
"Falling in love?" said the Ajahn. Suñño shook his head vigorously making 'whoo..aa' sounds and the monks both laughed together.

After tea, they had a hot shower, some convivial conversation with their host Rumi, then the monks were led to a surprisingly clean, tidy, small and almost empty attic room in this grand old country house. There was one camp bed with a collection of 1970's records piled on top and a guitar leaning against the wall.
"The stuff belongs to an Irish girl who went to America more than five years ago

and never came back," said Rumi. "This place collects all sorts of junk, waifs and strays. Nobody stays all that long except for the argumentative ones!" He added as his wife shouted up the stairs, angrily urging him to be quiet. "Forgive me, Ajahn, the boss is calling." Smiling he left.

Suñño sat for a long time in the moonlight contemplating, whilst his companion sat meditating. His shiny head was almost glowing in the tiny window. It was surprising for the young monk to see how upset the Ajahn was when Rumi was describing how poorly the previous monastic guest had been behaving there some years before. Playing a guitar and entertaining the residents or joining them in the swimming pool. The suggestions made a visible, physical impression on the Ajahn who was usually fairly cool. It seemed that Ajahn Hitessi had become interested in following a psychotherapeutic path that had led him out of the monastery. He followed an independent route and then found it difficult to keep up the training rules. He seems to have been much loved and respected and received a lot of support; therapy sessions were offered free and accommodation and food was supplied by various friends. But he realised getting about and meeting appointments were often a problem and he found himself being a burden; attending to this monk's special needs was obviously becoming a strain on the families around him.

The Ajahn described the last time he saw Hitessi was when he came to the monastery to disrobe. He was clearly very distressed and actually wept during the private little ceremony with his preceptor. He had been a monk for almost 17 years. Apparently after all these years of practice, he had come to the conclusion that he had suffered a very difficult birth, which had been a radically traumatic experience for him, and the only way he could see of resolving this was to disrobe. The Ajahn joked 'Only he wasn't interested in climbing back into his mother's womb!' Shortly after disrobing, he married a strong and independent woman who ran an alternative health clinic. Now it seems the relationship had collapsed and the ex-monk is back to seeking his own way again, living alone and training to be a therapist himself.

Suñño looked over at the music collection and thought about the Irish girl. The possible coincidence seemed too far fetched but the memory was close. Debbie, another drifter looking for happiness and contentment in things which could never provide it. The young monk felt extremely grateful. It was good to be spending this chilly night under a roof, having showered and refreshed himself, although he was now very keen to be getting out of there in the morning. This house may be huge but, in his mind, it was quickly turning into a cage.

"We develop a different kind of seeing.

The mind which is aware remains still
and the countryside moves,
as if through us."

Abbey Madness

Approaching the ancient abbey ruins, both of the monks were pleasantly surprised at the warm welcome they received, especially so as the lady at the gate waved them in without any request for an entrance fee. Suñño's somewhat spaced out expression may have either confused her or impressed her with an image of monks who had abandoned this place some 500 years before. However it was, the young monk sailed through the entrance gate as if he owned the place. She wobbled for a few seconds then beamed a beautiful smile and just said, "Welcome!" The Ajahn followed and began making apologetic gestures and expressing that he was unable to pay but she repeated her welcome and invited the monks in to look around.

"Wow, what an amazing place!" gasped Suñño. "These stone walls are so tall and the arches! How old is this place?"

"Probably built about 800 years ago," said the Ajahn. "Did you see the entrance? There is a little gift shop and a lady selling tickets."

"Hell no! Should we go out?" Suñño turned and went straight back to the ticket window. "I really didn't see you there. I am sorry but we can't pay, we have no money, perhaps we should leave now?"

"What's an ancient monastery without monks? It is good to see you. No, please take a look around," said the white-haired lady at the window. Just then a family group were leaving and a boy offered the monk their guidebook without a word. Suñño stood for a moment to take it all in, smiles reflecting in all directions. He looked at the book.

"Great! It's in Spanish, this I can understand, well... mostly!" he said.

"Would you like to leave your bags in the office with me?" asked the lady. "I dare say you'd like to put them down for a while."

"You are so kind and thoughtful," said Suñño as he passed his bag through the side door, then he went and relieved the Ajahn of his.

"You must be Buddhists," she said when he returned. The monk nodded and chuckled to himself. "Please stop by for some tea before you go, I'd like to talk with you," she added. Suñño held onto the office door handle, swinging the door to and fro a couple of times in a joyful and playful mood.

"Sure! That'd be great," he chirped in pure Californian. Closing the door mindfully, he bounced off to join his friend.

"Feeling lighter?" grinned the Ajahn who was cupping his hands under the drinking water tap and then took his fill. It was a hot and sticky afternoon. The after meal rest was postponed until they reached the Abbey ruins but now they had arrived, a new surge of energy had overcome the young American.

For an hour or two, the monks wandered about the great walls, tidy paths, lawns and terraces which was all that remained of the monastery. They amused themselves at the artist impressions of the monks in their quarters, dining hall and infirmary. But something else was attracting the attention of the senior monk. For quite some time, a group of teenage schoolchildren had also been scouting the place. Their interest was not very much centred on the piles of stones but on the strange looking robed men who lurked about the chapel. There were three adults or teachers who struggled to keep them in line, calling them back and telling them to be quiet. Eventually, the Ajahn decided to stay put as they charged into the old cloister and stood uncomfortably, giggling at the monks.

"Please excuse us!" called the teacher, a large and sweaty man in a black suit. "The boys and girls would like to ask you some questions if that's all right with you?"

"Ok," replied the Ajahn who took a seat on a wall and invited the students to sit on the lawn in front which they did. Suñño moved a few steps away to another wall and sat cross-legged, completely unaware that just beneath him was a large sign saying 'Keep off the walls'! This brought some smiles and grins of approval from the boys.

"Can anyone tell us what kind of monks they are?" asked the teacher. Suñño now feeling like a specimen in a zoo decided to close his eyes, leaving all the talking to the Ajahn.

"They are Buddhists!" came a girl's voice.

"Very good Jenny!" said the teacher.

"We did Buddhism in year seven sir!" said another girl.

"Boring!" said a boy and they all laughed.

"That's enough Daniel!" barked another adult voice, a woman this time.

"And what school of Buddhism are they from?" asked the teacher in a slow and deliberate voice, "Come on now you should know." The students shuffled about and mumbled to each other. One voice whispered 'Tibetan' several times but he was ignored.

"Venerable sir! Would you kindly enlighten us?" probed the teacher in his deliberate tone. The youngsters were clearly amused at the teacher's plea and continued to giggle and murmur for a few moments. The Ajahn remained silent, scanning the faces of the crowd assembled beneath him, then he turned to gaze up at the great Gothic arches towering above them.

"I expect you are wondering what a couple of Theravadin Buddhist Monks are doing wandering about this old ruin too eh?" said the elder monk, quietly and after a long pause. "This spooky old place, long abandoned from a great monastic tradition which arose and died like a flash in a pan. And do you know why?" There was a stunned silence. "Because the monks here became involved in power and politics, so, let that be a warning!" and then he roared with laughter. The students now completely quiet, glanced at each other, then at the teacher who didn't move.

"See this robe?" said the Ajahn as he tugged the rolled folds resting on his left shoulder. "This comes from a living monastic tradition which dates back, unbroken for over 2,500 years!" He started to point a finger at the children. "Do you know what that means?" a gentle chuckle bubbled up from the monks chest. "It means that we know how to look after ourselves!" then laughing "And so now we have learned how to look after each other!" Suñño, also amused began to shake gently on his seat.

"He's right!" said one of the boys looking at his illustrated guide. "All gone in 256 years, what a waste."

"Typical greedy Christians!" came a girl's voice.

"Yeh, always fighting," came another.

"Perhaps a little misguided," commented the Ajahn.

"Perhaps we could ask the monk another question?" the teacher jumped in with his booming and measured tone, the students looked irritated at him.

"Buddhists believe in reincarnation, don't they. Do you believe we may come back as a dog or even an insect?" The teacher looked almost victorious with his question, standing with his hands on his hips. The students remained quiet, waiting for the monk who was pausing.

"Well, let me answer in this way. Firstly I cannot speak for all Buddhists so I will give you my personal reflection as a Buddhist monk." The students nodded. "Secondly I would like to warn you about this word 'believe'. I don't like to use this much at all. As Buddhists, we are more interested in knowing things as they are, not just believing in what someone else tells us. You may believe your home is just the way it was when you left it but you don't know now, do you?" Some students shake their heads. "But you know we are sitting here now, don't you?" Some nod in reply. "Good! This is the kind of knowing, I am interested in."

Suñño opens his eyes and notices the Ajahn has the kids' full attention, smiling he closes them again.

"So if we are going to spend some time talking together, I don't want you to just believe in anything I am saying! Ok?" The Ajahn looks for some clear understanding and receives some enthusiastic and surprised expressions in return. "There is a famous story about the Buddha. Just after giving a teaching, the Buddha asked his most famous disciple if he believed in what he had just said. The disciple said he did not because he had not yet tested and examined it for himself. The Buddha praised this disciple as an excellent student. So I ask you to question what I say, don't believe a word of it, see it for yourselves. Check it out, until you know it!" The monk looked intently at the young faces who beamed a clear silent reply.

"Reincarnation" reminded the teacher.

"Yes of course. Well this was an idea which was common to most religious thought in India long before the Buddha. One might say he also adopted it as part of a cultural heritage. It still remains true to many different traditions today, not just Buddhist. Personally I certainly wouldn't rule it out!" The Ajahn laughs. "To believe in it, well..., it might not be all that necessary."

"So you don't?" interrupted the teacher.

"Let's look at it scientifically?" continues the monk, getting into his stride. "You have been studying matter in school haven't you, atoms, molecules and all that stuff?"

"I am doing 'A' levels!" said a boy.

"'A' level eh? Well I dare say you could teach me a thing or two by now so please correct me if I am wrong." One boy took out a notebook; the Ajahn continued. "Everything is in a continual state of change, is that so? All things are continuously on the move, arising and ceasing. Look at the food chain. We eat some cheese sandwiches, the body extracts some of the nutrient but most of it goes straight through and back to the ground, via a toilet!" They all laugh. "From the ground, we grow wheat, cows eat the grass, give us milk and by and by, the sandwich comes round again!"

"Then our bodies end up in the earth too, like my Grandad did!" said a girl.

"Now he's feeding worms!" replied a boy.

"Oh shut up!" cried the girl.

"That's it! Continual recycling!" adds the monk. "When it comes down to it, you can't make anything disappear, can you? Water in the drink, to water in the blood, to water in the earth, to water in the river, to sea, cloud, rain and back to the water in the orange juice! So what happens if you burn something?"

"The elements break up and disperse, water evaporates leaving carbon. We are mostly water and carbon actually!" added a girl. "Yes it changes but all the elements are still there, you are right, nothing really disappears."

"So according to present evidence, can you see anything that appears from nowhere, continues for a while, and then changes into something else which then remains in that state for ever? Never changing."

"No way!" said the girl. "Nothing is like that."

"All particle physics shows that everything is all just elements changing positions, we do this in class," adds another boy.

"So, according to present scientific evidence nothing else but reincarnation makes any real sense?" asked the Ajahn. "It certainly looks that way does it not?"

"I've never looked at it like that" added the lady teacher. "Very good and perfectly sensible explanation." The students liked it too.

"But what about the soul?" chipped in the big voice of their master.

"Oh boring!" a familiar chant goes on from a boy at the back.

"Quiet Daniel!" the teacher jabs a stern look at the boy.

"The soul, yes, excellent. I am pleased you brought that up," replied the monk.

"I'm not!" said Daniel.

"That's enough!" shouts the lady teacher. "One more word out of you and you'll go back to the bus."

"Suits me," said Daniel who gets up and turns away.

"Please wait," pleaded the monk. "I'd like him to stay." Offering a hand, he said "Please stay a little longer. You see Daniel reminds me of someone. I reckon he has a lot to offer us really."

"Who do I remind you of?" asked Daniel as he turned around.

"You remind me of myself! I always felt that school was a totally boring waste of time too, so actually I completely agree with you." The kids grinned at the monk's frank approach. "I also gave my teachers a pretty hard time!"

"Now you can get what was due!" added one very round boy, looking straight at the monk. "Now we can give you a hard time."

Suddenly the monk stopped. He became very still and silent for a few moments, returning a very long and loving look at the plump young lad who stayed transfixed in his gaze. Venerable Suñño detected a change in the mood, opened his eyes and noticed the Ajahn's lip quiver. The old monk wiped a tear from one eye and simply said, "Bless you" and there was silence.

"Bless you, young man!" the monk continued, getting back into his flow. "Yes please give me a really hard and testing time, it would be good for me."

"He wants to know about the soul," said Daniel, now picking up the subject. He had returned and sat down right in front of the monk.

"The soul. Well I suppose we need to come to some kind of agreement as to what the soul really is? What does it mean? It is a Christian concept I guess. Perhaps one of you could help me, tell me what is the soul?" the monk looked about the students and teachers for an answer. The youngsters squirmed and rolled about on the grass, mumbling and chuckling to each other but nobody spoke up, except the teacher who was giving all sorts of encouragement but still no satisfactory answer.

"It's a kind of spirit," said a girl.

"Well maybe, but I'm not sure I understand what a spirit is either? What do we understand the soul to be?"

"Is it the person?" added a boy. "No, no" said a voice from behind.

"Sir, sir I know sir!" called out an enthusiastic lad with long blond hair.

"Yes Cutter?" the teacher prompted.

"Isn't it some kind of flat fish sir?"

Then there was chaos for a few minutes. Even the monks and teachers could not resist joining in the laughter.

"I thought that Buddhists don't believe in a soul?" said the teacher but he had pretty much lost control of the class. No one was paying him much attention. The monk raised both hands nodding and smiling and order was quickly restored.

"It's a pretty difficult question, isn't it?" said the monk.

"I have a better one!" interrupted a voice from the front.

"Yes Daniel?" asked the monk.

"Well, I'd like to know who you are, how you live and why you are a monk?" asked Daniel and a simultaneous cheer came from nearly all the students.

"Much more interesting!" said the lady teacher.

"This concept of anattä or 'not self' is a fundamental Buddhist concept." Then turning to the teacher, the Ajahn said "this will take a little more time and I'm not sure how much more we have together?"

"What about you?" asked the teacher in return "Are we disturbing you?"

"I have all the time I need. We aren't going anywhere and I am certainly not disturbed, are you venerable?" the Ajahn turns to his friend who shrugged his shoulders and smiled.

"Please tell us a bit about yourselves," the lady teacher spoke gently. "We don't meet monks very often, I'd like to know more too, like Daniel. We'll have to be going back to school before long."

Suñño sat motionless for a while as the elder monk described how they lived and told a couple of stories of their current pilgrimage adventure. Occasionally the young monk gazed up into the stone shadows and watched the rooks as they flapped about, sometimes squawking so loudly the Ajahn had to shout or wait until the wild birds calmed down. The immense structures supported all kinds of life, not just birds but delicate ferns and mossy ridges in greens and browns. Then some almost white circled patches on the high vertical surfaces drew the monks attention away from the group sitting around him.

The students and staff were full of questions, the usual things about robes, choice of food and not having money, then the conversation took an interesting turn. The Ajahn was explaining that one of his duties, especially in the monastery, was to be the receiver of things. He said they were sometimes given things they could not really use, like shampoo! This amused the youngsters a lot. He explained that he has very little in the way of personal possessions which means he could be packed up and moving on to another place in just a few minutes. He liked to keep all his stuff to a level whereby he could carry it all away in just two hands. Although he confessed that after several years in one place, he probably now needed a case with wheels on. He had recently received a collection of books written by an old college friend, which he was glad to have but he realised that he was not going to carry them around for the rest of his life so he would have to find a good home for them somewhere. Because monks understand everything they own is freely given, even land on which to build monasteries, great attention is given to accepting things, to their care and distribution. Monks can't really own very much at all, not even the monastery they live in, certainly not as personal property.

"We have lots of rules about all this," exclaimed Suñño.

"What would you do if someone gave you a million pounds?" asked a boy.

"I wouldn't go near it!" smiled the Ajahn.

"What if someone gave you a nice new car, like a Mercedes, all taxed and insured. Would you take that?" asked another boy.

"Well I'd need a driver, and how would I pay for the petrol?" The monk thought for a few moments. "I suppose if the other residents of the monastery and the lay supporters felt we could use and maintain such a thing, perhaps I might. If I moved away, the car would have to stay there!" He paused. "For myself, I'm not interested at all!"

"What is the most valuable thing you have ever been given?" asked a blonde girl.

The Ajahn smiled and considered his reply, taking his time. "Well..." There was complete silence. "I could say that the most valuable things I have been given are my robes and bowl."

"Oh wow," said the blonde girl, and they all turned to look at Suñño who had coughed quite loudly, as if he had something to add. Which he did.

"I'd say the most valuable thing I have ever been given is my sīla," said the younger monk.

"What does he mean?" asked the blonde girl.

"That is beautiful venerable," added the Ajahn. "Absolutely right, but I'm not sure they would understand what you mean."

"Tell us, tell us!" another girl called out.

"Sīla, the moral discipline, you could say means the rules he keeps. He says that is the most valuable thing he has been given!" explained the elder monk.

"So strict!?" said a boy at the back.

"Good grief, he is one hell of a serious monk!" exclaimed Daniel. Suñño laughed and beamed a bright smile straight back at Daniel who was obviously quite shaken at the idea.

"Seriously happy it seems to me!" added the blonde girl.

"Wow that's really cool," said one.

"Kind of scary," said another.

"Amazing, these guys are for real!" added another.

"He really wants to do this... blows my mind!" exclaimed Charlie Cutter. "Blows my flat fish clean out of the water man!"

They all began to stand. The teachers tried to gather them together, directing them back to their bus but the kids protested, talking and scattering in all directions. The older lady teacher approached the Ajahn and said, "That was wonderful, thank you so much, I have never seen this lot so attentive. They are always loads of trouble but I think you touched them very deeply, thank you, thank you."

The students and monks milled about the cloister walls.

"Thank you venerable," said the Ajahn to his friend. "You reached out further than I dared, that was precious."

"Inspired by the moment, just as it is," replied Suñño and the monks bowed their heads to each other.

"Why can't you be our teacher?" Daniel asked the Ajahn. "You could come to our school, couldn't you?"

"Well, I could come and visit sometime," replied the Ajahn.

"When? You could come tomorrow couldn't you?" pressed Daniel.

"I don't know how you are fixed but I am sure it would be great if you could come to our sixth form assembly tomorrow. We can provide you transport and even feed you, if that's ok?" the older lady teacher asked. "It would be very exciting for the children. We are close to the end of term, exams are over and some of the children are leaving us. It would be great if you would come."

"Yeh! Oh please sir, mister monk sir!" pleaded Daniel again. His sentiment was picked up by some of the other children. "Oh please!"

"Where is the school?" asked the monk.

"Brookdale! It's about 15 miles east. I could drop you back here afterwards if you like," said the other teacher. "Sometime after school, about 4 o'clock."

"15 miles east sounds about right to me. Don't you think so Venerable Suñño?" replied the Ajahn. The other monk played about for a few seconds, giving thoughtful looks into the sky, rubbing his chin and making humming sounds.

"15 miles... east... tomorrow... mm... sounds fine!" Suñño grinned at Daniel who leapt for joy and hugged the young monk's arm.

Sorting out the logistics took some time. The bus driver would not take the monks with them due to some insurance problem which upset the teachers because there were empty seats. Additional plans were made, pick up times agreed and some ideas for accommodation for the night discussed but still uncertain. The Ajahn seemed totally unruffled by their scattered behaviour and unsettled plans. They wanted to continually reassure the monks that everything was fixed and certain when it was obvious it wasn't. The Ajahn kept trying to set their minds at rest by saying uncertainty was ok with him but any ambiguity seemed a big problem for them. The elder monk eventually stepped in to say it all seemed perfectly clear to him and he would go with what had been decided, only nothing had been decided; but the firmness and clarity of the Ajahn's statement seemed to throw a fire cracker into the confusion which brought all the arguments to a halt, instantly.

Just as the teachers were about to board the bus and the monks were going to have their long awaited tea with the ticket lady, all the kids came piling out of the bus again, much to the teachers dismay.

"Group photo!" cried Charlie Cutter waving a camera.

"Ok children but be quick now," said the large teacher in a suit who Daniel introduced as 'Mister Manslaughter'! They later found his name to be Jeremy Manthorpe.

"Do you mind?" asked the older woman teacher who Daniel introduced as Auntie Margaret, who actually turned out to be Daniel's auntie.

"Not at all," said the Ajahn glancing at his friend, who looked away.

It was another 15 minutes before all the cameras were passed about. The bus driver was roped in to take the last few shots. He kept apologising to the monks about rules and regulations, then nervously dropped Mister Manslaughter's camera on the road. Cross, hot and bothered, the boss eventually drove his flock into the bus and they were gone, almost everyone waving as they went.

"Do you really think they'll be back to pick us up?" asked Suñño.

"The odds are pretty good I'd say," said the Ajahn, "but they might not... we'll see."

They went over to the ticket office and souvenir shop where they were given seats at a small desk in the back room just behind the booth. The lady there was very chatty and managed to keep several different conversations going at the same time, serving in the shop, at the window and tea for two. Whilst she was busy the monks were silent until the Ajahn spoke.

"I notice you struggle whenever the photo opportunity comes up."
"Yeh, I really don't like it," replied Suñño.
"What's the problem?"
"Feeling exposed I guess. I mean you really don't know what they'll do with it. I could end up in some sleazy magazine or pasted up on some dodgy internet site!"
"Right! We don't even own our own face!"
"Everything becomes so public."
"Our real refuge is in knowing, not in becoming," smiled the Ajahn.
"Knowing... ?" Suñño became silent again, against the background hum of the Abbey office he was drifting off into an inner world of contemplation.

"When the beautiful view
suddenly makes its impression,
the pain vanishes instantly.

Which just goes to show,
you can't trust the mind!"

Different Wavelengths?

Mrs Hopper was the second lady teacher they met the previous afternoon. She had returned to pick up the monks from the Abbey quite late and by the time they arrived at the school, the students had all gone home. She had been hoping to invite the monks to her home for the night but the conversation in the car revealed that she was living in a small flat with two grown up girls and no husband or partner. She wanted the Ajahn to talk to her daughters. He convinced her that it would be better finding another solution for accommodation so the school gym was suggested; perhaps they could meet again after school the next day.

They were taken to the school gym to meet the caretaker who offered them a place to sleep in a cosy staff changing room with hot showers, comfortable chairs and rubber mats to sleep on. The very familiar stale sweaty smell which hung over the place and some of the athletic paraphernalia reminded Suñño of a starkly hostile and competitive environment he was now so pleased to be free from.

The monks awoke quite early as usual, not long after dawn at about 4:00. They had been invited to join some of the staff for coffee and breakfast at 7:30 so the young monk took himself off for a walk in the grounds. He found a delightful spot by a stream which lay in a hollow between woodland and playing fields. The sun soon climbed up above the grassy banks and warmed his back as he sat in meditation, listening to the gentle trickle and burble of flowing water. The trees were full of bird life singing their hearts out, squirrels chattered and argued, peering excitedly at their early morning human visitor who sat motionless, just a shiny bald head poised upright on a pyramid of brown cloth, very much awake with eyes gently closed.

After an hour or so, the monk needs to stretch himself but just before he does he detects a different sound which alerts his attention. Footsteps perhaps but definitely not human. Then he hears some breaking twigs from the direction of the woods. Very slowly he opens his eyes and instinctively holds his breath. Just a few paces up-stream standing in the bracken by the waters edge, he sees two deer, presumably mother and youngster. They too are completely still, staring back at the monk with ears pricked up. Nothing moves, even the squirrels freeze in anticipation. They are so close that the monk can almost smell them, their smooth brown flanks twitching almost imperceptibly. Their eyes sparkle, glancing away for a millisecond then back scrutinising the monk. Suñño recalls a passage in the ancient Buddhist texts where the Buddha describes this very sense of alertness and attention.

'... In just the same way, the Bhikkhu trains himself, alert and mindful like a wild forest deer...'

Very slowly these two beautiful and graceful creatures lean forward and then down, bending their front legs a little and drinking silently from the stream, their attention so sharp and yet their movements are calm and steady. Suñño is gripped, his breathing has stopped, his thinking stopped, mind bright and empty, at the same time completely filled with the moment, pure, with nothing added. The mother deer quickly raises her head, the youngster moves just a little, its black nose just an inch above the water, the mother checks the scene for a moment then lowers her head, they both continue to take their fill. The only all-pervasive sound is birdsong, high pitched, angelic and ringing loud and clear from all directions, even from deep inside the monk's own mind. First, the adult deer begins to lower herself, the little one a moment later, a second's distinctive tightening of her muscular frame, then suddenly she leaps and takes off into the air with the foal a few moments behind, its head outstretched. It reaches the top of the grassy further bank in one leap. In another, they are both gone.

Suñño hasn't moved a muscle except his eyelids. The deer had leapt out of his field of vision and he makes no attempt to follow them with his head. Transfixed his eyes close again where an action shot picture of the young animal remains captured in his mind for a while then it slowly disappears until all is bright and empty. He allows his mind to rest in this state for some time. Timeless time. Now, not caught in mental proliferations, free from concerns about physical feelings, awareness of time enters the timeless. Slowly he is aware of taking one enormous slow and deep in-breath which he holds effortlessly as if afraid of losing it; then he is fully aware of a very elongated exhalation which doesn't appear to end. Attracted by a plastic or almost metallic and definitely unfamiliar buzzing sound, which his senses tell him is alarmingly close, he ventures to open his eyes again.

Directly in front of his nose, only a foot away hovers a giant dragonfly. Wings beating in a perfect steady rhythm, this metallic greenish-blue and monstrous insect elevates an inch or so, maybe taking a better look at the monk, then it drops a couple of inches as if the thread holding it had just released its slack. It stayed just hovering there with bulging eyes pointing directly at Suñño. Without any noticeable preconception, the monk discovers his right hand is floating up from his lap. He gradually twists his wrist and instinctively finds the opening in the front of his robe which is draped about 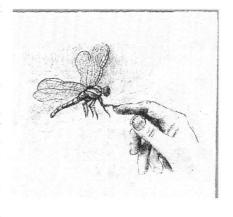 his shoulders. His right hand reaches up, led by a lightly extended index finger towards the dragonfly which remains hovering in exactly the same spot. In a few moments of silent appreciation, a kind of blessed communion, the young monk lifted a front leg of the magical creature with his finger-tip and he actually shakes hands with the dragon. Suddenly the dragon flies backwards a few inches, bobbing up and down a few times in space then it flies around Suñño's head in a clockwise direction three times and disappears vertically upwards like an arrow. Then there is only birdsong and sunlight.

* * *

At 7 o'clock the Ajahn stood watching Venerable Suñño as he was absorbed in meditation by the stream. Many wild flowers of various colours surrounded the young monk as he sat so peacefully. Keeping a respectable distance, the Ajahn coughed gently to attract the attention of his friend but he received no response. He stood there waiting for a while enjoying the picture. A voice pierced the air and the Ajahn turned around to see the school caretaker walking towards them. He greeted the monk warmly and courteous morning greetings were exchanged.

"You have to go and sign in at reception. They'll give you a visitor's badge which you have to wear at all times, then I'll take you to Mr Manthorpe's office for breakfast. They are expecting you," said the caretaker in a rich Scottish accent. They turned towards Venerable Suñño who had suddenly appeared standing behind them. The Ajahn could see immediately the kind of space his friend was in, glowing with sympathetic joy he smiled in resonance, nothing needed to be said.

They walked back to the gym to collect their things, which were already packed, then, making a wide loop about the school grounds, the caretaker took them on a tour before reaching the main entrance. Walking behind, Suñño could see that the Ajahn was wearing his feigning interest face as the little Scotsman rattled on in a continuous commentary about every kind of bush or flower they passed, how the children are continually wrecking the place, the old building, the new building, the not so new building, the fire regulations and many references to 'all the goings on in there' or 'all the naughty goings on in here'. He barely took a second to suck in an in-breath, then all the out-breath was fuelling a battery of almost incomprehensible chatter. The Ajahn was nodding from time to time saying just 'Oh?' or 'I see'.

The school receptionist wasn't in yet so a passing teacher spent a few minutes pacifying the speedy caretaker saying that the monks could check in later and it was ok to pass the second doorway without a badge. He would see the head teacher personally about the matter. They were escorted to Mr Manthorpe's office only to find it locked which sparked the caretaker off on a diatribe about teachers and office keys and classroom or pass keys, their positions and regulations pertaining to their use. Mrs Hopper appeared from a staff toilet opposite with one eyebrow painted and one unpainted, flapping about everything being a little too early, then ushering the monks to the staff room for breakfast, the caretaker showing two rather amused looking monks the way.

Passing the reception desk a second time, the staff were in so large 'visitor' badges were issued. The monks signed in with time and date recorded on the appropriate line and in the right box. Mr Manthorpe's name was put in the box for him to sign but still nobody was able to locate him although he had been seen in school earlier. The staff room was quite huge, filled with easy chairs in small groups around low tables. The walls were lined with tables cluttered with bags, boxes, books, computers and cups. The far wall was covered with notices. A magnificent window to one side of the room looked out over woodland. On the other wall hung several modern works of art, presumably from the students. Hardly anyone looked up as the monks entered. Even after an introduction from Mrs Hopper who bustled in behind them, only one or two faces looked up in acknowledgment. At first glance everyone looked tired, dull and heavy or stressed and irritable.

"Have you seen Jim?" asked a young man with a neat trimmed beard. Turning to the monks, he continued, "Mr Manthorpe has been talking to me about you, yes... very interesting, he wants to see you privately before the class."
"Please have some breakfast!" cried Mrs Hopper as she hopped out again. Two tables were strewn with buns and pastries. Some people seemed to fly past and grab something but most went straight to the tea urn or coffee machine and helped themselves. The monks stood for a moment then took seats by the buns and waited but they were ignored. After a few minutes Mr Manthorpe came bowling in.
"Good! I see you've had breakfast," said Jim Manthorpe, head of RE in the school, then he turned to the Ajahn. "Look, can we talk privately for a minute?" he added.
"Sure," said the Ajahn who was quickly led away to Jim's private office. As they left, a booming voice called out "Mrs Hopper will look after you." Suñño sat observing the staff room alone.
After a while, several other teachers came to introduce themselves to the monk sitting quietly in the corner. They sat engaging him in friendly small talk, munching on cakes and biscuits as they did so but nobody ever offered him anything so he had none. Once he hinted that they looked good, once he asked if anyone can take one but everyone seemed to be operating on a different wavelength, broadcasting and not receiving. Daniel's lovely auntie Margaret came into the staff room and immediately joined Suñño; she was clearly excited to see him.

"I am Margaret Smith," she said. "Shame on us for not introducing ourselves yesterday, it was so rude!"
"I'm Suñño"
"Have you had enough breakfast? We have to be in the hall quite soon," she asked.
"Not yet," said the monk. "You see I don't help myself."
"Of course! Oh please let me help," said Margaret piling things onto a plate and handing it to the monk, "I guess this lot are so used to looking after number one, typical! I am sorry, why didn't you say?"
"Nobody asked I guess," said Suñño.
"Oh wonderful! What about tea or coffee? I guess nobody asked either?" said Margaret, raising her hands in despair.

The atmosphere suddenly changed as a strange buzzing alarm rang out across the school and everyone became mobilised, dropping cups, plates and newspapers and making for the door. "Oh dear, registration already. Look, you have a few minutes to eat before Assembly, stay here and I will collect you in a mo, ok?" she said in a sweet motherly tone. Suñño nodded and bit into a jam doughnut, looking playfully at the lonely coffee machine on the side table.

The headmaster introduced the two visiting monks to the school at the morning assembly as friends of Mr Manthorpe, explaining they will be spending time with his classes that morning and that the monks would be leading the sixth form assembly and discussion group in the afternoon. The monks sat with the teaching staff on the stage whilst about five hundred children looked back at them. Suñño assumed that the Ajahn had organised a programme with Jim but things were not so clear. There was an initial plan that the elder monk would talk to that morning school assembly but the headmaster and Mr Manthorpe had some complicated and rather hushed disagreement on the stage in front of the school, leaving everyone puzzled and feeling somewhat embarrassed. The headmaster then invited Mrs Hopper to give a Bible reading for which she was completely unprepared so she gave a brief story of how they met the monks the day before at the abbey, which seemed to annoy the headmaster. Eventually they were saved by the bell and chaos returned as the school disbanded for the first class of the day.

"Mr Manthorpe's class will join mine in room 19!" bellowed Mrs Hopper as they dispersed. "Please come with me," she said to the Ajahn. As they were leaving the stage by the back door, the Ajahn moved in between Mr Manthorpe and the headmaster as if to try and make some apology or understand what problems there might be.
"It's a bloody mess!" grunted the head teacher as he marched out and turned away.
"I'll catch you later Ajahn," said Jim Manthorpe and he turned to follow the headmaster to his office.

Suñño followed the group to room 19 with Mrs Hopper leading the way through crowded corridors milling with uniformed teenagers. For a few brief moments, the monks were reunited as they moved along. It seemed that Jim was in a bad way. He was really falling to pieces which was fairly obvious to Suñño but now the young monk was also feeling that maybe this school visit was turning into a disaster for them.

"I think it's all ok," assured the Ajahn as they entered the classroom. "We'll see what happens next. The headmaster seemed pretty happy to see us; his problem is with poor old Jim," he whispered to Suñño as they waited for Mrs Hopper to finish her introduction and get the children settled in a classroom intended for half as many pupils.

The first three sessions were both irritatingly short and comprising of much

115

younger children who were very new to the subject. The monks became more and more impressed when watching Mrs Hopper in action at the front of the class. She facilitated quite a good debate, however short, and kept the pupils engaged with great skill. This was certainly her vocation. Jim returned looking very drained and visibly shaking at the end of the third session to invite the monks for their meal break, which he had remembered much to the younger monk's surprise. As they left, Jim walked straight into the closed door and banged his head very hard; the children shrieked with laughter. Jim looked as if he was about to burst into tears but managed not to. As they walked out, Suñño offered the teacher a piece of tissue paper; his forehead was bleeding.

Waiting outside the classroom was their good friend Daniel and the blond girl who introduced herself as Donna. They had brought the monks' bags from the staff room and offered them with broad smiles. They were taken to a courtyard surrounded by beautiful flowerbeds, which opened out to a grassy bank and then to woodland. Standing in the courtyard were all the children they had met at the abbey plus some new friends. Each one was holding something to eat. The monks are invited to walk Alms Round in the garden and they ask the monks' advice as to how to do it. Suñño sets up two seats with sitting cloths, bowl-stands and cups at each place on a raised bank to one side. The Ajahn instructs Jim who lines up the donors in a large circle. Slowly the monks walk along the line as apples, pies, sandwiches, chocolate bars and all sorts of tasty offerings are placed in their bowls by youngsters who looked so pleased and yet tried to look quite serious.

The monks took to their seats and the pupils sat in front as the Ajahn explained a little about their chanting. Meanwhile the headmaster came out of a door behind the children and stood next to Jim Manthorpe, putting a reassuring arm around his shoulder. Jim started to cry silently to himself and quietly moved away. The monks chanted the blessing in Päli, the headmaster, teachers and children listen fascinated. The buzzer-come-bell rang again and the students moved away as the monks tried to make some impression on the mountain of food they had received.

After they had finished their meal, the Ajahn explained to Suñño that Jim had been confiding in them the nature of his own personal nightmare. His wife and family were leaving him because of some totally unfounded accusations of improper behaviour from a student who seemed to have had a problem with Jim's own children. He was close to a complete nervous breakdown and had taken to drinking in order to drown his sorrows, which had led to a further disaster the previous weekend. The headmaster had been Jim's best friend for years but had now mistakenly bungled a meeting with a policeman which had made matters much worse.

The monks were offered a couple of hours break before the sixth form assembly. The Ajahn spent it in Jim's office and Venerable Suñño took to the woodland, alone.

The afternoon session was very different. Their meeting was held in the music room which was quite large and had a small stage. The Ajahn arrived early with Jim who was looking brighter. They had both spent some time setting up the room. All the furniture was piled to one side and some carpets were spread on the lino floor. A framed picture of a Buddha image and a vase containing some flowers were standing on the piano. When Suñño arrived, the Ajahn was sitting and meditating on the stage with Jim who was also sitting on a chair to one side with his eyes closed. The bell summoned the students in from the recreation ground and a steady hum of voices echoed from down the corridor. Suñño positioned himself slightly behind and to one side of the Ajahn and took up a meditation posture. Staff and students came ambling down the narrow passage bringing with them the social and lively energy of the playgrounds. However, as soon as they walked into the room, they changed. Within a few more paces, they stopped talking and found a place to sit on the floor; no instructions were necessary. The Ajahn held this silent space for the room for as long as he felt it was needed then he began to talk quietly with his eyes still closed.

"In meditation practice, we develop our ability to be aware. We refine this awareness to a point where we can clearly see the way things really are so we are no longer deluding ourselves, no longer confused. We develop wisdom." The old monk spoke quite slowly and clearly; nobody moved. The silences held peacefully in the acoustically designed music room.

"So who do you think you really are?" he paused, "or should I ask what do you think you really are... have you ever really thought about it?... are you really happy with whatever that might be? Most of you are probably thinking you are your body... are you sure?"

The Ajahn asked the students to contemplate their bodies. He pointed out that they had been sitting there for about five minutes and already they are restless. He asked them to see how long they can simply be still. Pointing to the other monk, he asked,
"How long do you think he can be still?" There was no answer from the students, who sat rigid.
"Two, maybe three hours maximum," said Suñño.

There was another pause for a few minutes and the Ajahn pointed out that they were already shuffling about.

"You see! If you found the most comfortable chair or bed, how long could you stay there before you'd have to get up? The body has its own business, doesn't it? It has to be fed, cleaned, it gets too hot, too cold and it wants to go to the toilet at the most inconvenient times! And can you ignore it? No, of course not. It gets sick without asking your permission. It is always wanting something, isn't it; never really satisfied. Furthermore, it is constantly changing, isn't it?"

The Ajahn continued to ask them to investigate these questions in their own experience. The Ajahn described that from his own experience, when surrounded by a group of teenagers, he can easily recall what it was like to be 16 or 17 years old. He said it feels exactly like it does right now; in his mind he doesn't experience being any older. Although he suspects that if he was to join the boys for a game of football, his body would quickly remind him that it is now in its 50's! If he looks down at his hands and feet (feigning surprise), he is amazed to see they are not teenage at all.

"I expect you lot have seen some extraordinary changes in your bodies! Now the smart clothes you had a couple of years ago won't fit anymore. Did you ask your body grow? At your age, your bodies are boiling with hormones, changing shape, sprouting hair and making all sorts of new and different messes! Can you stop it?"

The Ajahn looked around the room and collected their attention. Shaking his head, he received many shaken heads and broad grins in reply. "So how on earth can you call it you and yours?" and he laughed. "It won't even do what you want, so how can it be?"

Just then a loud fart clearly penetrated the brief silence.

"You see we only have fairly minimal control over it. It goes on growing, breathing, sweating and smelling regardless!" he laughs again and the students join him.
"Then it grows old, gets sick and dies... guaranteed. Only we can't be sure about old age and sickness for everyone, but death is certain." He smiles and shrugs his shoulders. "You might say we are like temporary crew members of a sinking ship!" The youngsters whispered together for a while as the monk receives a jug of water and a glass from Mrs Hopper who then sits down on the floor with the students.

"Now I expect many of you have the crazy idea that you are what you think!" said the Ajahn pointing at his head, "I mean you associate the thinking process as belonging to you."
"What else?" asked a voice.
"What indeed!" said the monk, "so let's try an experiment... I invite you all to sit quite still for a couple of minutes, close your eyes and stop thinking altogether, just don't do it. No thinking for a couple of minutes please..." He waited for a while.
"So... How is it going? Have you done it? Can you do it at all, completely stop the mind from any kind of thoughts, verbal or imaginary?... No way eh!" the Ajahn chuckled. "So how can this be you and yours? If it was you, you could control it, couldn't you? Ok listen to your own thoughts again for a bit." Some of the youngsters sat transfixed with eyes shut, some fidget about.
"So boring, isn't it!" Now he had a teasing tone to his voice. "Always the same old stuff, isn't it? Nothing really new or interesting is it? Same old stuff going round and round, don't you find?"

Some of the staff begin to laugh amongst themselves and the youngsters pick up on the playful mood.

"Don't you ever get fed up with it? Wish it would change or do something useful like come to a sensible resolution?" he continued. "And still we reckon all this nonsense is me, mine, possessed by me but it's totally out of our control as well, isn't it?"

Several small whispering conversations begin in the large room but most of the attention is focused up at the front.

"Maybe, when the stuff really hits the fan, a whole committee move in to sort it out! All prancing about in the muddled little mind, several different views and opinions, several voices all pitching in and what's more... which one is really you? Any of them? You may think this is crazy but we all know it, don't we? We know we are out of control!" the Ajahn chuckles and looks about the room. "Trust me, you are not what you think! Definitely not!"

After a few affirmative comments from the group and a couple more gentle wind-ups from the Ajahn, the monk suggested an opportunity for the students to stand and stretch their legs for a moment, which they did. Then he invited everyone to sit down again whilst he guided them in a short meditation session. He encouraged an attitude of being the observer of the body, the breath and then the activity of the mind; to notice there is thought and activity and there is also a quality of attention or awareness, which is aware of the activity and yet not party to it. Being the knower of thought but not the thinker. He encouraged them to notice their changeability; that nothing remains static except the knowing of it all. This he suggested did not change.

"Don't believe in what I am saying. Question it. Explore this for yourselves. Maybe you have never looked at the mind in this way?... Notice I call it the mind and not your mind or my mind. The mind. You may find it useful to see it this way. Experiment with it and see... You may well find everything becomes a great deal clearer and naturally more peaceful if you develop this kind of attitude to your own inner world. When the heart and mind are at peace, everything is at peace. Finding real happiness and contentment all starts and ends with the mind, with a wise and clear mind...."

The room remained silent until the electronic bell rang to announce the change of class. It acted beautifully as a closure to the meditation session.

"Fortunately, we have a double period!" said Mr Manthorpe with a broad smile, "so we have plenty of time for questions and discussion. Firstly, I would like to thank Ajahn for opening this very unusual sixth form assembly in such a wonderful way. Now, has anyone have anything they would like to say?"... Nobody moved. "I think you have them stunned," said Mrs Hopper in a quiet and playful tone. "I don't think that by just watching my mind I am ever going to make it calm down very much, there must be something else I can do?" said a girl from the centre of the room.

"Well, yes, you have it! Absolutely!" said the Ajahn who then paused for a moment to consider his reply.

"Yeah, I can't just sit there like this all day!" came another voice.

"I suppose what is most likely going to help us is if we understand what it is that gets the mind so stirred up? Why can't we settle it down? We could ask, 'what is it that winds us all up in the first place?'" asked the Ajahn. "Maybe there is a common cause?"

"Sir!" called a boy in the back of the room.

"Yes, Bobby Collins," prompted Mrs Hopper.

"Isn't this what you Buddhists call dukkha?" said Bobby.

"Dukkha, yes that is it!" said the Ajahn.

"Please explain the meaning of dukkha sir? I have seen so many different translations and uses of the word, I am no longer sure I understand what it is?" said Bobby. "They say something like suffering but of what kind?"

"Any kind really!" smiled the Ajahn.

"Well I don't suffer!" exclaimed a girl.

"Neither do I," came another voice.

"Really?" said the Ajahn. "Well, I would say this means you haven't yet really understood what dukkha means. The RE syllabus does cover the four noble truths, doesn't it?"

"In principal, yes," said Jim.

"The bottom line is what we call taêhä or craving. Wanting to have something you don't have, wanting to be away from something you have and don't want, wanting to be someone you feel you are not, or wanting not to be someone you feel that you are, this kind of thing," said the monk.

"So we shouldn't feel anything or want anything? It sounds really depressing to me!" came another voice and some negative and approving comments followed.

"If you look at it like that, it does!" agreed the monk. "Let's try and look at it in another way?" The Ajahn scanned the faces and tried to connect with these youngsters on their level. Seeing how they are dressed and presented themselves, he continued. "So at 16 or 17 years of age, you are basically for having fun and enjoying yourselves, I guess? Perfectly normal and ok, right? We all agree on this?" said the monk who received clear and positive responses from most of them and some quiet, discursive chatter followed. A girl directly in front of the monks said quietly,

"Don't you fancy me then? Sweet sixteen they say, don't they?"

The monk raised his hands to call attention and Jim called out "quiet please!" in support.

"And where is the best fun and pleasure to be found? Where does the world tell you to go looking? For love, sex and relationships I guess? Pretty popular I imagine?" added the monk, much to the surprise of many, especially Venerable Suñño who looked startled at his friend who was being so bold.

"Ok, very good, but let's really examine this in detail together, shall we?" said the Ajahn looking directly at the young temptress sitting in front of him who blushed.

"How good does it really feel?" he paused again. Everyone was back on board, fully with him. He leaned back and closed his eyes...

"Imagine... Imagine... you win the attention of the partner of your dreams... you enjoy one or two thrills and spills together... and you figure they are yours?... How does it feel?... Now how long is it going to last?... Afraid of losing it?... Yes?" Some giggling came back in response.

"Imagine... Imagine... you see your best friend and your new lover fooling about together at a party, kind of secretive but probably perfectly innocent... How does it feel now?... Maybe a bit jealous?... Perhaps you start to hate your friend?... Mistrust them?... How does it feel now?... You may be completely wrong but can you be so sure?..."

"Imagine... Imagine... the partner of your dreams breaks up with someone else and comes to tell you that you are really the one for them... and you reckon you are!... Oh so happy!..." The Ajahn chortled and it is echoed by the class. "Then your new lover's ex tells you of all the times he or she had cheated on them... How does it feel now?... Are they really going to see their granny this weekend?... How is it now?..."

"Imagine... Imagine you have found the love of your life who says so many beautiful things... totally breaks your heart... then you find a novel in their bag with all the lovely things they said, not their words at all!... So maybe you now wonder what they really feel and think?... what are they really after?!.. Maybe you don't care and want to try it out with as many partners as possible?... Ok... Then what happens when the perfect partner finds out that you've tried it out with everyone else already?..."

"Imagine... Imagine you win the partner of your dreams... you get on really well, no arguments, you trust each other completely, then they have to go away for a while... Oh dear... crying into your pillow at night!" he pretended to wail.

"It hurts when you win, and when you lose... Isn't it more like this?"
"Oh he can really read my mind!" came a cry from a girl at the back. The Ajahn chuckled.
"The Hollywood romance ends when the couple get together, doesn't it?" continued the monk. "But things have the nature to change, don't they? How many of your parents are still looking adoringly at each other over the breakfast table each morning?"
"So messy, confusing and depressing!" said a young voice.
"Well this is dukkha! Do you know what I mean now?" the monk laughs. "Does anyone here not know this one fairly well for themselves by now?" No hands are raised.

"But we can't all become monks, can we?" came another comment.

"Not at all. I'll come back to that in a moment if I may?" said the Ajahn. "So what would you say is the common difficulty in the examples I was giving you to consider?"

"Wanting?" said a boy.

"Not wanting to lose someone. Err, fear of loss?" said another.

"That's it! Attachment," said the monk.

"Buddhists believe we shouldn't be attached, don't they?" added Mrs Hopper.

"Actually this is a very common and complete misunderstanding," said the Ajahn. "I have never seen any reference to the Buddha saying we shouldn't or must not become attached. What he did say on numerous occasions is that attachment leads to suffering."

The Ajahn went on to point out this is not a judgment but an observation. In the same way, we could say if we sit out in the hot sun we will get burnt. The sun will do that. That is its nature. If we don't sit there, it won't. We understand the forces of nature. If we take on a new pet dog or cat, we become wise enough to understand that these creatures, lovely though they are, still don't live so long and eventually we lose them. When we see this, we are not feeling personally betrayed when we do lose them because we knew they were impermanent all the time. Still it hurts us when they die but have you noticed it doesn't hurt half as much if a neighbour's cat gets killed? Why is this? Because you are not so attached to the neighbour's cat as you are to yours.

He repeated again. "This is not a judgement. Not that we shouldn't be attached, just to notice that when you do, you must expect some grief will follow; it is like the bill you have to pay for having got it! It comes with the deal! When we realise that we can't really own anything for ever, we can begin to appreciate all that we have. I suggest one of the reasons we are so hard on each other is because we do expect them to be around for ever, so we begin to abuse them. We say things like 'Oh Dad, he's always like that!' or 'Mum is always going on about it!' But they are not, I can assure you of that."

"Recognising impermanence we see the value of everything much more. We won't take each other for granted anymore and our responses are much more likely to be kind and compassionate. Naturally, we won't have to try to be kind because we won't be able to do anything else. We understand the true nature of things. We look for partners who are interested in developing the same qualities as us. Becoming clear, wise and trustworthy. If you really trust me, then I don't need to worry too much about us because I can already really trust myself. I know where I am at!" Then the Ajahn became silent.

"Relationships with our partners is what most of life is all about," Suñño said gently. "Understanding how to live beautifully and harmoniously together means we just have to understand how to live wisely."

"Common sense I suppose," said a girl.

"This is Dhamma. Yes it is obvious. If it is not obvious, it is not Dhamma!"

praised the Ajahn. "Dhamma is a word sometimes used for 'The Teaching' of the Buddha but more literally, it means 'the way it is' or natural truth."

More questions began to arise from several directions all at once, so the teachers intervened and the session changed shape. The classroom broke up for a while with some youngsters talking to the Ajahn and some to Venerable Suñño who moved to a chair at the back of the hall. The convivial conversations continued until the bell sounded and Mr Manthorpe stood up on the stage.

"Well, I can see that you have all very much enjoyed the session this afternoon. Before we all depart, I'd like to suggest we thank these two monks for coming to see us," said Jim and all the students applaud loudly with cries of "Thank you! Thank you!"
"I would like to give a very personal thank you to you Ajahn who has been helping me through a very difficult period in my life. You have been the best friend I have ever had, only we just met yesterday." Jim was visibly quite emotional and the children were quite captivated and moved by their teacher's openness.
"Please give us some final words Ajahn?" asked Mrs Hopper.
"Yes please," said a girl's voice. "I'm not ready to go home yet anyway."

The older monk stood up next to his friend Jim and took his shoulder.

"Maybe we can begin to let go of our attachments. Not let go of the things but of our blind attachment to them so we understand their true nature. If we see our practice in terms of letting go of stuff, of foolishness and confusion then we will find peace, a natural peace in the mind. We don't have to become monks or nuns to understand this. We don't have to acquire or be anything really but we do need to let go. Our teacher from Thailand, Venerable Ajahn Chah, used to say,

If you let go a little bit... you'll get a little peace
If you let go a lot... you'll get a lot of peace
If you let go completely.... ?
Then you will begin to understand what the Buddha is pointing at!

Wishing you well, we will chant you a blessing."

The Ajahn put his hands together and began to recite verses in Päli. Suñño joined in after a while and the monks chanted together. After the monks had finished their chanting, Mrs Hopper was astonished to see that not a single child rushed out of the door as they have always done in the past. Slowly they filed out.

"How do I become a nun?" a girl asked Suñño.
"When it is time, you will know how. Maybe now you can see more easily what you need to look for, for when you are ready?" said Suñño.
"Yeah... maybe... I reckon," she said.

"I expect that everyone
will eventually leave me...

Therefore I am grateful, happy
and never feel lonely...

Contented."

Expecting The Unexpected

After some time of travelling together the monks' conversations became increasingly single pointed, brief and focused on spiritual practice. It was clear to Suñño that the Ajahn had little time for small talk although with the lay folks he would go along with discussions about the weather, the cost of living or even in debating religious doctrine but only for a little while. He would always try and bring it around to something more immediate and profound as soon as he could. Sometimes he showed interest in the life story of his younger companion. On fewer occasions he would talk a little about his own past, usually in order to illustrate some aspect of Dhamma which he was trying to explain. He would keep reminding his friend that the past is a memory, the future is just a dream, the only place really worthy of full attention being the present moment. As their time together was coming to a close, the elder monk seemed more anxious to be guiding and instructing his friend. He would often use expressions like 'This is the nature of the mind' or sometimes, 'This is the way of the world, the way of Dhamma is different'.

When Suñño was on a high, blissed out on some wonderful insight he thought he had, his teacher often appeared unnervingly cool and unimpressed, replying with a simple long and drawn out "Oh?" Then when Suñño dived into a desperate or even angry state of mind, he would approach the Ajahn with his problem and receive exactly the same long and drawn out 'Oh?' and very little more. Once, one evening after a long and arduous day, the Ajahn said, "Pleasure and pain are both the same really, aren't they? High or low are extremes which can both be deluding and captivate our attention. Noticing feelings from a truly mindful perspective means we know them for what they are, without taking it all personally. In a sense, we give up trying to control and live peacefully with what is." He quoted a famous rhyme which he loved, calling it good old English Nursery Dhamma,

> Whether the weather is cold
> Or whether the weather is hot
> We'll weather the weather whatever the weather
> Whether we like it or not.

More baffling than ever for the young monk, he was stopped in his tracks when the Ajahn said,

"Don't get snared up in trying to be a good monk or trying to be anything at all!"

"So what do you mean Ajahn?" asked Suñño. "You are often telling me how things should be done, like looking after my bowl, robes and so on. You are often correcting my behaviour; about my walking, talking, relating to people and stuff and pointing out all the monks training rules for me. Now you tell me not to try to be a good monk?"

"Trying is just that, very trying!" laughed the Ajahn. "Neither the robes or the rules are going to set you free if you grasp them with ignorance. They can even take you to misery."

"How then?" asked Suñño, "by not trying at all?"

"Ah now you are grasping again! Trying to be someone you think you are not, trying not to be someone you think you are, it's the same thing really," said the Ajahn.

"So what would you say the monk's life is all about?" said Suñño.

"We can be perfect looking Bhikkhus, beautiful in bodily action, beautiful in speech and reckon we are beautiful in our minds and yet continue to be critical and judgmental as ever, which then inevitably leads us to sorrow," said Ajahn.

"Sounds familiar," said Suñño.

"All these rules and observances are to be applied, not to take hold of unwisely and certainly not to be used as weapons with which we beat ourselves or others. You know what I mean?" the Ajahn smiled.

"Maybe."

"Using the form as we have been given it is a pretty testing experience that is clear. Many of these training standards are designed to frustrate the habitual outgoing nature of the mind. Using it wisely, we are simply following the form and continually reflecting or evaluating the effect it has on the mind. I would say the holy life is really about practising humility and renunciation, whilst aiming for liberation. If we use it to become something new then we may be missing the point, don't you think? Attaching to or becoming anything at all will inevitably lead to suffering. Seeing Bhikkhu Suñño as anything more than a conventional truth is going to lead to what?" asked the Ajahn.

"I guess Luang Por named me 'emptiness' for a good reason!" laughed Suñño.

"Wearing the robe properly or keeping your belongings tidy isn't going to liberate the mind from all its misery, that is true. These observances help us to be present with what we are doing. They sustain feelings of gratitude and appreciation for the support we receive and guard the mind from becoming scattered or worried. This leads to inner peace and contentment and a clarity which enables our practice to deepen; the mind then trusts this clear seeing, knowing itself well. So when I forget something, I notice I am becoming distracted and bring the mind back to the present moment, in much the same way we follow the breath in meditation. This way everything becomes a meditation practice," said the Ajahn as he handed his friend his bag. "Which reminds me, I think I've left our toilet roll in the bushes!"

As the elder monk walked back to recover the toilet roll, the young monk stood watching a group of crows in a tree. The penetrating noise of their squawking startled Suñño. It appeared to him that the birds were involved in an argument which had led to a lone member of their group being singled out and punished. This victim was pinned to the spot, in a hollow beneath the great oak tree, whilst all the others swooped down and screamed insults or threats at it. A few moments later, they all suddenly flew off in a violent flurry leaving the poor victim on the ground. Suñño moved over to the fence and peered at the solitary creature which seemed to be looking back at him as if it was looking for sympathy. Then it swooped up and perched for a moment on a branch just a few inches from the young monks face, which made him duck, then the solitary bird disappeared back in the direction of the group.

* * *

A few days before, the monks had come across a couple of young boys hiding out in a church porch smoking cannabis. The Ajahn was very friendly with them, laughing and joking for a while, even telling them a little about his dope smoking past and crazy exploits with hallucinogenic drugs. His art student days.

"I have some friends who had their first insight into altered states of mind under the influence of drugs, which later led them to investigate meditation," said the Ajahn.

The young lad then offered the monk a puff on his joint. The Ajahn leaned forward, very close to the boy, pressing his hand onto the boy's arm until his smouldering joint stubbed itself out on the bench.

"Imagine what it would be like if you had spent many years half starved and lost in an underground labyrinth, locked in with a bunch of madmen who messed you about so much that you just wanted to die. Then someone appears and sets you free, takes you to a beautiful place by a beach with delicious food and lovely company... Would you be persuaded to go back into that hole?" The Ajahn's face was incredibly stern and stared directly into the young lad's eyes who just froze, his jaw dropped, leaving his mouth wide open. The monk held the boy for a few moments in his gaze, then as he began to smile, the young face smiled back.

"The real high comes from being completely awake, stone cold sober and brilliantly clear... and it is absolutely free!" and the Ajahn laughed, turned and walked away without another word. They hadn't gone far before the second, taller boy came running after the monks, full of questions.

"Yeah, I remember," said Suñño. "I used to think that getting stoned was peaceful too, then once I had a taste of a pure mind on a meditation retreat, I just lost interest in getting high with artificial aids. In fact, it didn't feel like being high anymore, really much more like being doped up. Pretty dull actually, like having my mind stuffed with cotton wool, comfy but dark and claustrophobic. I also didn't like the feeling that something else was in control of me anymore."

"So are you in control now? I mean, are you always so happy?" asked the boy and Suñño laughed.

"Being happy is ok if you are still attached to such a thing," replied Suñño, "but being free is much better!"

"Free of what?" asked the boy.

"Free of wanting anything!" smiled Suñño who then stopped walking for a moment and took the boy's shoulder "Free from fighting shadows, free from getting lost while looking for something else to please me, for that hit which can't possibly satisfy me at all; freedom from delusion."

"You seem very happy," added the boy.

"Yup, it happens!" laughed the monk. They looked up the trail to see the Ajahn was waiting for them, sitting on a bench, so they joined him. They talked a little more, not much, just enough to pass on the monastery address and a couple of useful contacts which may help the boy. Just as they were about to move off, they saw the other boy approaching.

"I'll bring Dogs to the monastery with me," said the boy.

"Dogs?" enquired the Ajahn.

"That's what we call him, Dog's Breath. It's a nick name, it kind of stuck," replied the boy. They waited for Dogs to come closer but he kept his distance. "He is pretty shy," continued the boy. "His dad beats him up and his mum is half mad, yet he's great once you get to know him. He's really deep man, brainy, writes cool poems and plays a mean guitar!"

"So what's your nickname?" asked the monk.

"Dad," said the boy.

"Why Dad?" asked the Ajahn.

"Because it is usually only me who keeps his head when all the others are freaking out on a bad trip or something!" said the boy who ran off to join Dogs who remained motionless fifty yards away. A few moments later, the two long-haired boys turned around and walked away, deep in conversation.

Later in the afternoon, the monks encountered a gang of bikers. First they saw only one on a large black classic bike with stretched forks and long handlebars. The rider, dressed in black leather, slowed down as he passed, waved at the Ajahn then sped away. Then a few miles further down the road, a group of about six bikes, some with two riders, came roaring up behind them. It was a quiet country lane with no surrounding houses. Suñño tried to pretend he was cool and confident as the black leather brigade surrounded them but inside he was shaking with fear. The bikers all switched off their engines and one tall thin man riding pillion dismounted from behind an enormous figure with an eagle design made of studs on his back. The tall fellow struggled with his helmet for a moment then, much to Suñño's relief, out popped Dad.

*"In some areas [in Thailand], he was served silk worms, basically a blue
maggot curry, or grilled locusts..."*

Both aware that the evening was drawing in ... they were beginning to fly.

*The Ajahn took a seat on a wall and
invited the students to sit on the lawn in front.*

*The young monk lifted a front leg of the magical creature with his finger tip
and he actually shakes hands with the dragon.*

*Slowly the other helmets revealed an assortment of hairy grins
and respectful nods.*

"Hi!" said Dad then pointing at the big guy with the eagle. "This is my brother Menace, that's Moggs, that's Wedge and the girl over there is my sister Smudge." He pointed to the other side, "Cheech and Chong, Jaws and the Spotlight Kid."

Slowly the other helmets revealed an assortment of hairy grins and respectful nods.

"I just want to ask you something?" said Dad.
"Ask away," said the Ajahn.
"Are you the head monk at your place?"
"No, I am not the Abbot," said the Ajahn.
"Oh... Do you have to pass any exams to be a monk at your place? I mean can anyone join?" asked Dad.
"Well right now, we have the usual mixed bunch I guess," said the Ajahn. "Let me see... we have two college dropouts, a waiter, a builder, an electrician, a doctor, a philosophy lecturer, two school teachers, a painter and artist, a drummer from a punk band, a millionaire's son, a nurse, a lawyer and a computer programmer."
"And an army officer and a beach bum!" added Suñño.
"And they come from all over the world," added the Ajahn. "Having the right attitude is really all it takes, a great intelligence is not really necessary, which is a good thing for me at least!" and he laughed.

Resounding laughter and appreciative smiles were shared all around. Nothing else was said, helmets were pulled on, fastened, engines kick started, a loud roar and they were all gone.

* * *

"I like surprises!" said the Ajahn as they settled down for the night in the garage of an old vicarage, "especially when they prove me wrong."

He told a story of a previous tudong a few years ago when he was walking in a similar area close to where he had spent his youth.

"I was walking past a field of strawberries whilst the farmer and his crew were hard at work picking their harvest. I had lasting memories of strawberry picking over thirty years before when I was a schoolboy. A backbreaking job if you stand up all day and bend double or you end up crawling about with painful knees on stones and squashed strawberries, always in hot sun with wasps buzzing around and threatening to sting you. I recalled the old farm ladies who seemed to simply hinge in the middle and filled their trays with amazing speed. But I always struggled in pain and made very little money. The farmer regularly scrutinised his produce and criticised me for damaging the fruits. For many years after that summer, I could not even smell a strawberry without feeling sick. I resented the farmer for being mean and stingy and hated the workers for poking fun at me. Many of these memories naturally came to mind as I walked along the hedge and fence which separated the field from the road. I remember that as I passed the gate, I stopped for a second and watched the farmer loading trays of fruit onto a tractor trailer. There were a number of young people working there although, unlike in my days, none of them seemed to be speaking English. 'Typical,' I recall thinking to myself, 'using cheap labour from abroad,'" the Ajahn said smiling. "I continued to walk past when my attention was caught by a voice which called out 'Please wait!' So I stopped and turned round. A gentleman wearing a tweed jacket with patched elbows, cuffs and a flat cap was waving to me. It was obviously the farmer, so I was expecting to receive some abuse from him and prepared myself in readiness. The farmer continued to shout at his workers so I turned again and moved on." The Ajahn continued, enjoying telling his tale.

"'No please wait!' came the cry again from the farmer. So I stood still, waited and very slowly this time, I turned round. To my amazement the next thing I noticed was the farmer was standing right by me with a small tray of strawberries held in his outstretched hand.

'Would you like these?' he said to me, a little out of breath.
'You want to give them to me?' I replied, obviously pretty stunned.
'Yes, if that's ok,' replied the farmer.

This put me in a slightly embarrassing position. As you know our training rule prevented me from receiving food in the afternoon, meaning if I did accept them I am falling into an offence which I would have to confess to another monk later. I was considering taking the strawberries and accepting the rap, purely for the benefit of the farmer, whose generosity certainly needed acknowledging. Instead I tried something else first."

The Ajahn changed his voice a little explaining that he said to the farmer, something like this,

"'Well, I am both surprised and very touched that you would choose to give them to me. Only as you can see I have no way of carrying them without making a terrible mess and I am not up to eating a tray of strawberries at this time but bless you for the lovely offer and I hope you will not feel offended if I do not accept them right now,' I said. Well, the blessing appeared to work well enough because the farmer smiled and even gave me a little bow!"

The Ajahn changed his voice again,

"'No, not offended at all, thank you,' said the farmer. Which proved my point. His offering was well received after all. As he returned to the gate my curiosity overcame me and I called after him. 'Excuse me,' I said, 'I do hope you will understand me asking, but what was it that gave you the idea to offer me the strawberries?' The farmer looked a little uncomfortable for a few seconds then looked up and smiled and said, 'Well, first I saw your friend walking by, an unusual looking fellow but I liked his style!' You see at that time, I was the junior monk, trailing behind my elder. The farmer continued, 'Then when you came by looking so tired and weary, I felt it was just something I had to do. Are you monks or something?' 'Yes, Buddhist monks,' I replied. 'Well, it was very nice to meet you,' replied the farmer and he walked away with a lively, almost dance like stride. 'Have a nice day!'"

The Ajahn said that he had never imagined such a thing could ever happen. It seems that the sign of the mendicant monk, although very rare in present day Britain, still has its natural place. An ageless and culture-free symbol, an ancient tradition which brings an instinctive response, in the same way that an animal might instinctively take care of another's abandoned young. Or conversely, the way a child is naturally fearful or respectful of a snake, even if they have never seen one before. This monk was certainly not misunderstood. He was recognised as a goodness magnet in ways he didn't expect.

"Another perception bites the dust!"
"What a relief."
"What a load of old bollocks!" came a voice from behind a pile of junk in the back of the garage.

Suñño jumped up, amazed to see a small boy emerging from a hideout in a packing crate.

"If you believe in all that, you're as mad as you both look!" he said as he climbed over the monks and opened the door to the back of the vicarage kitchen.
"James? Now don't you go bothering those nice monks," came the voice of his mother.
"Bollocks," said James.

"Have you noticed that the trees
in the forest grow twisted.
They need to bend
as they compete for the light.

Whereas trees which grow in an open space
are grand, balanced, magnificent."

A Secret Hell

The ancient Pilgrim's Way seemed a reasonable path to follow and the cathedral was to be the end of their pilgrimage. At times the route wandered, as it does, but the monks had often maintained that their goal was to reach this enormous medieval cathedral, built from the time when the earliest Christian missionaries came and established the church in England. Suñño had visited one or two old churches in London on his way to the monastery but this place was especially awesome for a young man from LA, California. There was a brief history printed out on a notice board by the entrance which said that the building began in 597 AD when Saint Augustine came to England on instructions of Pope Gregory in Rome to convert the pagan Saxon people to Christianity. It said that the Pope was struck by the beauty of the Anglo slaves he saw in Rome and decided to exploit them. The building is gigantic even by today's standards and still towers above the city after hundreds of years. Built with extraordinary skill and refinement, it stands as a great edifice demonstrating the power and wealth of a religion which dominated the country for a long time. The monks wandered about for a while with the young American asking his English friend all sorts of questions about English history, most of which seemed to agitate the Ajahn.

"I came here many years ago," said the elder monk. "I was working on an exhibition in the crypt. It was just after I left art college. I remember I loved the silence here. I do remember researching some history which you don't read about in the guide book. Come I'll show you."

They walked over to the ancient 15th century tomb of a former king of England. The Ajahn explained that this king was a warrior knight who led many battles in Europe. He deposed the previous king who was a cousin and childhood playmate, locked him up and starved him to death. He lived in a very violent time, suppressing rebellions and ordering soldiers to destroy many places in his own country too. He was also famous for being a guardian of the faith and the first English king to allow the burning of heretics. He died from a nasty skin disease, probably leprosy or syphilis or both.

"Some extra trophies he brought from his crusades in the far east I guess," added the Ajahn with a smirk, "such is the karma of a warrior king!"
"I guess in those days they would have been barbecuing Buddhists," added Suñño.
"If you were lucky!" smiled the Ajahn. "Maybe you'd be tortured first. Yup, it was conversion by the sword, then extortion by the priests."
"You seem to have some pretty negative impressions of the church Ajahn," said Suñño. "I notice you are keen to point them out to me."
"Yes, I'm afraid you are right," replied the Ajahn. "It is a bad habit and I must be careful that it doesn't turn sour."

They moved to the centre isle under the majestic and towering arched roof and sat together for a while in silence as people milled around. Echoing footsteps, whispers and broken or distorted conversation reverberated through the air. Many different languages and visitors of all ages shuffled like tiny insects in an empty tomb. Suñño was still aware that a disproportionate amount of attention was aimed their way. He was feeling like a tourist attraction again. Next to him sat the Ajahn, bolt upright with his eyes closed, his facial expression quite empty, meditating. The young monk moved forward one row of seats and sat slightly to the side of his friend, giving him more space.

A raised section of the cathedral in front of them came to life as a group of schoolboys in uniform entered, barely visible from that distance, climbing some steps to the side. A few minutes later an organ began to play. Instantaneously the young monk felt goose pimples all over his body as the choir began to sing. They both sat motionless.

"Quite something eh?" said the Ajahn when the music finished.
"I liked it, amazing acoustics in this place," added Suñño.
"Yes, me too," said the Ajahn. "That's what Christians do best, music, architecture and nothing much else... Oh dear here I go again. I don't really mean to keep criticising but I do wrestle with my feelings about it."
"How Ajahn? What do you mean?" asked the young monk.
"It probably goes back to my school days. My studies of church history used to give me nightmares," said the Ajahn. "My classmates used to love all the gory details but they quite spooked me."
"Even now?"
"Maybe I witnessed a witch hunt in a previous life or maybe I have been executed numerous times before. Who knows? But for some reason, I am often haunted by violent images if I stay in a place like this for very long - they often come up. This building is probably one of the biggest, if not the biggest, single room space I have ever been in and yet after a while it feels incredibly stuffy and claustrophobic and I feel a strong need to escape," the Ajahn sighed.
"So why do you keep coming into these places? We are always stopping in churches on this trip. I notice you are very quiet inside but I didn't realise you were so adverse to it," said Suñño.
"Well, I am not really adverse, you see. I don't trust these feelings and memories either," said the Ajahn. "There comes a point when I need to investigate these ghosts in the mind, so that I can be free of them. You know I have some very good Christian associates. You've met brother Herbert! We also had a Benedictine monk friend who regularly used to visit and stay with us in Hartwood. His beautiful presence and loving care and attention really touched me. He helped me a lot when I was a new monk. I regret missing his funeral. We used to discuss some of the great Christian mystics like Meister Eckhart and Saint John of the cross, real contemplatives who lived a beautiful life. Father Peter used to say that some of his Christian brothers found union with God despite the church. Bless him! If he was alive in the 14th Century, he would certainly have been silenced!"
"Greetings and welcome brothers!" came a voice from behind as a grand, robed

figure of a man approached the Ajahn. The priest exchanged pleasantries with the monks for a few minutes, which provided an interesting inter-faith photographic study for a couple of passers-by and for which Suñño turned his back.

The previous day, at a tea and cake stall in a small village church, two sweet ladies were enthusiastically offering advice for the monks' day in the old city. Abbey ruins, museums, gates and gardens were among the special attractions available. However, once the monks had walked into the city, finished their Alms Round and taken a customary rest for an hour or so in the park, there was little time or inclination for either of them to explore very much. Their guides had suggested, on at least a couple of occasions, that they would be welcome to approach a Franciscan monastery for accommodation in the old city.

That evening, standing in the cathedral, the Ajahn again received directions to the Franciscan place nearby. As it was getting late, they decided to give it a try. As was often the case, the place was not so central after all and the monks arrived very tired. It was another modern complex with flat roofed buildings made mostly of brick, paved in brick and walls in brick, with a neat garden at the entrance. 'There was a quiet and peaceful atmosphere' thought Suñño and, to complete the picture, there was a robed monk sitting on a bench in the front garden, hunched over with elbows on his knees, his dark brown hood obscuring his face. The Ajahn approached the Friar, crouching down low so to see his face, he gently introduced himself, then moved to sit next to him on the bench. The Friar looked up and walked off with barely a word. The Ajahn re-joined his friend.

"Doesn't look good," said the Ajahn. "I thought these people were famous for their kindness and hospitality."
"Maybe they don't like us heathen, non-believers," added Suñño. "Let's walk on out of town; we still have some daylight."

They spread their well used and faded map on a wall by a flowerbed and studied it for a while until a large and energetic Friar with a strong Irish accent came to greet them. It was immediately clear that this was the senior incumbent in the place. He ordered another brother about as he approached and then offered an open hand, saying,

"Welcome! How can we help you?"

The Ajahn came straight to the point explaining that they are Buddhist monks from a monastery in West Sussex, on a walking pilgrimage and they were looking for some shelter for one night.

"Look, there is a guest house opposite," said the Friar. "They usually have space at this time, and they are very reasonable."
"I see," said the Ajahn. "We are very limited for choice because we don't have money, we don't handle money."
"Don't have money? So how did you get here?" asked the Friar.

"We walked," said the monk.

"Walked! From West Sussex! Extraordinary!" exclaimed the Friar. "How long did it take you?"

"Two weeks."

"How did you survive?" asked the Friar.

"By going for alms in the towns, sleeping rough sometimes, invited into homes sometimes, that kind of thing," said Suñño.

"Why... splendid!" cried the Friar. "Look, of course you can stay here, though I am not sure we have any rooms free. Please... I invite you to stay here with us."

"Anything will do," said the Ajahn, "a store room or garage is ok." The Friar disappeared for a few minutes while the monks put away their map and sat on the bench in anticipation.

"We are in luck!" cried the Friar on his return. "Two of our brothers are away for a few days so I can offer you their rooms for the night. I hope you don't mind if they are not quite prepared, with other personal stuff and all?"

"Not at all," said the Ajahn. "I trust the occupiers won't mind us sharing their space in their absence."

"No, no I'll deal with that!" cried the Friar. "Look perhaps you'd like to change your clothes and join us for supper?"

"Well, we don't have any other clothes," said the Ajahn picking up his bag.

"Is that all you have?" asked the Friar. "Extraordinary! Oh you must stay."

"And I am afraid that we don't take food after noon," added the Ajahn.

"You don't eat after noon?"

"Only between dawn and noon."

"Extraordinary!" gasped the Friar. "Well look, you really must stay with us and have some breakfast in the morning."

They entered the building and made their way through corridors to find their rooms as others went in search of keys.

"Look, perhaps you would like to join us after supper, in the lounge. Do you like to watch the telly?" asked the Friar.

"I am happy to talk but I can do without the TV," said Suñño.

"You don't watch telly?" said the Friar, shaking his head and looking at the other Buddhist monk who shook his head in reply. "Oh you must meet the others though. Maybe we could just talk? I'll have to see."

They arrived at their rooms. Another fellow joined them with keys and unlocked the doors. The Ajahn was shown into the first door, Suñño into the next.

"Adjoining rooms!" said the Friar. "Now, I do hope you can join us later."

He led Suñño into a small room with a large bed, cupboards, a desk and chair, a washbasin with a large mirror and a window looking out into the garden. Every surface including the windowsill was cluttered with the personal belongings of a stranger which was beginning to make the visiting Buddhist feel a little uncomfortable.

"Oh what a mess!" said the Friar. "I am sorry I'll have to have a word.. Oh dear.. Look oh dear!" The bed was grimy, the pillow greasy and the duvet cover was spattered with semen stains. "Oh disgrace! Shame. Shame. I'll change the bedding for you."

"No need, I'll sleep on the floor," said Suñño.

"Look, no I'll change it! This is awful."

"Really, we always sleep on the floor," added Suñño. "Besides I don't want to embarrass the poor fellow anymore. Please leave it."

The Friar left Suñño alone in the room having explained where he can take a shower saying he would be back with a clean towel. The dank and stuffy atmosphere in the room engulfed Suñño giving rise to a mild panic which he tried to alleviate by opening the window. To do this, he had to move several objects from the windowsill before he could reach the catch. Leaning over the desk, he was careful not to knock over bottles, cups and glasses. He took off his robe, which tends to snag on things, but could not see any place that he felt suitable to lay it down. Folding his robe neatly, he balanced it on his bag which stood on the grubby carpet. There were enormous robes on wire hangers, hooked on the cupboard door which was slightly ajar, various articles of clothing spilling out of the crack. 'This poor fellow must be massive' thought Suñño. Piled to one side of the desk were various catalogues of priestly apparel, the top copy was open on a page displaying gowns with gold trim and fine embroidery. Among empty biscuit and cake wrappers, a vast range of hair products covered the desk and sink; shampoos, creams, sprays, two combs and a hair dryer which was plugged into the socket. Then scattered about were bottles of aftershave of various brands leaving a pungent aroma that made Suñño feel nauseous. The clean towel arrived and the dusty young monk went straight to the bathroom. He met the Ajahn on the way who ushered him to take his shower first.

Suñño returned to the room and to the sound of a vacuum cleaner. As he entered, he met the Friar who was madly wielding a 'T' shaped object on a hose. Still apologising, he made a quick exit. The bed had been stripped to the mattress, the empty wrappers, dirty cups and glasses had disappeared, the cupboard door was closed and most of the perfumed paraphernalia had gone. On the floor lay a small white rug, just the right size to lie on, and a new looking blanket was placed, neatly folded, on the chair. Feeling refreshed, Suñño took the blanket, placed it on one end of the rug as a pillow and stretched himself out on the floor to take a few moments rest. Then the other secrets were exposed. Wedged in every conceivable space, previously concealed from above, he spotted the colourful packaging of biscuit packets, soup packets, chocolate bars, cakes and potato crisps; all poking out from under the mattress, the sink, the desk drawer, even under the chair. Then against the wall, right at the back of the bed, sticking out from a suitcase were several bottles of spirit and a plastic bag with something mouldy spewing out onto the floor. The young monk closed his eyes and sat bolt upright holding his breath for a moment, trying to erase the vision from his mind. He was consumed with visions which brought him feelings of deep despair, imagining what it might be like living with a mind which could become so obsessed as the man who lived in that room. Secretive, passionate and lost in sensual desires, frustrated, confused and obviously miserable. The young monk crossed his legs and sat motionless, pulling his robe around him.

Back at the monastery, his teacher used to encourage everyone to leave their living space in such a way that anyone could move in at anytime; their rooms were not locked and every space was shared. This discipline with its strict attention to detail, although sometimes perfunctory, certainly supported one important thing thought Suñño; peace of mind and freedom from remorse. He realised that if he suddenly died or could not return to his home base, there would be no hidden secrets to haunt him. During his student days, there were hidden girly magazines, drugs and maybe books pinched from school which used to weigh him down with fear, guilt, shame or remorse, although he liked to pretend they didn't. Now he could really taste the difference for himself and he felt a profound contentment. Reflecting further, his mind became blissful and bright. He knew the blessings of a pure life.

Strangely enough, he felt very grateful to the grubby monk whose privacy he had inadvertently invaded. This experience had clearly demonstrated the life Suñño had chosen penetrated deeper than he realised. For a few minutes, the young Buddhist tried to share the merit of his discovery with his Christian brother, wishing him well. Hoping that this discovery may support a deeper realisation into his private world and a more fruitful movement towards an inner understanding, bringing him further peace and contentment in his practice too. Wishing indeed, that this lesson did not reinforce the evidential poor self-image he burdened himself with and lead to further pain and suffering for his Christian friend whoever he was.

Suddenly, there was a knock on the door. For an instant Suñño wished he wasn't there, fearing the resident had returned. Then he heard the voice of the Ajahn. He stood up and went to greet him. The passage was deserted. Suñño went to the Ajahn's room next door and found the door open so he knocked gently and entered. The elder monk had just returned from his shower, his room was clean and tidy, completely bare except for a shelf full of books and the Ajahn's things which were neatly laid out on the bed.

"The Abbot wants us to meet with the brethren. Are you up to it?" asked the Ajahn.
"Sure," replied Suñño.
"What's all the fuss over your room?" asked the Ajahn.
"Rather embarrassing actually..." said Suñño. Just then there was a knock on the door and the Abbot's bright face peered in.
"Do you drink?" he said.
"Some tea or fruit juice would be fine, thank you," answered the Ajahn.
"You don't drink," said the Abbot in a flat tone then he paused. "Look... I'd really appreciate it if you would come and meet with the brothers here. We have finished our supper and we won't turn on the telly, maybe you'd find it interesting to chat a bit over coffee? I am sure they will appreciate it."

"I'd be happy to," replied the Ajahn. The Bhikkhus put on their robes and they were led to a dark common room with sofas and low tables. The Abbot ushered them in and introduced them in his lovely rich Irish accent, his voice lively and playful.

"Look... these are Buddhist monks. They have walked here all the way from West Sussex, a very long way. They don't touch money, they don't wear lay clothes, they fast every afternoon and night, they don't watch telly, they meditate... and they don't drink. You should listen to these guys, you could learn something from them!"

The Ajahn introduced himself and his American friend to a silent group of about six gentlemen who lounged before them, most wearing lay clothes and all looking rather heavy. Throughout the evening, Suñño barely noticed the grey figures as they melted into the soft blue furnishings, the entire space being dominated by a slender African brother who appeared from the kitchen bearing refreshments. This dark and quietly spoken priest had a brightness and energy which glowed. He joined the two visitors at a low table, offered the tea and engaged them in stimulating conversation for an hour or so as a mostly silent audience observed from the gloom just a few metres away.

Some brief discussion about their monastic discipline revealed the Franciscan friars used to follow very similar observances of alms mendicancy and renunciation. However, they had decided to abandon many of their rules as they were seen as not applicable or suitable for today's modern society. They would only now wear the robe in the monastery, feeling they are 'more effective in spreading the word' if they live closer to the world. So it is easy for them to wander into the town at night or engage in a more social life. The church is quite wealthy so despite the ideal of living modestly, most of them 'do rather well' as the African brother pointed out.

"It looks as if we might have acted a little rashly in our modifications of monastic life," mumbled one of the friars.

"Thrown the baby out with the bath water," smiled the Ajahn for which he received a few dismissive huffs from the distant onlookers as one of them stood up and walked away.

Their lively Christian brother told some interesting stories of his own. He had survived two attempts of assassination at his place in Africa, one from a nine year old girl who pulled a gun and shot him in the stomach; she had been bribed with a television set to kill the priest. He seemed proud to be 'living in the front line' and enjoyed meeting the challenges.

"Why would they want to kill you?" asked the Ajahn.

They talked around the subject of violence in that part of the world but the question remained unanswered. The Buddhists looked blankly at their hosts when questions about believing in God arose or in discussions concerning spreading 'the word' or about missionary work. It was as if they were talking in different languages. They seemed to be getting nowhere. Suñño was beginning to feel very uncomfortable and wished they had never come to stay there.

"So what do you believe in?" came a voice. There followed a long pause which rattled some of the onlookers who seemed inpatient for an answer. Suñño daren't say a word as the replies had been coming thick and fast, his mind disturbed by the pushy atmosphere he was perceiving.

"I believe in a peaceful coexistence within the world around me, in awakening to this peace, and in supporting it in my fellow brothers and sisters," said the Ajahn finally.

"Do you believe that Buddhism is the only way?" asked the voice.

"I really don't know," replied the Ajahn. "I can only speak from my own experience... it seems to work pretty well for me, so far!"

"So you have doubts?" said the African.

"Sure! I sometimes doubt if many people are really going to be able to understand what the teaching is all about," smiled the Ajahn. "I think that few really do!"

"Do you think everyone will become Buddhist?" asked the voice.

"I doubt it, and even if they say they'd become Buddhists, I doubt if many would really understand it!" the Ajahn laughed. "Few practice it anyway!"

"That's the same for any religion, I suppose," smiled the African with a chuckle.

"Even the Lord Buddha himself doubted if he would be able to get his message across at first," said the Ajahn. "He understood that the realisation of truth was difficult to see, very subtle and complicated to explain, so he wondered at first if he could find anyone capable of getting it. Then the story goes, that another being could see the question arising in the master's mind. He begged the Buddha to try, saying that there are people in the world with just a little dust in their eyes, pleading with him to teach for the benefit of them. So he first taught some old friends with whom he'd been practising for some time and they understood the point! So he gained confidence and it kind of snowballed from there but he didn't seem to be out to win everyone over, only those he thought would understand. He'd try to help anyone who asked. However, he wasn't always successful. At least that is what our scriptures say."

"He did not want to try to save everyone?" said another voice.

"Maybe he was wise enough to see his limitations," smiled the Ajahn. "He taught for 45 years, in which time he formulated a teaching. He set up a monastic community and a discipline which would continue to support people after his death and it is still going more than 2,500 years later."

The Ajahn went on to explain something which he said was important for them to understand. The purpose of a Buddhist monk's life and training is essentially for the realisation of liberation, for enlightenment. They are not ordained as priests but are contemplative monks who practice a strict path based on purification, simplicity, renunciation and meditation. The monastery acts like a school or place of learning where people can live within a precise discipline and receive support from a lay community who then gather benefit from their learning and example. Most Buddhists are not monks or nuns, not many take on the training and it is rare that anyone takes on the monastic life for very long. They do not take life vows. Some of them may take up some teaching if they want to but it is not expected.

"We are certainly not priests," said the Ajahn. "In fact, we are not allowed to preach without being invited." Then he laughed. "You had to indicate that you were interested in what I may have to say first! So I thank you very much for inviting us to come and meet with you tonight and I must ask you to forgive me if I have said anything or done anything by body speech or mind which may have offended you; it was certainly not my intention." He put his palms together in salute.

"Oh not at all!" came an Irish voice from the back of the room. "Look, I think we have learned a lot this evening. I thank you for your time and patience. I am sure you must be very tired and would like to rest now."

The Ajahn wondered if the Abbot was very quietly seated there all evening. He had not noticed him at all. The dark and shadowy characters in the armchairs seemed to have thinned out. Only two were left and they too slipped away quickly as the Abbot turned the main lights to bright.

"We have an early morning prayer service at 7:00," said the Abbot, "but you are welcome to join us for breakfast later."
"Yes, I will prepare it myself," said the African, "in here at about 8:00?"
"Fine, thank you," replied the Ajahn.

As they departed for their rooms, the Abbot explained that their group that evening had consisted mainly of brothers from various places; some from abroad who have been struggling with their practice and had come there to receive support. He asked the Buddhist monks to forgive their rudeness but they had not really understood how to receive them.

"God bless you for coming," came a gentle Irish sigh and a warm shoulder hug as the Ajahn reached his room. After a few minutes the Ajahn went to knock on Venerable Suñño's door.

"I fancy going to join them for their prayer thing at 7:00," he said.
"Ok I'll join you," replied Suñño.

* * *

The young monk woke at 4:00 am as usual. Before retiring, he had carefully carried the mouldy sludge found under the bed to the toilet, flushed it away and mopped up the puddle on the floor with toilet paper. In the morning, the smell still lingered so the monk sat up on the bed for his meditation, opening the window wide. An enchanting morning chorus rang out and brightened his mood immediately. One little bird continued on and on with a simple little song which

Suñño's playful mind interpreted as saying 'keep going, keep going'. Memories of the previous evening occasionally flowed through his thoughts, uncertain whether their hosts were really as hostile as they sometimes appeared to be. Their Order were famous for their hospitality but he couldn't help feeling the Abbot had felt obliged to help and then felt resentful, certainly embarrassed at the state of this room. And why would someone vomit into a plastic bag then stash it under the bed before leaving? There was a sink in the room. He must have been in a hurry, certainly distressed and where was he now? Slowly, the young monk's attention rested on the gentle flow of his breathing, seeking peace and clarity, then a different kind of energy flowed through his upright body and everything fell perfectly into place. This present still place where just the breath would 'keep going'.

A gentle tap on the door alerted Suñño who stood up and put on his robe as if it was done in a single movement with perfect co-ordination and mindfulness. He seemed to arrive at the Ajahn's room in a split second.

"Good, let's go!" said the elder monk as they swiftly headed barefoot to the chapel.
"No shoes?" said a figure at the door of the chapel. The monks both looked down as if they were surprised themselves. In their own monastery they would never wear shoes inside.
"Is it all right," asked the Ajahn, "to enter barefoot?"
"Of course," came the reply from a puzzled looking friar in a long dark habit and sandals. "Please come in. You are welcome."

The Ajahn and Venerable Suñño sat quietly at the back and observed it all silently. The African friar was the last to come in and almost jumped for joy when he saw the Buddhists sitting in the back row. With lots of enthusiastic smiles and nods, he took the chair next to Suñño. The service lasted only a few minutes. The congregation stood in front of their chairs for much of the time reciting and chanting texts from books held in their hands. They sat in prayer or meditation for a short while, many of them with heads bowed. The ceremony seemed to come to an abrupt end when everyone stood up and turned towards the door at the back, thereby facing the two visiting monks who remained seated.

"Please wait a moment," whispered their African friend. Suñño almost held his breath for a few seconds as he became aware that they were all looking directly at him. He wanted to look away but resisted the urge and held them in a kind of loving embrace, just for an instant, then the picture broke up and everyone began to move away.

"We have our own breakfast arrangements this morning. Sorry you will not be able to join us. Please come to the refectory and I will serve you," said the African. As they moved out to the passage, one of the brothers who he had barely noticed before, walked up to Suñño bowed a little and took both of his hands.
"God bless you Brother," he said. "And thank you." He then turned and moved away. Suddenly, some animated expressions from smiling faces met the young monk as heads turned round to share an intimate moment of brotherhood before they also walked away.

After breakfast the Ajahn and Suñño returned to their rooms, packed their bags and prepared for their departure seeing nobody else about. As they stepped out of the entrance into the tidy courtyard garden which had greeted them the evening before, they noticed the same friar sitting on the same bench. He stood up and approached the departing visitors.

"It is a shame you have to go," he said, looking at the ground.

Then the lively Irish Abbot came bowling out of a side door. "Look, are you sure you can't stay a bit longer? I can offer you a different room if you like?"
"It is very kind of you. I truly appreciate your offer and I think we have both enjoyed your company," replied the Ajahn looking at Suñño who nodded in agreement. "But we must be making our way back to our monastery now. Hopefully, we can hitch a lift or two or I will be in trouble!" As they hauled their bags onto their shoulders, some other friars came out to see them off with smiles and words of appreciation.

"Tell me, why do you do this?" asked an elderly fellow, looking at Suñño's damaged feet. "I mean it is terribly hard isn't it?" The monk waited for a reply.
"I do it as a test of faith," said the Ajahn. "Not my faith in Buddhism or my faith in the monastic form but to test my faith in the innate goodness of human nature." He smiled. "The fact that we have been able to walk some 200 miles with nothing but a robe and an alms bowl just goes to show there are many beautiful people in this part of the world who will support us, even when they don't understand what we do or who we are."

"Praise be to God," said the old man. "May you find the enlightenment you seek, dear Brother."

"May your God go with you," said the Ajahn. Everyone standing in the garden gave little bows of their heads, smiled at each other and then went their separate ways.

"It must be a hard act to follow," said the Ajahn, as the cathedral came back into view. "I mean, I think their role models, the first saints, died in the struggle to spread the word. Their basic practice seemed to be martyrdom, to die for the cause, so once they had won the people over, what was there left to do? Just beat themselves up for being miserable sinners?"

"Original sin, yes, what a downer," said Suñño. "The whole world takes on a completely different shape when we begin with original blessing."

"Thank goodness!"

"I think that Saint Francis was different though wasn't he? Famous for being gentle, especially with animals," said Suñño.

"Yes, maybe I should look him up again sometime. I liked those friars' humility and gentleness. I don't understand their practice of prayer though. I am sure they'd be happier if they knew how to find peace and contentment from studying their own hearts and minds."

"Yes, I couldn't make out what they were reading this morning," said Suñño. They walked back to the garden by the cathedral and rested for a moment.

"What was all that chaos about in your room last night?" asked the Ajahn.

"Well... I think I'd like to keep that between a certain unknown friar, the Abbot and myself," said Suñño.

"Fair enough," said the Ajahn. "That Irishman told me he thought you were wonderful in the way you handled the situation, whatever it was. He said you had shown him a lot!"

"He did?"

"He did. He said you were an excellent teacher," said the Ajahn, "and an outstanding monk."

"Really? I hardly said a word."

"Not like me then, eh?" said the Ajahn with a grin.

Beautiful Prisoners

Their return journey was taking shape. The Ajahn had been talking on the telephone that morning and a meeting place had been set. Venerable Suñño deliberately tuned out of any conversations concerned with going back to the monastery. He was considering himself a real tudong monk by now and wished it would continue. Trusting in uncertainty and feeling relaxed within chaos was becoming much more natural for the young monk.

"I get a real buzz out of not knowing where we are going, not knowing what day it is or any idea where we will sleep or even if we will eat anything. The days all seem to blur together. Time and place take on a completely different meaning," he explained to a young boy who was watching closely as the monk packed away his things. The boy was quite mesmerised, studying the magnificent figure of a real monk who happened to be spending the night in his bedroom. Last night the boy was certain it was just a dream but this morning it was never more true and real.

"Do you have TV?" asked the boy, who was wearing bright blue pyjamas. He was slowly growing more confident and sat bolt upright on his bed. The monk was kneeling on the floor.

"Nope. Nor radio either," said Suñño.

"You didn't sleep on my bed," adds the boy. "Why not?"

"Monks don't sleep on beds."

"So I won't sleep on beds anymore either," said the boy in a very definite tone.

"Would you like to be a monk too?"

"Maybe..." There followed a long pause. "Do you play football?"

"Nope. No games," said Suñño.

"It sounds very boring... girls, any girls?"

"No girls," grinned Suñño. The boy began to smile and nodded in approval.

"Don't you like girls?" enquired the monk.

"Some. Mostly they're silly and don't play fair!" replied the boy and immediately received a jolly chuckle from the monk.

"It'll change, things do," added Suñño as if talking to himself. He took up two small books and placed them in the middle of a square of cloth, then began to fold the cloth around the books. Taking a long cord, which was sewn onto one corner of the cloth, he bound the parcel tight.

"What's that for," asked the boy.

"They're my books," said the monk. "I keep them safe like this."

"What's in the books? Can I see?"

"Ok," said Suñño and unwrapped the bundle. "One is a chanting book. They are all texts I am trying to learn. The other is a notebook."

"Please show me!" asks the boy. He took the first book with surprising reverence thought Suñño. Opening it at the first page then slowly turning a few more leaves, looking very studious. "It's not English is it?... Well some bits are, what does it

145

all mean?"

The monk explained, "They are ancient Buddhist texts, special verses in the Päli language."

"Wow! What about the other one?" asks the boy again. A careful exchange of books took place. Suñño was impressed at the poise and gentleness of the boy. His room was very tidy with lots of toys and some pictures of football heroes on the wall. He never touched any of the monk's things before now. He now received them with extraordinary attention. The boy giggled as he opened the note book,

"I like this! Did you do this?"

"Yep," said Suñño.

"Did you do the drawings too?" Suñño nodded. The boy turns the book around so to share it with the monk.

"Wow... Brilliant! Is this your friend with a dog? Gosh that looks scary!" Suñño nodded again.

"Will you read it to me, I can't read your writing," pleaded the boy.

"Well they are mostly just notes. Maybe I'll make them into a story one day," mused the monk.

"Please tell me a story."

The boy slides down off the bed onto the floor with a bump, still firmly holding on to the notebook. Then a different voice entered the room. The soft tones of the boy's mother came in through the open door.

"Come along Edward. Let the monk alone now, they have to be off soon."

"Oh mum! Why?"

"Because Daddy is going to give them a lift into town on his way to work and we don't want to make him late, now do we?" She stepped into the room and reached out a hand towards a now very truculent looking son.

"Oh why? We were just making friends. He was going to tell me a story. He is so clever you know. I don't want him to go right now! Please mummy!" Edward started to cry.

"When I write my story book, I will send the first copy to you," said Suñño.

"Will you?" sobbed little Edward.

"I promise," said Suñño, "as long as I know where I can find you." The boy was led out of his room, still crying, as the monk added, "Only you may be a married man by then!"

Packed and ready, the monks were seated in the car watching the last minute farewells and hugs through the side window. Edward was held firmly in his mummy's right arm, his legs wrapped around her bulging waist. One quick kiss on each cheek and a flustered daddy climbed into the car with a big sigh.

"It's a shame you couldn't stay longer. But if I am late for this meeting, the guys will kill me!" The young father's speech was very speedy and his accent was still a strain for Suñño to follow but the Ajahn seemed to flow along with him just fine.

They had all been talking quite late into the night. What an interesting evening it was.

On the face of it, this was the ideal young, happy and successful business man. He had a beautiful wife, bright and talented son, spacious country house, beautiful garden and a fancy fast car. Plus there was a big car for his wife, son and expected baby. However the harsh reality of their situation became evident as the evening had revealed. Their host had been enlightening his visitors to the world he lived in. Following persistent pressures, mostly from a successful and ambitious family, the young father had embarked on a career involving law and property development. Very much, life in the fast lane. So much of his sales act relied on portraying the right kind of image. This had been impressed on him right from the start. So he went for it, studied hard and borrowed a lot of money. He ingratiated himself with the 'jet set' and developed a new circle of friends. Still only in his early thirties, he proved to be a gifted player in full-scale real estate transformation. His dad was really proud of him at last. Monopoly was kid's stuff, now it was for real. Or so he thought.

Last night, after his wife and son had gone to bed, he described his own experience of success. He described it as 'living on a knife edge'. On one level, he appeared to own many valuable things but in fact it was all owned by a series of banks and money lending organisations. One loan was supporting another. Each project he undertook put more strain on his complex attempts to keep up a falsified balance which appeared stable to his clients and investors. He described it as if being pushed along a tightrope over a bottomless pit by a mad axe man while monkeys threw coconuts and bunches of bananas at him from both sides. And the tight rope seemed to be endless and going nowhere! There was no going back, no standing still and the way forward seemed very bleak! He saw that through sheer exhaustion, there must come to a point when he will not be able to keep his balance anymore and he will fall into disaster.

After this graphic description, his eyes welled up with tears. He wasn't sleeping well and he was rapidly losing touch with his darling wife who felt she had already lost her husband to his work. He was terrified to take a holiday because he could not trust his partners anymore. Furthermore he had been discovering evidence of some underhand dealing which had forced him into making some regrettable decisions which could end up putting him into prison if he was found out.

"I had no choice!" he said again and again. "I dare not tell my family either. You are the only person I have ever spoken to about it. You are the first person I have met who I feel I can really trust, I don't know why!"

The Ajahn listened attentively. He had also been in business before he chose the monk's life. In fact, he used to be in a similar trade and was able to sympathise and even crack the occasional joke, which managed to raise a smile or two.

"You know," said the elder monk, "when I was in business, I also felt pressurised into buying a house. The first thing that occurred to me was that I never did own that house, in fact it owned me!" They both laughed. "Well I couldn't take it anywhere. It required a lot of my time and attention, not to mention a large proportion of my income for a long time to come! I felt as if I was tied to it, like an enormous weight about my neck."

The Ajahn went on to ask his generous and stressed out host several questions about his experience of ownership. Did he really own anything? Could he really see anything which could be permanently his. Or was it always just a temporary relationship with these things, all of which are in a constant state of change. Eventually he would have to relinquish it all anyway?

The monk and the businessman found they shared a lot in common that evening. Both came to a close and intimate understanding of each other, of the blessings and illusions of life and through seeing its instability, a greater sense of gratitude was found and a much broader perspective was recognised. The young property tycoon was seeing some things about himself and his predicament which now excited him. He went on,

"It often felt like I was still just playing some silly childish game of monopoly! But I was too scared to ask myself the questions that you have asked me. I am glad you did though. Everything has its own kind of reality as well as its falseness, doesn't it?" The Ajahn nodded in reply. "It still seems, I am just playing with bits of paper with numbers on. It is all true. And yet it seems the real source of the problem is in the way I relate to it, isn't it?" said the young father, the realization hitting him so hard that he reeled about in his chair as if recovering from a blow.

"This is your 'get out of jail free' card!" laughs the Ajahn, pretending to hand him something.

"Oh yes! 'Go directly to jail, do not collect your £200!' I remember it now." They both grinned at each other. The Ajahn continued,

"Letting go, yes. Our teachers tell us that we are not to be 'getting rid' of attachment, this often turns to aversion, which is pretty much the same as attachment only moving in the opposite direction. We just recognise attachment leads to suffering! It is not a judgement, it points to the way things really are."

"What do you mean?"

"Well, if I put my finger into this candle flame, it will be painful. If I don't, it won't. It is not that I shouldn't put it in the flame. I must simply expect it to be painful if I do!"

"Cause and effect. Common sense! Very sound! Only very deep... Wow. Yes."

"What you do keep though is the results and memory of your actions. The inner world of fear or freedom, of freedom from remorse. Looking back at your life with no regrets. If you look after what you put in here," he said pointing at his head, "you will always be free from a troubled mind and you will always have friends who will trust you," instructed the Ajahn.

"Yes, I will remember what you said about being clear and feeling good about my intentions. In that way, I won't be neglecting the family anymore. Trusting in goodness... definitely." The young fellow was looking much brighter and then suddenly very tired. "I reckon I'm now ready for bed."

"Put good things into the mind and you will get good things out. Pretty simple really," adds the Ajahn. "I wish you all the best in clearing up the mess and in wining back the trust of your partners!"

"I am so happy to have you stay in my house. It is as if the angels had sent you here, although I really don't believe in all that sort of stuff," he added as he climbed the stairs.

"And it all began when your little son invited us in for a cup of tea!" said Ajahn as they retired. "Amazing how things can turn out!"

After a rushed and simple breakfast, they were being driven off to a new destination and a prearranged meeting with another one of the Ajahn's friends.

"So what are we doing today Ajahn? I feel you have something different planned," asked Suñño.

"Well, we'll see. It all depends on a few things. I don't suppose you have any official kind of ID on you, do you?" asked the Ajahn.

"As it happens, I do have my US passport! It's a kind of habit. Us Americans are very uncomfortable travelling anywhere without ID!" replied Suñño.

"That might do it. The problem is I don't have anything with me but I suppose you could go in without me," said the Ajahn.

"Go in where?" enquired Suñño.

"Prison," said the Ajahn. "You might find it very interesting!" They all laughed.

"Make sure you have a 'get out of jail free card'!" added their speedy friend behind the driving wheel. "Interesting you should be doing this after our talk last night!"

"Going to prison?" asked Suñño. "Where, why, who?" The Ajahn explained,

"We are going to meet an old friend of mine who is a certified Buddhist prison chaplain. He supports Buddhists who are inside with meditation instruction, encouraging them in their practice and so on. Sometimes he invites me or another monk or nun to join him. I like to go from time to time just to offer him a little support." The Ajahn turns around to Suñño who sits behind. "The trouble is the prison authorities usually insist on some official ID. Only I have come unprepared. So maybe you could go in without me. Tony will look after you."

"But I am no teacher! I won't know what to do," pleaded Suñño.

"Just be yourself! You'll be fine. You don't have to go of course. We'll meet Tony in the town and see what happens. I only spoke to him this morning so he is uncertain if we will be able to go at such short notice but he is keen and will be talking to the Prison authorities to see what can be done." The Ajahn turned to their driver. "Bless you for the food and shelter and for the interesting evening. I trust we did not create too much of a disturbance for you!"

"It was such a pleasure! Yes, sure it was disturbing but in exactly the right way. Just what I needed. You know I didn't tell you but the past few weeks have been hell. I have often been obsessed with the idea of throwing myself off the office roof... now I think I am just about ready to let the office fall!" He stopped the car and looked at the monk directly in the eyes, a quiver in his voice "I can't thank you enough!" The Ajahn saying nothing, just took his hand. Their friendly host just added,

"This is the bus station, I have to leave you here."

The monks clambered out into a busy street. There was no more time for words. Just a friendly tap on the car roof as it sped away.

"Did you get their address or phone?" asked Suñño.

"No, he didn't offer it. I don't think we even know his name either! But they have ours. We'll see, eh? ...Very intelligent, kind but not very wise," said the Ajahn.

"Do you think he'll break out of it?"

"He seems less committed to following his dream world. Or rather his nightmare world! He certainly picked up a lot last night. Imagine living like that?"

They crossed the road in search of a cafe with a red lion outside; Tony's meeting place. The red lion was obscured by scaffolding so the monks walked up and down the street a few times before they realised it was just next to the place where they were dropped off. There was no sign of Tony so they stood outside and waited. It was still quite early and most people were in a hurry to get to work.

"These people have a very different energy to the ones we usually see out shopping later in the morning!" observed the Ajahn. "They are hardly looking at where they are going as if they are striding along in auto-pilot!"

It was a startling and accurate observation thought Suñño. Within a few minutes, he was bumped into twice by men who had their attention fixed to the ground just a few feet ahead of them. Most people's faces looked grey and lifeless, their senses appeared quite dull to him. Simply following a daily routine. Suñño imagined that in their thoughts they were still living in a late night television world. Just off the train or bus. Probably having spaced out, subdued or distracted their minds in some pointless entertainment. From one dream to another. Now just emerging from an attempted escape into a magazine or newspaper. The monks were unnoticed by the commuters who drifted by in their trance-like state or maybe nobody had the time, space or awareness to pay any attention to the odd looking strangers. Out of the crowd came a young couple of Asian origin with enormous back packs, which towered above their heads and extended well beyond their shoulders. Obviously lost. Until then, they were the only passers-by who seem to have noticed the monks standing there. They appeared very excited and went directly to speak with Suñño.

"Are you Buddha's?" asked the man who was considerably shorter than the monk as he looked up from under a long peaked baseball hat with a large Nikon label.
"Buddhist monks," replied Suñño.
"Take picture?" said the Nikon man, as the woman wedged herself between the monks, grinning a cute smile at both of the monks whilst nodding frantically and turning from side to side.
"Feels very Monty Python!" said Suñño.
"Enough said," replied the Ajahn, struggling to retain his composure.
"Ajahn!" came a call from the road. It was Tony who had pulled up in his car just behind them.
"Let's get out of here," whispers the Ajahn and they both instantly bolted for the car, leaving the Nikon man struggling to pull his camera from his belt pouch, completely unaware the monks had gone.

Within a few minutes, Tony had them sitting comfortably in a quiet park on the edge of town with a flask of tea and biscuits. It had begun to rain, just a few drops but quite heavy. The simple bandstand they sat in provided a perfect refuge. Suñño took an immediate liking to Tony. At first, he seemed remarkably short and timid for someone who worked with criminals. However he proved to be an inspirational fellow practitioner. There was a brief discussion about the kind of situation they might expect in the prison. The prisoners who attended the Buddhist meetings did so entirely voluntarily. They meet in the prison chapel every week to meditate, share their insights and occasionally discuss their problems together.

"You'll be fine!" assured Tony again.

They were to go to a high security prison on an island nearby. Tony explained that the usual security procedures might be the main problem. Although he had been visiting there every week for several years, he is supposed to clear extra visitors a good week in advance, which he had not done. It also seemed to depend on who was at the gate, what security level they were operating on at the time and if the prison governor was involved. Fortunately, Tony had a very good relationship with the governor here.

"So, I have a packed lunch for you both, if we don't get you in," said Tony. "But if we do get in, we are invited to take a meal in the prison officers' mess." Tony looked at his watch and beckoned them towards his car. "What happens if they don't let you in, Ajahn? Should I leave you both outside? I should be out in good time to join you for lunch."

"I know how much the prisoners appreciate our visits. If Suñño is happy to go without me, I am happy to sit in the car for a while," said the Ajahn. "Let's wait and see."

Suñño had never been anywhere near a prison before. It was much bigger than he had imagined. The sight of the immensely high and very long walls was quite chilling. There was a great grey rounded hood balanced on the top of the yellow brick wall, which looked to him like an enormous fat grey snake, instead of miles of barbed wire, which the young monk had expected to see. The only green was the well-mown grass and a few well groomed flower beds by the entrance. Not a tree in sight.

A threatening looking storm was looming overhead as they pulled into the car park. Very dark grey clouds were building up. It was quite a walk from the car to the entrance, which looked like a tiny window in a red and yellow cliff face. Walking quickly as the oncoming rain looked heavy, they were joined by several white-sleeved, uniformed officers; men and women who were on their way to work, most of whom offered smiles and greetings of 'Good morning'. The first door opened automatically as they approached. It led into a small lobby. Most of the walls were made of heavy smoky-grey glass and shiny stainless steel, just one side was painted brick. A uniformed officer stood behind a small steel sliding hatch in a narrow steel countertop. Behind him were numerous black and white TV monitors, shelves with many files and hundreds of keys in pigeon holed compartments. The monks peered through the window at the officer who looked back at them with an expressionless face. Between them was thick armoured glass.

"Prison chaplain," said Tony waving a tag on a chain. "I phoned through. I have two visitors for the chapel."
"Chapel keys!" called the officer. He started scanning through a book and several sheets of paper clipped to a board on his desk. Suñño could not make any sense out of the conversation between the officer and Tony. It was all in some code, 'Have you a B36?', 'Did you clear it with so and so?', 'We're on black and the governor is checking J31s (or something like that!)' They discussed names and times, all within a few rapid moments and then the officer pushed a book through the sliding hatch. Tony started writing in the book straight away.
"ID?" came an electronic sounding voice. Suñño gave Tony his passport and it was passed through the hatch with the book with some words of explanation from Tony about the lack of any ID for the Ajahn. The monks stood back whilst the decision was made. The Ajahn seemed very cool thought Suñño; he just waited. However, Suñño was feeling some pressure since they now had taken his passport. Could he change his mind? His confidence was waning fast. Another officer came to the window who seemed to recognise the Ajahn. They nodded at each other. Then the first officer shook his head and Suñño's spirit fell into a silent inner mild panic. Meanwhile another group, who were standing

behind, were acknowledged by the guard and a great glass sliding door into a kind of airlock opened automatically and they went in. The door closed. After a few moments the inner door opened and the monks watched as the group disappeared into the next room. Some more incomprehensible talk between the guards and Tony continued with the uniformed figure behind the glass waving his finger about, leaving Suñño wishing he hadn't even come in this far. Moments later the air lock opened and people walked out.

Without a word, Tony led the two monks in through the sliding door. They were joined by an enormous officer with biceps like superman who wished them a jovial 'morning'. The sliding door moved shut and all was silent for a moment. Then the other side opened and they entered into another lobby area. Here, Tony was issued with his keys which were fixed onto a chain and belt. The monks were issued with 'visitor' tags on silver chains which were to be worn around their necks. Still the monks remained silent, taking it all in. Just shaking their heads when asked about mobile phones, knives or drugs. They carried no bags and were not searched. All communication was still carried out through armoured glass and small hatches. There was a constant stream of people coming and going through the airlock doors; collecting and depositing keys, signing sheets and passing friendly greetings. They were all very familiar with each other although every step was meticulously followed, watched and recorded on closed circuit camera.

Tony led the monks through the first pair of doors. One solid door with a small window at face level which opened inwards. Then immediately another gate made from very heavy steel bars, which hinged outwards from the same doorframe into a yard. Each door had no handle, just a keyhole. Each door was unlocked, followed by the gate which was also unlocked, then held open as the key was put back into the other side of the door, which is then locked shut. The key is removed and the gate is then locked shut before moving into the yard. This laborious procedure was repeated numerous times as they moved into the prison centre, through covered passages, corridors and across yards. A real maze, thought Suñño. Tony said it took him a while to find his way around. They hardly met anyone as they went their way, just a few officers. The large chapel had a few simple offices adjoining it. The monks were introduced to a grey-haired Catholic priest and an Arabic Muslim imam who both welcomed them with warm friendliness.

Tony prepared the chapel by moving a number of chairs away from one corner and setting up a Buddha statue on a table. Stashed away in a storeroom, they had a number of meditation cushions, which were placed around in a semicircle. There was only one prisoner present who was introduced as 'the orderly'. He was very quiet and was asked to prepare some tea by the priest. They were to expect a group of twenty three that morning. Phone calls had been made to various wings and numbers were verified. Only then were the prisoners escorted to the chapel, arriving through a door from an upper level. Suñño was told that most of the group were serving life sentences, which filled him with apprehension. The monks sat in chairs and composed themselves as the doors opened upstairs. The low mumble and chatter of voices came closer. Suñño felt scared. A fascinating collection of characters entered the room. All ages, many nationalities, some big and strong, some looking frail and sickly. Some of Asian origin who did not appear to speak much English. They all took off their shoes and entered quietly. Many walked straight over to the monks wanting to shake their hands.

"Thank you for coming brother!" said a big Jamaican fellow.
"Good to see you again," said another to the Ajahn, in a very upper class accent.
"Very happy to see you man!" said another, putting his palms together in a polite salute. They all quietly took their seats. Some sat in chairs, some took cushions and sat on the floor.
'Extraordinary,' thought Suñño to himself. 'I have never been made so welcome outside the monastery. In fact their greetings seem friendlier than many of the people I live with in the monastery!'

Two officers came in, counted the prisoners then left again. A distant clap of thunder rattled through the featureless and very spacious brick chapel. Very high up there was a roof light, a raised ceiling centre with a narrow vertical window providing a distant halo of daylight although the light was now fading to dark grey. There was a constant sound of voices, even some intense shouting. Although quite distant, it easily penetrated the mind and always, the sound of banging doors or heavy footsteps echoing along the passageways. After a brief introduction, simple devotional chanting, the lighting of candles and incense, the Ajahn began a guided meditation session. The elder monk's voice was gentle and slow. He encouraged everyone to open to the experience they had. The noise, the restlessness and stresses, both internal as well as external. Slowly, he encouraged them to extend their awareness to contemplate the environment outside and beyond, exploring senses of attraction or aversion as they did so.

As the meditation theme developed, so did the storm outside. For a few minutes, the thunder, lightning and intense rain pounding on the metal roof became almost deafening. The Ajahn fell silent as a 'heaven sent' crescendo brought a really dramatic climax to his theme of dwelling in the present however painful it may be! For a few seconds, Suñño was convinced the roof may actually fall in. It was so intense. After the meditation and a very short talk there was an uneasy quiet, so it was suggested they take a short break for tea or coffee. One of the prisoners came over to Suñño and sat on the floor next to him. Looking up, he tried to say something but instead, just hummed a few times. Together they looked up into the roof light. Suñño could see large hailstones piled up against the glass. No wonder there was such an incredible noise! Remembering he was actually still on tudong, he looked at the young fellow sitting beside him and said,

"Wow! Look at those hailstones! I wouldn't have liked to have been caught out in that!"
"I would..." said the prisoner, looking directly at Suñño.

"Oh... I am sorry," said Suñño.

"So am I," said the very sad face which looked up at him. Then there was silence. Suñño swallowed hard. He was just beginning to arrive in the prison himself.

Their meeting just lasted a couple of hours but for Venerable Suñño, it may have been days. He saw so much suffering and so much courage and fortitude. These were beings who were indeed living in a hell realm. They discussed many personal and complex difficulties. It was hard for many of them to face the monsters in their own minds. Mostly they did not seem to be violent men at all but now they are forced to live in the violent world of seemingly endless incarceration. Desperately trying to escape an aggressive and threatening environment which surrounded them all the time. These weekly meetings were a rare chance for them to get together with some fellow peace seekers and like-minded friends who were also striving to etch out some refuge in a threatening and depressing environment. The Ajahn encouraged them and praised their efforts. Some of the inmates were visibly stirred by the monk's kind words. It was very evident they did not receive praise often. Their exchange of energy and inspiration touched a very deep place for everyone present, especially for the young monk. At the end of the meeting, many of the prisoners expressed beautifully their appreciation and gratitude to the monks. One big strong guy came straight up to Suñño and squeezed his hand.

"Wow, man. You're so beautiful and peaceful, man. I don't know how you can do it! You know I don't think I could do it at all. I am so pleased to meet you, man. Those guys on the wing reckon I am losing it, you know. They don't understand how I feel when I see a Buddha or a monk. I don't understand why I am like this! But I'm not like them anymore. I'm sick of fighting. Been fighting all my bloody life, man. Those guys don't get it, they don't really see it, why I should change?"

"You want them to change too?" asks Suñño.

"Yeah, but no 'fing chance! They don't see what I see. They reckon I'm goin' soft but it's much harder not fighting, isn't it?" His grin showed several missing teeth.

"And now you feel better about yourself?"

"Much better! Well.. sometimes! Only me mates aren't the mates they used to be. They don't get it. The first time I saw a monk in this place, I knew I had to come but I don't know why."

"I think the reason you recognise a good thing here is because you can clearly see the goodness in yourself," said Suñño.

"Me? But I am not a good guy! Why look at me, I'm a bloody mess!" replied the big fellow prodding himself firmly in the chest. "A danger to society!"

"If you didn't have goodness in your own heart and mind, you would not be able to recognise it in others, would you? It's because you do have it, that it enables you to see it. That is why you are here," added the monk.

The big man reeled back a pace or two as if he was avoiding an invisible punch from the monk. A second later he is right back, fascinated, ready for more.

"I never wanted to get into trouble or hurt anyone, just felt I had to! Well you would if you grew up where I did!"

"I expect a lot of your mates are just the same, eh?" asks Suñño. "Really, underneath it all, we all want to get along OK, don't we?"

"Yeah, we do. It's just that living cooped up in this rat hole brings the worst out in some people!" said the big fellow who was becoming softer with every breath. Suñño took hold of both of his enormous hands.

"But it can bring out the best in some of us, can't it? eh?" he said. They squeezed each other's hands affectionately. "Or should I say, it has great potential... Keep up the good work my friend, it is hard but the benefits are literally out of this world!"

"No shit," said the big guy. "You make me want to try... to let go ... to be at peace brother."

"First, we learn to be at peace with ourselves," said Suñño as the big fellow walked away. He turned, put his hands together in a beautiful salute and disappeared.

As they were leaving, Tony explained to Suñño that almost all of the inmates in the group who were serving a life sentence for murder, were not hardened criminals but first time offenders. He reflected on this and could see that in many ways, they were exactly like him. He could recall events in his own, not-so-distant past when he came very close to causing actual physical injury himself because he had been so mad with anger but he managed to restrain himself. Some of these guys probably felt they were being pushed a little too far and then really lost control. Perhaps another lover's tiff which had gone horribly wrong. As they stood in the air locked exit, they were joined by a couple of guards. Together they waited a few moments for the sliding door to open.

"Being locked up in a deluded mind," uttered Suñño, audibly but to himself. "It's much more difficult to escape from there, even if you have the key!"

A well built and stern looking guard peered at the monk with a puzzled but interested expression.

Suñño looked directly into his face and said,
"The most frightening prison cells are the ones which have walls that you can't see."

Block Head

looking at the world thru rose tinted glasses!

Four And Two Halves

The walking was rapidly coming to an end. For the last couple of days most of their travelling had been by car. Now, the monks were moving at the invitation of various friends who were galvanised into action whenever the phone rang. A message was spreading about the neighbourhood that the Ajahn and his friend were visiting. Suñño was learning the true meaning of Sangha; of spiritual community. Although he had been living in the monastery for three years, he had not really appreciated until now, the complexity and scale of support the monastic community received from friends scattered all over the country. Senior monks and nuns were sometimes going out to visit lay groups locally. The young monk was aware of this but he was surprised at the continual array of new faces which came to greet them. Each time offering respects and kind words in much the same way that close friends or families would after having been separated for a long time. Many of them recalled with love and gratitude meetings with monks or nuns who have long since moved away or disrobed. Now they were treating these two newfound robed figures as if they had known them for years.

This morning the monks were quite eager to meet up with two of their sisters, fellow community members from another of their branch monasteries. These two nuns had been walking tudong in Ireland and were also making their way back to their home base. Then by some strange coincidence, an invitation to attend a weekend retreat, led by their sisters, came to the house where our monks were staying. So the Ajahn and Venerable Suñño had been toying with the idea of making a surprise visit, just walking in at the mealtime. The monks had laughed about it for a while but soon realised that such a surprise may not necessarily be well received as it would almost certainly disturb their retreat. So the Ajahn and his friend organised a surprise phone call instead, early in the morning. Smiling and holding the telephone receiver away from his ear, the Ajahn shared the delightful and enthusiastic tones of Ajahn Muditä as her slightly muffled voice rang out into the kitchen. After a few minutes of slightly puzzled and confusing introductions, their venerable sisters made a definite invitation for them to join the meal offering. It was to be a picnic; the final part of a weekend retreat with a large group of friends.

The monks had stayed with an elderly couple that night. Rupert was a retired army officer and Jane was once a schoolteacher. Jane had been a long-term friend of the monasteries but her husband showed no interest in the monks at all. He seemed to just about tolerate her fascination with Buddhism. She explained that they had spent most of their lives in separate worlds, tied together for a short while by their children who had long since left home. Rupert was close to losing his temper when they eventually drove into the car park near the picnic ground as they had become lost a number of times. The tense atmosphere in the car would probably have exploded had they made one more wrong turn; fortunately they didn't. Slightly shaken and yet relieved, Jane and the monks were hurriedly dropped off and tersely dismissed.

"Thank you darling!" cried Jane as they stepped out of the car. "Carol will bring me home." Their grand old Bentley swept off towards the Rose and Crown Pub, Rupert's second home.

A well-made gravel path led from the car park through dense trees, diminished by strong winds, into a field with a magnificent view of a long and winding river. However there were no sisters or anyone else in sight.

"Are you sure this is the right place?" enquired the Ajahn, leaning on a tree. "Yes, yes this is it. Carol's Land-rover was in the car park together with Ben's old bus. They must be around here somewhere," replied Jane. Then they heard cries of "Ajahn!" from another rise above and behind them. So they crossed a style into another field and turned to see a group of maybe thirty people sitting round in a neat and tidy gathering with two dark-brown robed figures standing in the centre. The nuns carefully stepped their way out of the group. Ajahn Muditä, the elder sister, towered over her friend, Sister Sanghamitta, as she gave instructions to their friends who began to disperse in all directions. A pile of bags and boxes, a grand picnic indeed, came into sight beside a hedge as the monks climbed the hill to greet them all.

"Suñño, Suñño!" came two little voices as Lilly and Richard burst out of the crowd and came running towards the monks. Then suddenly they stopped and ran back. The Ajahn spoke to Jane for a moment as she stopped to take a breath. Suñño watched the children with a real flutter in his heart. He realised these were very special friends now and he was quite moved to see them again. He felt almost tearful and grateful that they now know him by name and not as 'the pink one'. They reappeared with cartons of juice in their hands. Running in a wild and wobbly way that only small children can manage, both screaming loudly. Little Richard ran straight past the monks starting to make skidding noises as he applied his special brakes. He stopped, changed into a lower gear and purred up to Suñño from behind.

"Seen any more monsters?" asked Lilly.

All Suñño could do was laugh, and laugh some more with tears rolling down his cheeks. He tried to speak but nothing came out. He had to squat down and hold his aching belly.

"It looks like Suñño's lost the plot!" mused the Ajahn as the sisters walked down to join them.

Eventually, the young monk had to come up for air. With a carton of juice in each hand, he wavered, caught his balance and stood up. The children were running circles around them.

"Well, what a pleasant surprise!" said Ajahn Muditä in her rich Slavic accent.

"Welcome to our picnic!" said Sister Sanghamitta who was standing to her side. They made little bows with hands held, palms together, in front of warm hearts. The nuns radiated gladness.

"Uncle John!" cried the children as the Ajahn's old friend arrived to take the monks' bags. He carried one on each shoulder. Then both children helped by lifting each bag from underneath and pushed him up the hill to a prearranged blanket laid out on the ground.

"So, how was Ireland?" asked the Ajahn.

"Wonderful!" replied the elder nun.

"It was hell," said the younger nun who then paused. "Wonderful sometimes, but mostly hell!" Then she laughed.

"How long have you been out and about?" asked Suñño.

"Three weeks in all, actually, twenty two days, twelve of them in Ireland, some in Wales and now, I think, three days here," said the younger sister in her gentle New Zealand voice. This was the first time that Venerable Suñño had met Sister Sanghamitta. She had a great reputation for her gritty stoicism and strength despite the fact she was of a very slight build. Her head only just above Suñño's elbow as they stood next to each other.

Suñño knelt down on the blanket and unpacked the Ajahn's bowl first before attending to his own. Sanghamitta sat at a good distance on another blanket with their nun's bowls and sitting places already set.

"Gosh!" said Sanghamitta, "Is that all you have? Only one bowl bag!"

"We have our yam's[9]- too but we try to keep to one bag using the other for extra food on pindapat or for packed lunches if one should arise," said Suñño.

"Wow, I am impressed!" said Sanghamitta. "I couldn't do that, it seems too risky."

The Ajahn's both stood for a while looking out over the rolling hills. He said very little and stood on one leg whilst she chattered on gesticulating with wild excitement, pointing out their intended route across the hills to their next intended rendezvous with friends. The monks and nuns sat at their places as their lay friends took it in turn to offer their venerable friends an extraordinary range of culinary delights. They had brought enough for everyone. Each item was first offered to the Ajahn monk and then passed along. The monks and nuns would take a bread roll from one, a chip or two from another and so on until after a few minutes all the food was massed to one side and the faithful lay friends waited for the Sangha to chant their blessings. All except little Richard who was already tucking into a chocolate muffin.

The Ajahn gave a short talk about the Sangha, the Buddhist community. He said that there are many more Buddhists in this part of the world than he had realised. He spoke about how little Richard and Lilly had 'saved their lives' a couple of weeks ago on the Downs and how pleased they were to see them again at the picnic. Mostly, he wanted to point out that there are a lot of kind and generous

[9] *yam - Monk's shoulder bag*

people who share in a natural goodness, regardless of their beliefs. An instinctive generosity which often goes unnoticed until we have the chance to help other people reveal it in themselves. He talked a little about their retreat coming to an end and advised them on the importance of being mindful. Suñño noticed that his elder companion was looking very tired and weary. His words seemed clumsy and he rarely looked up at anyone. After they had eaten, John took the monks' bowls away to wash them and a growing circle of friends surrounded the shaven headed and brown-robed figures who sat upright, bright and peaceful in the centre. The inevitable tudong stories emerged.

Venerable Suñño related almost all of the highlights of their trip with a confident Californian style that had everyone laughing, crying and asking all sorts of questions. He would occasionally turn to his Ajahn for comment but received little response. The nuns were an unlikely looking couple. Their characters are completely different. Ajahn Mudità was describing in detail the beautiful scenery of the Irish countryside whilst Sister Sanghamitta was clearly unimpressed. They inadvertently performed a delightful and hilarious double act as they described their frantic search to find a spot to pitch their tent in a wild Irish bog in the dark with a failing flashlight whilst being rounded up by a mad and lonely sheep dog. Sanghamitta described her meeting with Christian nuns in a convent school. Some details of the story were obviously completely new to her Ajahn who also delighted in listening to her version of the story. Like some of the experiences of the two monks, it was easy to see how two people may have different views or memories of the same event. Most moving of all, the younger sister told the group about how she dealt with going without any food at all for three days as they crossed some wilder parts of the country. They stood in one small village for a couple of hours and collected only rainwater, lots of it. Describing in some detail the fatigue and confusion which had gone through her mind; her doubts, her anger and frustration and then ending the tale with a beautiful smile saying, 'It was wonderful really!' Chuckling to herself she lifted up the carton of fruit juice her friend had passed her and said, 'There was a time when I felt prepared to kill someone for one of these!' Then she laughed.

"But now I can only feel gratitude," said Sister Sanghamitta. "I'll never forget the old man who emptied the entire contents of his basket into my bowl that morning and said 'Praise the Lord' as he did so." Then her eyes filled with tears.

Ajahn Mudità told her story about their going to the wrong mountain or was it their friends who went to the wrong mountain. Anyhow the planned picnic offering that day didn't happen.

"My goodness, how many days did you go without food?" came a voice from the crowd.
"Four days," said Mudità, "...actually four and two halves."
"Yes, once we had only a little bread and once just a bag of sugar and an apple," said the younger sister.
"Oh but it was so beautiful!" said the elder sister. "We went to a Tibetan temple,

way up on a cliff, with buildings like they have in Tibet. We were really blessed to have met a senior Lama who was staying there. He gave us such a welcome. Oh, he was really bright and radiant and gave us many gifts!"

They explained how they'd met an artist who invited them to stay in her studio, which sounded like an amazing place, and performed a blessing ceremony for a daughter's marriage. The nuns had put quite a bit of effort into some Irish networking before their trip so they had met with various Buddhist groups and supporters over the country who treated them very well.

"Muditä is aptly named," said the Ajahn as they packed their things away. "It means the opposite of envy, a sense of rejoicing in the gains of others. We don't have a word for it in English." A smaller group of supporters stayed close to the monks as the sisters went to pack their bags by the hedge. The Ajahn said, "She has an extraordinary gift for attracting dozens of generous supporters who love her dearly. She eats almost nothing and yet she has the strength and stamina of a horse... and the grace of a young deer." The Ajahn talked to them as Suñño skilfully wrapped and folded, wiped and dusted, sorted and slotted all their things into two neat little bags. Richard and Lilly were watching silently, quite mesmerised.

"She is so kind!" said an elderly lady who stood nearby. "She really helped my daughter after my granddaughter died. She is so compassionate and understanding."
"What are we going to do now?" asked Suñño. "Are we on foot or do we go by car?"
"I guess it depends," said the Ajahn, sitting cross legged he poked a foot out from under his robe and started to rub it, wincing slightly.
"Something wrong with your foot?" asked Suñño as he came to take a closer look.
"The car ran over it," said the Ajahn as he massaged between the toes with one hand.
"Did what?!" cried Suñño.
"It was my fault. I stood too close and Rupert drove over my foot," said the Ajahn.
"Why didn't you say!" called out another lady.
"Is anything broken?" asked Suñño. "Do you think we should get it seen to?"
"The Ajahn is hurt!" called out another. 'The Ajahn is hurt!' repeated the children and commotion ensued.
"It looks a little swollen," said John.
"It is a bit grey, maybe bruised," said Suñño.
"Just the tyre mark!" amused the Ajahn.

There followed a frantic meeting which seemed to involve everyone discussing what to do with the Ajahn's foot. Should they take him to the hospital or the doctor or back to the monastery or bandage it? Should he take a homeopathic remedy or rub tea tree oil or tiger balm on it. Maybe take a hot bath or a cold bath? Many more offers and suggestions followed.

"Now you see why I waited until after the meal to mention it," smiled the Ajahn.
"Is it painful?" asked Suñño.
"It was but now it is easing off," said the elder monk as he moved to a kneeling position, reaching out to Suñño for an arm up. "Let's see if I can put more weight on it now."

Standing for a moment, he rested his arm on Suñño's shoulder and smiled back at a group of anxious faces observing him. There were two simultaneous mobile phone conversations going on behind him asking advice or assistance for their Ajahn. The elder monk paced up and down a few times, limping slightly.

"It is ok if I don't put much pressure on the big toe," he said. His friend John approached with a hot mug of tea and offered it to the Ajahn.
"Ah! Vitamin tea, I feel better already," he said, chuckling to himself. He went back to his seat, moving gracefully from a stand to a squat and then to a sitting position, "Good... first things first," he said, smiling and reaching out to receive the large mug. A second cup followed, brewed by another friend on a camp stove, down by the hedge. Suñño joined his friend drinking tea, silently gazing out over the valley below them. The two nuns returned bearing tea cups and sat to one side. They were also concerned that the Ajahn's injury was not serious, making sure he was properly taken care of. After a customary taking of leave, paying respects and well wishes the two nuns prepared themselves for moving on. They had their sights set on spending the night at a camp site about ten miles away with some of their friends.

"We now finish our weekend retreat with some walking meditation," said Ajahn Muditä as she beckoned her friends over to say farewell to the monks, "only I don't think it will be very silent!" Five ladies came striding over, all bearing large back packs, one of whom the Ajahn thought he recognised but she now had a shaved head.

"This is Anna, she is joining our community next month." Anna made a short bow and smiled,
"I was on your retreat in KwaZulu three years ago," she said. "Now I am living over here."
"Wonderful!" said the Ajahn. "I am sorry I didn't recognise you."
"Not surprising, Ajahn, I used to have loads of curly black hair and I've lost a lot of weight!" said Anna.

Two of the other ladies lifted packs off their backs and passed them to the nuns who both put out shoulders to receive them. Sister Sanghamitta's pack appeared to bury her when viewed from behind, just her lower legs and large boots protruding from underneath. As she turned around, her shining head and bright eyes glowed as they were framed by a great black sausage, strapped to the top of her pack.

"Don't you say a word!" she said to Suñño. "It's embarrassing enough... I don't know how it happened this way!"

"See you in Hartwood next week, all being well," said the Ajahn as they moved down the hill.

"They have sleeping bags, a tent, bed rolls, tea making kit, loads of first aid stuff, sun cream, and Ajahn Muditä has even brought a camera and a photo album to show her friends!" said John, "and tiny little lightweight alms bowls which you would hardly notice."

"It looks like quite a different kind of practice for you though Ajahn," said the children's mummy. "You hardly have anything."

"There is a noticeable difference in style. Do you think there is any difference in the way it benefits your practice?" asked John, remembering his days as a novice. "I mean travelling light is more risky yet the camping gear is really heavy. Goodness, look at those two! They have some guts!" Then the Ajahn's old friends joined the children down the hill before the Ajahn could reply.

"Yea, whatever happened to contentment with little," said a teenage lad who joined the monks little gathering. "The monk's discipline is very hard, what with all your 227 rules and all."

"Ultimately, of course, our practice is not about abandoning the stuff we carry in our bags but about the stuff we carry in our hearts and minds," replied the Ajahn quite firmly. "Letting go of ideals, views and opinions is much harder!"

"Yes Ajahn," said the lad. "but I think you are much braver than they are."

"Well, it is easy to be fooled by appearances, young man," said the Ajahn. "I have been walking through fairly familiar territory, easy terrain with many towns and villages quite close together. Those two brave women have been walking through rough country with miles of wild open space. It looks pretty wise of them to me."

"Yes, Ajahn," said the lad, feeling a little scolded. Kevin had known the Ajahn for as long as he could remember but now he was feeling quite grown up. He was almost an inch or two taller than the Ajahn now but still a little shorter than Suñño.

"As monks and nuns, we choose to go against the stream. We don't follow the way of the world but choose to swim against it. It means you need to be really alive, like the fish in the river. The dead ones are carried along by the current. Helpless, they are like people who just follow their whims and moods without even noticing what they are doing. You have to be really alive to move upstream, against the defilements which delude the mind," said the Ajahn. "Understanding this takes a lot of effort, patience and endurance. This is the point really. It is not about what you carry but how you carry it."

"What do you mean?" asked Kevin.

"Well... it's like an athlete who uses weights or machines to train his body for the race but when he is competing, he leaves the equipment behind. He reaps the benefit from having done the exercises and doesn't need to cart the training gear about with him along the racetrack," said the Ajahn. Pulling on the lad's sleeve, he said "Only you look a bit like me at your age... eh?... not quite athletic

material either. Maybe a champion chess player!"
"Yea I'm a brainy type but I'm fed up with having to be a winner all the time too!
Always having to be doing better at school, being on top, endlessly improving.
If I don't do well, my dad has a go at me. Then if I do, the kids in the class give
me a hard time or at least some of them do," said Kevin. "Win some, lose some,
I guess. Sometimes I just want to tell them all to piss off and leave me alone.
Maybe I should become a monk or something!"

The elder monk reached forward and put his hand on the back of the young
man's neck, pulling his head forward they gently touched foreheads. The lad
moved closer and sat to one side. Suñño was sitting on the other.

"All this competitive stuff is really tiresome, that is true. I used to think that
coming to the monastery, all that would be over too but I was wrong!" the Ajahn
chuckled, "I have met lots of extremely conceited and arrogant monks who liked
to prove they are tougher, brighter and smarter than the others. They would be
the first to criticise or complain about another monk's behaviour and really enjoy
strutting about, chatting up the lay people with impressive Dhamma talks and
getting high on their own self importance."
"Really? Even in the monastery?" said the lad and smiled.
"I am afraid so," said the Ajahn, "but the lovely thing is, they can't get away with it
for long without a load of suffering, which means they usually have to either wise
up or ship out eventually."
"How come? It doesn't seem right or fair to me sometimes. Why is it that so
many people seem to get away with things and others don't?" asked Suñño.
"Getting away with it, right and fair are viewed far too highly, aren't they? When
actually, they are all illusions," said the elder monk. "When monks live together
it is much harder to pretend anymore. If a senior monk talks eloquently about
compassion and understanding or about beautiful right speech in his teaching but
continues to gossip, back bite and insult people behind their backs, he loses the
trust of his fellow monks and finds himself rather lonely. Or if another appears
to know a lot about meditation practice and expounds in detail the blissful and
clear benefits it can bring them but later he appears to be profoundly depressed
and confused, usually tired and burdened with a lot of his own baggage, he also
loses face and receives less and less attention from his fellow monks. Monastic
conventions are set up in a way which seem to naturally guide us towards a
deeper understanding and contentment, providing we use it properly. If we are
preoccupied with foolish and selfish interests, life in the monastery simply gets
too uncomfortable or at least, that is what I have noticed myself," said the Ajahn
to his companion.

Just three figures, sitting together on a camping mat, with the Ajahn in the middle.
They were overlooking a vast landscape whilst the other friends flapped around
with their belongings down by the hedge.

"It is like everything else in life, I guess; you reap what you sow," said Suñño.
"The simplified monastic lifestyle tends to expose some of the deceptions and

illusions which are more easily hidden in the ordinary world," added the Ajahn, "which certainly stings a bit sometimes!"

"You seem pretty comfortable to me," commented Suñño. "At least it looks that way."

"Right now things are going OK, that is true," said the Ajahn, "but it hasn't always been that way! You can ask John down there. I'm sure he remembers the time I fell out with another monk over a shoe rack! I used to be pretty miserable in the early days with anger boiling up and spilling out all over the place... rather messy actually. I have a critical nature which can turn fairly nasty if I am not careful. There are things I have done and regretted for years afterwards and need not have done at all! Yes, this critical mind definitely hurts me just as much as others."

"How come Ajahn?" asked Suñño.

"For example, two years ago I decided to go and see a much more senior monk than me who I used to give a hard time at Hartwood monastery during my early days in the community. I was very idealistic and this Ajahn, who was trained in Asia, became the subject of my critical mind. We started off as good friends but I kept on picking holes in his behaviour until my degenerating image of him really haunted me. Then, when his practice clearly began to wobble, certainly not helped, I felt, by my disparaging input, he went back to the tropics looking very upset. I despised him then but a few years later I found myself appreciating the sort of challenges he was meeting in those days because I was there myself and a guilty shadow hovered over his memory. So, when I was in his part of the world, I heard news of his whereabouts. He had been living for several years on his own in a cave and refusing to see any visitors. I went to see him despite advice from other monks to stay away because I wanted to ask for his forgiveness. When I eventually found him, we actually wept with joy. We both felt we had things to be forgiven for. Neither of us could find reasons to criticise each other. There was now a distinct and mutual respect."

"So what changed?" asked the lad.

"I'd been beating myself up for years for being so fault-finding of him and then probably driving him away. Being critical of my own judgmental mind, I'd actually driven myself into a hole. My own thoughts had turned nasty and poisoned myself. When we met again years later, it appeared my friend had no unpleasant recollection of our friendship at all, just his own struggles with himself. He greeted me as a dear friend. I thought he would want to hit me!"

"I thought you all get along fine, living in perfect harmony like in the stories," said Kevin.

"You haven't read all the stories then!" smiled Suñño.

"I have met some beautiful examples," continued the Ajahn. "Monks who naturally incline to make a point of mentioning the good and outstanding features of another's personality or actions and make little of their own. Generous with their time and attention, mindful of their actions and carefully avoiding conflicts, internally as well as with their fellows. They are never short of friends, they are energetic because they feed on their own merits and have little or none of their own baggage to weigh them down."

"Like Ajahn Lee in Thailand?" asked Suñño.

"Yes, he was a delight to be with. He kept on reminding me of my own goodness, pointing out the wholesome and making little of the problems. He seemed tireless although he did sometimes become pretty exhausted but I never saw him irritable with anyone even when threatened or insulted which was very rare. Although he could be very dismissive with arrogant or dishonest people, he'd be kind and polite and then just cut them off. He was very perceptive. People were convinced he could read their minds. Then if they recognised their error later and returned with humility and honesty, he'd greet them beautifully as if for the first time," said the Ajahn with a sigh.

"I'd love to meet him," said Suñño.

"Well you might and sooner than you think," grinned the Ajahn as he climbed up onto his feet. "Come, help me young man," he said, reaching out to the lad. They prepared themselves to move on. Suñño rolled up the mat and handed it to their young friend who stood between them, then the Ajahn walked off into the bushes.

"I have never heard a monk talk like that before," said the lad. "It has me thinking... we all have the same sort of problems and yet the monks have a very special way of dealing with them. I always knew it was extraordinary but in the same way it now all looks quite ordinary and sensible."

"Logical really," said Suñño, "The appliance of science. Happiness isn't found in things but in realising how we relate to them. If I thought this cup of tea was going to make me happy forever, I would now be feeling very disappointed, wouldn't I?" said the young monk handing the lad his empty mug. "But I've wised up about tea and I realise that the pleasure it gives me is just that much. So I am not devastated when I get to the bottom. But there are many things in life which we expect to bring us lasting satisfaction, yet in reality provides no more than this cup of tea did. These things we have yet to understand, eh?"

"I understand," said Kevin.

"Easy to understand but difficult to realise," said Suñño.

"Realise?" asked Kevin.

"No longer a theory or an idea but real, like really real!" smiled Suñño. "Like it is obvious... A friend of mine, who was a medical student, thought he wanted to be a doctor so he could cure people of their sickness. The more he studied and began to practice medicine, the more he realised that everyone he knew was sick in one way or another. Some people believed they were healthy but he could only see some potential disaster looming for them sometime in the future. He realised that sickness was the normal state. He had just learned to discern various levels of seriousness and developed a few strategies in patching up things and keeping them going a bit longer. But curing the body of all illness, he soon realised, was impossible."

"I'll never forget the Buddhist family camp we went to a couple of years ago," said Kevin. "We went for a walk in the woods looking for signs of birth, aging, sickness and death. The Ajahn made us explore all sorts of things which I kind of knew in theory but I'd never really looked at. It blew my mind actually! Then the girl next door couldn't understand why I wasn't all that upset when my hamster died. She went to pieces. A total mess!" and he laughed.

"Yep, you are a pretty wise young man," said Suñño.

"The problem for me is when I am stuck at home on a lovely day having to try and learn a load of complicated mathematical theory when I really can't see the point in any of it!" sighed the lad.

"With the training in school, we are supposed to become intelligent and responsible citizens, ready to play our part as good little consumers in today's society. The Buddha's teachings encourage us to develop wisdom, which is quite different from intelligence, isn't it?" said Suñño.

"I guess it is!" replied Kevin.

"I have some friends who are not very intelligent at all but they are exceptionally wise and I have enormous respect for them," said Suñño. "I also know friends who are intellectually quite brilliant and yet they are often depressed, confused and miserable. They have little wisdom and mostly, they appear to think too much!"

"That's my problem," said the lad. "I think too much."

Suñño and the young fellow started to walk down the hill to rejoin the Ajahn and the rest of the group.

"A wise person understands how to use the thinking mind when it is needed, like picking up a tool to fix something. Then they can put it away when it is no longer required," smiles Suñño, "so it doesn't push them around when they don't want it."

"Can you do that?" asked the lad.

"Of course!" Suñño laughed... "but only on the third week of the month, as long as there isn't an 'R' in the month and only if it is a waxing moon between midnight and three in the morning or maybe it's a waning moon which means two and five... mm., now I am not so sure!" Suñño winked at his young friend who slapped the young monk on the arm in a playful gesture.

"Oh now you are just messing about!" said Kevin.

"Yea well, that helps sometimes too!" said the monk.

The Ajahn was set to continue walking for a while. From their vantage point on the hill, they could still just about make out the tiny forms of the two nuns and their friends down in the valley. Now the monks were to be following the same route to a church by the river. Ben would take his old bus there in an hour or so then wait and see if the Ajahn's foot is troubling him too much. If so, they would take them back to the monastery. John would walk with them and bring a mobile phone, just in case.

As the monks, followed by John carrying the Ajahn's bag, disappeared down the footpath, which hugged the hedge to the edge of the field and then swerved off to the right by a clump of ancient oak trees, the tall teenage lad sat watching them, cross legged and motionless. Little Richard and Lilly walked up slowly to stand either side of Kevin, connecting for a moment with his silence.

"I think Suñño is the best," said Lilly.
"He is funny," said Richard.
"I think his name means emptiness," said Kevin. "No nonsense from him, that's for sure!"
"That's for sure!" said Lilly.

Cloud Hoppers

With a deft manoeuvre, the Ajahn managed to avoid another lift and consequent invitations. The monks were back on the footpath and very happy to be there together again. This time they would be navigating without a map but the elder monk thought he knew the area well enough. They still had their compass so both were reasonably confident they wouldn't get too lost.

"Do you think Raja will be upset when he returns to find we've gone?" asked Suñño.
"Raja is one of the most generous and helpful supporters I have ever met," smiled the Ajahn. "I've known him for years. I expect he'll be amused that we've given him the slip!" Then he laughs. "We've been playing cat and mouse games before, now it is my turn to win one over on him!"
"That was a Sri Lankan breakfast and a half!" laughed Suñño. "I'm certainly happy to be walking it off rather than be sitting about again."
"This will be the last day we'll be walking together. Providing I can find David's place this evening," said the Ajahn, "we should be back at Hartwood in time for the meal tomorrow. It is not far, David offered to drive us there."

The footpath followed the river exactly as the Ajahn remembered but when they met the bridge and the main road, there was no indication where, or if, the path continued near the line of the river or not. The monks walked a mile or so north looking for an opening to the west but found none, which was visibly upsetting for the Ajahn who was convinced he knew of one. Venerable Suñño stopped to watch some small fish in the shallows of a pond by the road while his friend asked a lady for directions.

Staying in lay people's homes, riding about in cars and spending much more time in conversation with friends who live very different lives from those in the monastery, had a noticeable effect on the young monk. Memories flashed in disjointed patterns through his mind, darting about but coming to nothing. Mostly reverberating echoes from lay peoples lives who were so used to multi-tasking, their attention barely in the present for a moment before it is dragged off to follow another need or other. Spending time in houses filled with all sorts of objects which no longer interested him and conversations which usually left him feeling completely isolated.

On the other side of the pond was a well-kept garden with lawns, flower beds and hedges well placed and neatly trimmed. In the distance by a large house, he noticed a man who was busy working himself up into a frenzy. He had a small orange coloured machine with a long white spout laid in the ground before him. Placing one foot on the machine, he pulled a cord jerking his body backwards but the machine did not respond. So he fiddled with it for a moment and pulled again. Still nothing happened. This game continued for a while. Sometimes the man held the machine in one hand and pulled with the other. Sometimes he used a foot and used the other arm to pull. Audible cussing could be heard as he marched off to the garage for a moment, then he came back to fiddle, pull and cuss some more, all the time working himself into quite a sweat. Meanwhile the Ajahn was speaking with the man's wife. Stomping about and becoming more and more exhausted, he was disturbed for a moment while the Ajahn and his wife approached. They stopped a few metre away while the lady asked him to verify some directions for the monk. The man barked out a few words in an angry and frustrated tone whilst still pulling madly on the cord, then suddenly the machine burst into life with a deafening noise. Everyone jumped. The lady and the monk made a hasty retreat whilst the man marched off to his garage with his machine screaming by his side. In a second he was back, scrambling to pull a pair of ear protectors on, then he began to blast a sprinkling of hedge cuttings off the driveway back under the hedge, a process which took him just a couple of frantic and stimulating minutes. Then it was all over. The machine was silenced and the man, now looking very weary, took his beloved labour saving device back to his garage and put it on the shelf, next to all his other gardening gear.

The man reappeared and looked gruffly at the monks. Everything about his manner said that he was not at all approving of these strange shaven-headed looking layabouts. Turning about, he marched off purposefully, looking as if he was 'going to do something very important and useful with his life,' thought Suñño with a smile. Suddenly the man appeared from behind the hedge heading straight for the elder monk.

"We don't want anything from the likes of you!" he shouted, waving a fist.
"Please don't darling!" cried the lady.
"Shut up!" he shouted. "We don't need your sorts around here, certainly not in my garden. My wife may be taken in by your nonsense but I am certainly not! So kindly go away!"
"They are just a little lost, darling," said the lady.
"You are telling me they are lost! My God just look at them! We fought wars to free this country and just look what we have now!" the man started to physically tremble with rage. "And you can wipe that stupid grin off your face before I wipe it off for you!" Spitting as he spoke and growing redder in the face, he threw a threatening fist towards the Ajahn but standing a couple of paces away it doesn't reach.
"Please stop it!" cried his wife but she was pushed to one side by the fuming husband. The Ajahn remained still, almost expressionless but his face was pale. He slowly took three paces backwards into the road. Suñño was standing on the other side so the man glanced nervously in both directions at the monks. The Ajahn looked at Suñño, saying nothing but the message was clear, 'Stay where you are.'
"We are just passing by," said the elder monk in a gentle tone. "I am sorry if we have disturbed you."
"Sorry eh?!" said the man. "Well a pretty sorry sight you are, aren't you?" The

Ajahn made no response... "What do you think you are doing? I mean why would a grown man go about dressed like that? Come on man, answer me!" bellowed the man.

The Ajahn paused, smiled and said, "Well now, that is a very good question." Then he grinned at Suñño and replied in his best educated English. "Why would I leave a loving family, a perfectly successful business life, a house and fancy car, to be wandering about the country, penniless and dressed in rags for almost...err, twenty years now eh?... There must be something in it, don't you think?"

The angry man stood fixated, shaking his head in disbelief, huffing and puffing but no distinguishable words came out until an almost explosive "Madness!" burst forth. He swung around repeating 'Madness' to himself as he strutted off, back to his garage.

"I am so sorry," said the man's wife, as cool as a cucumber. "Gerald has never been the same since they forced him to take early retirement. He loved his work you see but now he takes to the bottle. So silly really, what with his bad heart and all."
"He does not look well," said Suñño joining them.
"Not at all," she said. "Anyhow you are on your way to Ashweald?"
"That's the idea," said Suñño.
"The best way to Ashweald Forest is by Huntingdene Place," said the lady. "And you really should pop in and see the people there, you'd be very welcome I'm sure."
"Where is this?" asked the Ajahn.
"You are meditators aren't you?" asked the lady. "You must have heard about it."
"We meditate, yes," said Suñño.
"Well, it is famous. They have been on television. I believe they even stood for local elections. They do some extraordinary things. We saw them on the news! I think they call it 'yogic flying', wonderful. All leaping about in full lotus posture!"
"Really?" said the Ajahn.
"Yes, my daughter used to go there for yoga," said the lady.
"Oh well, yes. Certainly," replied the Ajahn, "we'll have to go there."

Directions confirmed, they continued up the road for another mile and then turned left into a narrow lane. The monks walked in silence. After an hour or so, they came to a driveway with a footpath sign and a notice pointing to Huntingdene. The Ajahn pointed it out and called out enthusiastically, "Good this is it!" Marching down the driveway, Venerable Suñño started to have doubts. He couldn't believe that they would actually be going to visit this place; 'the Ajahn must be going mad' he thought. The drive led them to a yellow gatehouse where it turned sharply right but straight on there was an open gate with a narrower gravel drive and a fancy looking sign saying 'Huntingdene Place'.

"So this is it!" said the Ajahn. "We must make ourselves ready."

"What? Are we going in?" cried Suññø.

"We must!" said the Ajahn putting down his bag and tidying his robe. Suññø followed feeling very uneasy.

"There is one thing though," said the Ajahn. "Oh dear, this is very important."

"What?"

"Did you bring your licence?" asked the Ajahn.

"Licence?" said Suññø.

"Your flying licence," said the Ajahn pretending to fumble through his non existent pockets. "Oh bother, I don't seem to have mine!" and they laughed. The Ajahn picked up his bag and said, "Oh well, maybe next time." And strode off down an almost hidden footpath to the left.

"Mm... looks like another 'witty Ajahn' afternoon!" mused Suññø, following behind.

The forest was everything Venerable Suññø had dreamed of. His most prominent first impression was of enormous space, which reminded him more of his home country. Southern England is very heavily populated by comparison and divided into a tiny patchwork of fields, hedges, winding lanes and scattered towns or villages made up of quaint little houses. When he first came to live in the area, he saw it as a kind of fairy tale place, something from a childhood storybook. This parkland was quite different. It was close to Midsummer's day, the longest day of the year and the weather, for England at least, was quite hot. He could almost perceive a gentle heat haze earlier in the afternoon but now the air was clear, the sky blue and much of the grass a golden brown. The landscape was mostly heath land with vast expanses of heather growing in low tufts and rolling over gentle hills. The heather had deep green foliage with bright purple and crimson flowers, sprinkled in a fine layer, as if dusted over the surface. Some gorse bushes, standing taller with fine dark green and spiky foliage also displayed a sprinkling of bright yellow flowers. Small clumps of trees were randomly scattered about; mostly silver birch, light and airy with slender white trunks and occasional groups of giant oaks or beeches offering cool shade.

The Ajahn explained that David's house was just an hour's walk away. It was only mid afternoon and they had the place to themselves so, after a brief discussion, the monks decided to wander off alone until 9 o'clock when they would meet again at the point where the main track meets the road; a spot clearly visible from where they were standing. The elder monk made a beeline for a spot on a hilltop which he knew well. He had been there several times before with David. Many pleasant memories were drifting through his mind as he grunted up the hill, using one hand to shield his eyes from the bright sun.

Suññø watched his friend walk away for a few minutes then he took a different path which skirted along the edge of a pine tree plantation, steadily climbing a gentle hill to a grassy ridge. A narrow lane crossed the forest just below and on the other side of the ridge. The young monk could just see it winding its way through the bushes and trees. Sitting with his back to the side of the ridge, sheltered by a small tree, he found the perfect spot to meditate, secluded but with a magnificent view. Delighting in the wild enthusiasm of a skylark hovering above, he found himself in a celebratory mood especially as he was not yet plagued with hay fever. Everything was perfect. Closing his eyes to meditate, his mind entered a kind of dream state, just listening.

A car door slams shut, a few moments silence and another door bangs, then a click or two followed by some slow chatter. Sounds that rattled lightly through the gorse bush behind. Another vehicle, with a noisy engine, pulled up. The door squeaks open loudly and the itchy, scratchy and rhythmic thudding sound of pop music leaks out. Another door bangs and at least two more voices, all male, begin to mumble. Then all is quiet again except for the skylark and the muffled music which sounds as if it trickles out of a partly opened window. Thoughts drift back to his collapse on the Pilgrim's Way, again accompanied by a skylark, which all begins to fade until Suñño is physically touched by a sudden high pitched whine over to his left. His attention arrested again as this loud whine moved suddenly from his side, directly into the air and very quickly whizzed overhead to his right. The sound dulled a little, then it comes flying back in front of him. Suñño remained still, amused at the prospect of what might be happening in the world about him, entertaining himself with colourful interpretations in his mind. He became the master of the other world.

Then another little metallic dragon takes to the air and they both circle the space together, drawing patterns, perhaps plotting ancient symbols across the sky. The first baby dragon, its numerous delicate silvery wings beating so fast they are invisible, takes a low sweep in front of the venerable master in a graceful salute. The second dragon, bright green with a magnificent long tail follows in similar homage but then it comes to a sudden and dramatic stop.

"I'll go!" came a gruff voice from directly behind the master. Heavy footsteps smashing through the forest floor thundered close beside the master as Omakar the great dragon tamer strides out to the rescue.

"Oh, er sorry mate," said Omakar as he passed. "Excuse me!"

A great and immeasurable light engulfed the master as his curiosity overcame him. His eyes were opened. The master became Suñño again. Omakar was wearing US army boots, camouflage pants, green sleeveless vest, a white cap with a long peak and large wrap-around shades. He stomped over the flowering heather shortly followed by his friend carrying a grey box with dials, knobs and switches and a long extendable antennae poking out of the top.

"It's ok!" cried the first fellow holding up a beautifully made model aeroplane, painted bright green. The first model plane made a low level victory roll at lightning speed over the two fellows below. "Show off!" cried his mate.
"I'll get you, Red Baron!" came a shout from behind.

Blistered Feet, Blissful Mind

An elderly lady walked past just below the monk who was sitting close to the track. She was hauled along by a small dog which wheezed and spluttered saliva about. She stopped and peered at the monk for a moment then turned to the flying aces.

"Can't you see that some people come here for some peace and quiet!" she cried. "They don't want to be disturbed by all your silly racket!" Then she went on her way, red faced and furious. Suñño stayed put, closing visionary consciousness again but surprisingly undisturbed by the antics of the hobbyists who buzzed about a little more but for only a few minutes before serious battle damage made a necessary retreat to the workshop.

As early evening approached, the young monk strolled over in the direction of the Ajahn. Climbing a small rise, the landscape revealed a lovely hollow and an inviting path for walking meditation to some grand, standing oaks on the next ridge. He placed his bag under a tree and walked up and down for a while, allowing his mind to rest gently on the movement of his limbs. The ground was very sandy so he removed his sandals and walked barefoot. The shadows grew long and the sky was  beginning to take a subtle orange glow as Suñño took to a sitting position by the trees and took out his notebook.

The young monk had neither heard nor seen anyone for a couple of hours or more. Time was drifting past unnoticed. The voices of young women soon moved into his space, long before their owners arrived. Suñño stayed with his notebook but his attention was drawn as they stood just a few feet away, giggling to each other. They called out to the monk who made a momentary glance in their direction but deliberately avoided contact.

"Oh, come on Lisa," called one as she walked on. "Leave him!" But Lisa stood still.

Eventually Suñño looked up to see an extraordinarily beautiful young girl standing in the sunset, wearing a long lacy dress which appeared completely transparent in the back light. Standing looking directly at the monk, she was well aware of the exhibition she was presenting for him. Turning slowly and exposing the contours of her body, she made provocative stretching movements, smiling and flashing her eyes. The young monk was hooked for a few seconds then closed his eyes, clutching his notebook in both hands. Suñño was very much aware that she had come closer, a lot closer, but he did not respond.

"Hello," came a soft voice. Suñño remained still, eyes closed, collecting his thoughts. 'She is absolutely stunning and I am feeling as shy and confused as any teenager on a first date. I am not sure I can handle this without making a fool of myself.' Then her perfume touched his senses and his mind almost stopped. "Hello," she repeated again, more softly this time. The young monk considered what he wanted to say in his mind first, before opening his mouth...

'Look, I can see you are very beautiful and I do find you really attractive and I realise that you are having a very strong effect on me. It's nothing personal. I am very happy that you are the way you are. I can rejoice in your attractive features. It is just that the life I am choosing to live right now means that I can't afford the risk of getting close to you. If we end up getting involved with each other then we'll probably burden ourselves with a lot of responsibilities which I do not feel ready, able or willing to accept. This way I am seeking a peace and a love which is not born out of attachment but out of freedom. There was a time when I would have gladly gone with you but right now I really want to give this monk's life a good try. So I'm really sorry but I have to ask you to leave me alone right now.'

After a few moments more he was ready to face her. He opened his eyes and looked around but she was nowhere to be seen. Vanished, as if she was only ever a dream, which he thought she might have been all along. He sighed, deeply relieved. He remained seated for a few more minutes but the memory of the young woman had him really stirred up inside. He knew he had to get up and walk about for a while. Gathering his two books and putting them away, his attention was grabbed by something lying in the grass in front of him, just on the other side of his bag. Kneeling he rises up to look. Some fine pink, lacy cloth. Then he recognised it, fancy ladies g-string underwear. 'My dream was no dream at all!' he said to himself, standing bolt upright. Then a sexy giggle came out of the bushes behind him and there she was lying in the grass, rolling about with her dress pulled up high.

"Gosh you are taller than I thought," she said. "Do you speak English?... Though I guess it doesn't really matter."
"I must go," said Suñño.
"Oh come on. Just a bit of fun, nobody can see us here," she said, sitting up.

Stuffing his books and sitting cloth in his bag, his hands trembling, he tries as hard as he can to avoid looking at her. Mumbling all sorts of swear words under his breath, he curses the situation he finds himself in. 'Hell this never happened to me before. A while ago, it would have been a dream come true but why now?' The half glances he gives her, drawing his attention closer, became more locked as he became aware she was now standing and walking towards him, holding her skirt in both hands and swinging her arms gently.

"It's ok," she said. "I'm only little and I won't bite, you know... Maybe I can help you, if you are a little shy?"

"I have to go," said the young monk as he swings his bag onto his shoulder. As if by magic, a short Päli phrase started to echo through his mind, Namo Buddhäya Namo Dhammäya Namo Sanghäya, ... he found it anchored his scattered thoughts instantly, as if it was playing on a tape loop in the back of his mind. He turned and started to walk away.

"No wait!" she cried. "Let's chat a little at least. Oh come on! We can just talk a bit, can't we?" The monk slowed a little, the chanting still flowing in his mind. He stopped and turned round. This time he felt it easier to simply look at her straight in the face. She was a beauty, there was no denying it. He opened his mouth to speak but nothing came out.

"Is there something wrong with you?" she said as her face began to change, those seductive eyes were becoming very cold. He held her gaze for a moment, his mind was like an empty space. Instinctively, as if tugged from behind, his body turned away again and started to walk down the hill.

"Don't you just turn your back on me, you bastard!" her voice stabbed out this time. "If you don't stop, I'll scream the place down. People will certainly come then and I'll tell them what kind of a perverted monk you really are!" Shrieking this time, she was trotting behind him. Suñño walked a couple more steps but stopped as she started to pull on his robe. He half turned his face in her direction and said quietly but firmly,

"Scream baby, I'm out of here!"

She didn't really scream. She whimpered at first, stamping her feet. Then she cursed and swore at the monk for a moment. Letting go of his robe, she directed a barrage of abuse towards him. The young monk stared at her for a few seconds. This was worth recording in his memory. The perfect picture of a fairy princess had turned into a vicious demon, ugly and quite frightening. She had failed to seduce the monk and she was livid, probably humiliated and now wretched.

He left her crying to herself. He walked on, never looking back.

Echoes And Vibes

Their car bumped over the speed ramps by the forest gate and they turned onto the main road.

"David wasn't there," said the Ajahn. "His neighbour told me he's in Israel but I'm sure we would have had the details right. He wrote to me a few months ago."

"Never mind, Ajahn," said anagarikä[10] Matt sitting in the driver's seat. "In this world, people's lives can change completely, almost overnight, never mind months!"

"It is very good of you to come and pick us up," said Suñño.

"We received your phone message this morning, Ajahn. Where did you spend the night?" asked Matt.

"David's neighbour offered us the use of his phone but clearly didn't want us hanging around so we went back to the forest and spent the night in the open," replied the Ajahn.

"Wow, I couldn't do that!" said Matt.

"Yes you could," said Suñño, "and you'd have loved it as much as I did... once you get a bit of practice in first."

The car was about 15 years old and had been offered to the monastery by a retired doctor. It was well used. Some of the seats had holes in the upholstery and the carpet was always a little muddy. Although it had not rained for a while, the lanes by Hartwood monastery always seemed to preserve a few puddles. The monastery and mud seemed inseparable.

The Ajahn exchanged a little news with Matt whilst Suñño relaxed on the back seat. His attention was aroused when Matt mentioned they were expecting a couple of senior monks from Thailand to arrive that afternoon but unfortunately Matt couldn't remember their names. They are having an ordination ceremony the next day, which means a large gathering of monks and nuns from various branch monasteries will be converging at Hartwood. Venerable Suñño was accepted into the monk-hood in the same way nearly two years ago. Now he feels like he is returning to the community with something very different in his heart as many things looked different to him now. He was very eager to express his appreciation to his preceptor and teacher Luang Por Suvïro but he felt surprisingly cool at the prospect of seeing his other friends again.

Matt drove slowly through the village where the Ajahn and Suñño did their first Alms Round on their pilgrimage. The place looked smaller. A large hole and a pile of earth was at the spot were the monks stood outside the post office and the pub looked as if it had been re-painted. 'Is this a time warp or was it really such

[10] *Anagarika - Male (Anagarikä - Female) lay postulant wearing white robes and having a shaved head who lives at the monastery keeping basic monastic precepts, the first step in training before novice monk or nun ordination.*

a long time that we've been away?' thought Suñño to himself.

The narrow lane leading up to the monastery looked much greener and the horses that peered over the fence seemed extra friendly that morning. Climbing the hill, the ancient narrow road was carved deep into the landscape, probably by hundreds of years of horses and carts. Great tall banks rose up at each side with rocky outcrops and tangled tree roots. Many wild flowers shone through long grass as they reached the top of the hill and the monastery entrance. The Ajahn laughed out loud as he saw an old friend, another tall American monk who had lived at Hartwood for several years, back in his old role as premium organiser with clipboard in hand and ordering people about on the front lawn. Suñño spotted a couple of unfamiliar faces in brown robes by the door to the house as they pulled into the parking spot.

"Welcome back, Ajahn!" said a new monk, who was about the Ajahn's age, as he opened the car door and reached out a hand to take the Ajahn's bag. "Oh good, you are just in time for the meal, 'though I reckon we'll be running late today as Ajahn Lee has also just arrived."
"The Ajahn Lee?" gasped Suñño.
"Didn't you know he was coming?" replied the monk.
"A surprise for you Suñño," chuckled the Ajahn.

Suñño instinctively took in a huge breath, bit his lip, then suddenly tears flowed down his cheeks. Almost shocked by his own unexpected emotional response, he buried his head on his robe, pretending to look for something on the car floor. He had often dreamed of Ajahn Lee. He had heard several stories of him and not all from his tudong Ajahn either. 'If he can really read my mind then what on earth am I going to say to him?' Suñño thought to himself as he swiftly pulled himself together and climbed out of the car. With the Ajahn's bag on one shoulder and his own on the other, he was quickly instructed to go and set up for the meal in a specially prepared marquee pitched on the other side of the house. As a junior monk, he quickly jumped to it, leaving his Ajahn to be led into the house to meet with the other elders.

"The nuns claim the green tent in the north field was offered to them and they want to take it to their cottage. They have no space for guests it seems," came one voice to the left of the Ajahn as he slipped off his sandals at the door.
"The tables from the village hall are no good," came another voice, spoken with a strong Germanic accent, to the Ajahn's right.
"Sister Sanghamitta wants to see you urgently," cried another voice, female this time. The Ajahn walked calmly through the gathering crowd with his head lowered, saying nothing.
"Did you have a pleasant trip?" came the calm and friendly tones of Venerable Javano, his trusted attendant. "Maybe you could use a drink?"
"Ah, now there's someone who knows how to treat their elders properly," smiled the Ajahn quietly to himself.

He stood in the hall and re-arranged his robe onto one shoulder before walking into the shrine room. Kneeling down, he bowed three times before the Buddha image.

"Nice to see you Suñño," said his close friend Sāmaêera[11] Tappassī. "Did you have a good tudong?" They walked together to the marquee.

Tappassī came from the Czech Republic to study law in London but his studies became sidetracked after he met a Chinese girlfriend who introduced him to Buddhism. He had been visiting the monastery regularly for two or three years before moving in. Venerable Suñño was very much a mentor for him. They had both been working on several projects at Hartwood and had shared some rough times together.

"Have you seen Ajahn Lee?" asked Suñño.
"Not yet. They took him straight up to room one," replied Tappassī. "Then he had a shower. He has a couple of attendants travelling with him. One is an Australian monk who speaks brilliant Thai. I have met him but he is really quiet, kind of shy with a great smile!"

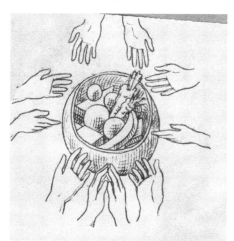

Together they quickly prepared their bowls and sitting places. Suñño realised this was to be the largest gathering of monks he had ever witnessed in England. There were more than fifty seats prepared on the monks' side and maybe thirty on the nuns'. A large red carpet was laid out in front of a makeshift shrine with two special, slightly raised seats with triangular backrests positioned in the centre. The rest of the floor was covered with a motley collection of carpets and rugs which was slowly being covered by lay people, mostly Thai, who sat waiting.

"We are expecting a large crowd tomorrow," said Tappassī.
"Are you nervous?" asked Suñño.
"Sometimes," replied Tappassī. Tomorrow will be his big day, together with two other novices. He will be taking full ordination as a monk. "Actually half of these seats are empty today. The others come just for the meal tomorrow so I guess we can move up a bit closer to the big Ajahn's seats."

A few of the other monks arrived carrying bowls and ushered the two friends to move up but Suñño was hesitating. A steady stream of monks entered through the narrow opening in the marquee wall to the side of the shrine, some bringing their bowls with them, some already had places prepared. Then Suñño noticed

[11] *Sāmaêera - Novice monk.*

a break in the flow and he looked up to see two unfamiliar monks, one Thai, the other western, holding the door wide open and lowering themselves as Laung Por Suvīro and Ajahn Lee stepped through. To Suñño's amazement, Ajahn Lee was much smaller than he'd imagined, really dwarfed by the huge American figure of Luang Por Suvīro, Suñño's preceptor. The elderly monks walked slowly and purposefully to their places as all the other monks gently moved from their seats and moved forward to pay their respects and bow to their elders.

"Come on," whispered Tappassī. "Let's see if we can get closer." Venerable Suñño was usually very circumspect and respectful when approaching elders. He would usually have given space for the more senior monks but by some kind of strange accident or coincidence, he was led right up close to the front. A rapid reshuffle took place for a few seconds as all the monks knelt in readiness with their palms held together in front of their hearts. A few glances to either side and then they all bowed three times in unison to each of the elder monks. As Suñño emerged from his third bow, he heard his preceptor say,

"How are you, Suñño?"

A little shocked that he should receive such special attention when there were so many others there, he looked disbelievingly at Luang Por, pointing to himself.

"Yes, Venerable Suñño. I hear you have had a splendid tudong. I've been hearing all about it," said his preceptor as the other elders laughed. Suñño felt a little embarrassed for a second but then he received a warm beaming smile from Ajahn Lee and he felt fantastic.
"Wonderful, yes thank you Luang Por," replied Suñño. "My Ajahn looked after me well and taught me a lot," he continued turning to his tudong companion. "We met some wonderful and generous people."

The monks all laughed again. A few other pleasantries were exchanged and the monks returned to their seats. Before the monks filed out of the enormous tent to collect their food, Ajahn Lee, Luang Por and a couple of other monks who Suñño couldn't see, were chatting together in Thai. They seemed to be pointing to Suñño and then to another figure in the crowd. Then they looked quite concerned. An uneasy feeling began to emerge in the young monk's stomach. They seemed to be pointing to someone in the crowd who was obscured from Suñño by a giant tent pole decorated with flowers. Then the figure moved forward a fraction to acknowledge the elder monks who all smiled and nodded in reply. All Suñño could see was a head of long blonde hair and a white top. 'Oh my goodness,' he thought. 'It's her! It was only yesterday evening we had that showdown in the forest! I didn't think she'd go this far. How the hell did she know how to follow me here. What a terrible mess! No wonder Luang Por was making such a fuss. I just trust they'll believe me when I tell them what really happened, although they seem to be supporting me. Oh my goodness, I hope she is not going to make too much trouble for us all but she did threaten to!'

"We have been admiring the new friend you met on your tudong," said another monk as they stood up to file out and collect their food.

"I can explain," stammered Suñño, feeling really sick at the very idea of eating now.

As the young monk walked out behind the others, he felt as if he just wanted to vanish. Out of the corner of his eye, he noticed the blonde figure was walking up behind him.

"Are you ok?" asked Tappassī. "You've gone completely white."

Once again, Venerable Suñño squared himself up to receive the monster, face to face. His friend pulled lightly on his arm but he just needed a couple more long breaths before he faced her, regardless of the fact he was holding up everyone. Just when the moment was right, he swung round. Beneath the blond hair was a wispy reddish beard and a young man's face. It was the quiet young dope smoker with the biker friends that they had met many days ago.

"Dogs!" cried Suñño loudly, "Wow what a surprise!" A great cry of laughter bubbled through the community.

"Dad told me all about it, 'though I kind of knew about it all already," said the young hippy. "I want to stay, if it's OK with you."

"Sure!" replied Suñño as he followed the others out of the marquee, now feeling a little dizzy, confused and wonderfully elated, all at the same time.

"A great mob of bikers turned up a few days ago and delivered the hippy boy. He is quite a character!" smiled Tappassī. "It seems you have a new disciple!"

"Oh no! He is the Ajahn's disciple. I'm not ready yet," said Suñño.

The first few hours back at the monastery were uncommonly bewildering for Venerable Suñño. On one level, he noticed his mind was remarkably calm and steady even when he made the mistake over the blonde girl at the mealtime. Everything was happening on a different timescale; very clearly, almost in slow motion. Although, on another level, his emotional sensitivity was moving off at a hair's trigger. He virtually wept at the sight of the magnificent spread of food laid out at the mealtime and practically any close or friendly contact with friends moved him deeply. However, all this was happening at quite a deep level and would have been completely unperceivable to almost everyone, except for 'those in the know'.

He was given the choice of accommodation by the lodgings monk, 'For tonight, you can share the attic with five other visiting monks or you can use the old grey tent in the north field.' Suñño chose the tent, gathered his things and headed out there for a short rest in solitude. There were a number of tents there but it was quiet. There was only one old grey tent, slightly mouldy with a broken zip at the entrance. The faded blue plastic groundsheet crackled as he stretched out flat. Lying still for a moment he found a hard lump in his back so he moved. Then there was one in his shoulder, then his thigh, then he surrendered to lumpiness and slept for just a few minutes.

When he awoke, he noticed the warm summer sun had moved the shady camping spot into full solar glare and his tent was rapidly becoming an oven. The young monk crawled out gasping for air only to find his long-haired hippy friend sitting outside in the shade.

"Well, Dogs, my friend," said Suñño. "Is that really what I should call you?"

"I'd prefer Andrew actually," came a big smile in reply. Suñño joined him in the shade of an old oak tree near his tent. They just sat in silence for a while.

"I've brought you something," said Andrew slowly pulling a camping mat from behind him. "The ground here is a killer, all stones in the long grass. This will help you sleep tonight."

"Thanks Andrew. That was very thoughtful of you," said Suñño. "Where did you find it?"

"That is not important," said Andrew. "It's clean."

"Ok then. Err, I guess it is," smiled Suñño. They both silently watched young Tappassï and a very much older Venerable Cägänando approach from the far side of the field. The older monk was an artist and extraordinary craftsman who had been living at the monastery for years. He had made an immediate connection with the young hippy. Tappassï brought a sleeping bag for his friend and the elderly monk carried a bottle of water. As they sat down, the old monk pulled out a small pocket set of watercolour paints and handed them to Suñño without a word. A gift from one artist to another. They enjoyed each other's company for a while but Suñño was keen to see Ajahn Lee again. Cägänando said they were still in the marquee, chatting with the Thai visitors.

"I stayed for a while but I couldn't follow what was going on, so I left," said the old monk. "That old Thai monk has some energy, I can tell you. Like a 100 foot tall lighthouse! It is lovely watching him and Luang Por chatting together. Pure magic!" he called out as the three youngsters walked quickly back towards the house.

The marquee was deserted apart from a couple of anagarikä's who were tidying up. Suñño was reluctant to go and pursue Ajahn Lee to his room. He would probably be resting now after the long journey. Besides, there was no guarantee there would be a translator available. They walked around the side of the house and then Suñño heard his Ajahn laughing. It seemed that the Thai monks were feeling cold in the huge tent, which Suñño found amazing as he felt pretty warm in there. So the group of elders had moved to the conservatory which was partly shaded in the afternoon but sweltering nevertheless, even for a southern Californian.

Luang Por had gone to rest at the Abbot's residence leaving an empty seat. Ajahn Lee sat cross-legged, high in a wicker chair looking like a giant, happy bullfrog on a lily pad. The others sat on the floor around him. As soon as Ajahn Lee saw Suñño at the door, he beckoned him in enthusiastically. Following Thai custom, which meant walking on their knees, the young monks, Suñño and Tappassï, moved into a space in the middle of the floor. Andrew sat leaning against the

doorframe at the back. A tall and extremely skinny Australian monk sat on one side, dutifully attending to Ajahn Lee and translating for him. There was a box of coke cans under the chair, which were passed out to all arrivals as directed by Ajahn Lee.

For the first few minutes, Suñño just sat silently taking it all in. This was a much more intimate gathering. Mostly monks filled the room which meant the Thai lay friends stayed outside. A couple of nuns were sitting by the doorway leading to the house. All the attention was centred on the master in the high chair who was glowing with life and vitality. Sometimes Ajahn Lee appeared to completely ignore a question as it was translated for him. He would make no sign of acknowledging the questioner and continue a reply to a previous person. Then maybe several minutes later, he would suddenly move all his attention back with a concise and direct comment or sometimes ask another question in return. Occasionally, he could round up several different issues into one point, capped off with a lovely story or a joke.

The way he juggled with so many things at once reminded Suñño of a circus performer he knew who was able to keep three eggs, a frying pan, a top hat and a burning torch in the air for some time. The juggler would pass things between his legs and behind his back without dropping anything until the finale when the top hat falls on his head and the eggs smash themselves into an open frying pan held in one hand over the burning torch held in the other! Like a magician, he had everyone spellbound.

There were a few western lay men who were quizzing Ajahn Lee about refined states of consciousness and supernatural powers. Mostly he avoided very much involvement with them. He kept encouraging them to investigate these things from their own experience and insisted they are not issues which should be held on to.

"Please, I'd like to ask the Ajahn a question," called out a grey-haired gentleman leaning on the wall at the back.
"Please do," said the translator.
"I have heard many good reports of your monastery and of your teaching venerable sir, but some people still doubt it. Pray tell me, are you actually enlightened or not?" he asked in a very upper class accent. The question caused some amusement to the monks, some even chuckled. Everyone turned to see

the master's response as the translator passed it on.

Ajahn Lee looked a little taken back for a second, then smiling he gazed up into the sky for a while. The room was silent as he scanned the faces which surrounded him, holding a particularly long look at Suñño, which sent ripples through his mind.

"Well, it is like this," said Ajahn Lee. "I am like a tree in the forest. This tree produces a lot of fruit and many birds come to feed themselves from it. Some of the birds say that the fruit is sweet, some say the fruit is sour but for the tree, all this is nothing but birdsong."

Most of the time Ajahn Lee wanted to emphasise a simple life for the monks and warned them not to get caught up in seeking comfort. He said there is a lot of danger in trying to make a perfect monastery where everyone is happy all the time. He pointed out such an ideal is foolish and will only lead to trouble. 'It is good enough!' or 'Patient endurance, you can do that' or 'Look and see for yourself' were phrases he continually repeated. After a couple of hours, the mood suddenly changed. Ajahn Lee uncurled his legs and put his feet on the floor. He pointed his chin mentioning 'Tan Suñño' as he gave instructions to his attendant.

"Suñño, he wants to stretch his legs and asks if you will show him around the grounds," said the attendant as everyone prepared a path for his exit. First the monks asked permission to pay their respects, so the Ajahn returned to his seat and received their bows.

Just outside the conservatory door, the other Thai monk was waiting with a blanket which he wrapped around Ajahn Lee's shoulders whilst another guided his feet into sandals placed strategically on the ground in readiness.
They had only walked a few paces when they were approached by a youthful looking middle-aged man with neatly trimmed hair and beard, wearing a white jacket. He introduced himself as a meditation teacher from a large vipassana retreat centre.

"I would like to ask permission if I could come and study with you for a while in your monastery in Thailand?" asked the teacher.
"It is not the place for you," said Ajahn Lee, looking out over the fields.
"I hear that you are a great teacher and I am sure I could learn a lot from you," requested the teacher.
"Not the place for you," said Ajahn Lee.
"But I am sure the monastic experience would support my practice," said the teacher putting his palms together.
"He said that his place is not for you," said the attendant trying to press the message home as Ajahn Lee turned to walk away.
"I am a genuine practitioner Ajahn. I take refuge in the triple gem and I keep the precepts. I am sure you can help me!" the teacher moved to block the Ajahn who

stopped and looked directly into the man's face as he listened for the translation. Then he said something directly to the teacher with a firm yet kind expression. "If you come to the monastery to die, then he said he can help you," said the attendant.

The teacher was dumbstruck. He stood motionless for a moment, a tiny tear welled up in his eye but he did not break his attention with the monk.

"Thank you," said the teacher quietly, holding his hands together in respect, then he turned and walked away.

The tour of the grounds was very brief. The elderly monk pottered along while Suñño tried to explain a few things about what they saw but they showed no interest in any more information. Ajahn Lee's attendant said they had had no rest for over 38 hours and he was straining to keep up with the translating. So then they walked in silence. Suñño and his friend Tappassī were both searching their minds for a question to ask the wise old monk when they were in the conservatory but could not find one. Now they were just happy to be in such a master's company.

Ajahn Lee showed some interest in a gigantic chestnut tree which was slowly dying. He pointed to it and said it was similar to the Sangha (Buddhist monastic community) in Thailand, spectacular and impressive but largely dead wood. Most of the useful stuff is high and out of reach or very hard to find. Then he compared it to a young sapling, which he said was like the Sangha in the West, small, fragile but full of life and great potential. He said that many of the great teachers in Asia believe that the real Dhamma, even the next Buddha will arise in the West. Traditionally, a Buddha statue would always face East but there are teachers in Thailand who have built their temples with the Buddha facing West.

"So, do you think this way of life will continue to benefit people here in England?" Suñño asked.
"The signs are favourable!" replied Ajahn Lee through his translator. "You have all you need here. It is up to you to use it well now that you know how."

With this final comment, Ajahn Lee beamed a lovely grin at Suñño and turned off the path making a beeline across the meadow for the house. A short comment was passed onto the tall Australian as he marched off.

"Oh good," he said. "He's told us to go and take a rest... And he'll see you again tomorrow." The tall skinny monk trotted off after his Ajahn. 'This seemed to be an enormous compliment that this eminent master made me,' thought Suñño. 'It is up to me to use it well, now that I know how... Wow I'd better be careful not to let this go to my head!'

It was mid afternoon when Suñño returned to his tent feeling highly charged.

He propped himself up against the oak tree and took out his notebook and pencil for a while. Looking through the many notes and drawings he had made on his journey, he then picked up the colour box and the bottle of water and boldly added a new coloured dimension to his memoirs, in the same way that the pilgrimage had added a new level of understanding to his practice. The colours almost mixed themselves as memories and feelings flooded through him.

The angry and threatening woman who made such an incredible transformation was the first who came to mind. The little plastic peppermint box which her daughter had offered now contained a handful of his hay fever tablets and a treasured memory.

The lovely death of the old man and the completely scattered life that family led. There seemed to be so much pretending, clinging to their past and not the least bit aware of the deep suffering they were making for themselves. 'So wrapped up in their delusions those guys!' he thought.

Suñño laughed to himself as he recalled the delightful childish innocence of Lilly and her little brother. He could still see them crying as they left to continue on their trail in the morning. 'Yes they will be shedding a good many more tears as they grow older. What comes then has to go away.'

There was that large extended family with a lot of children who all looked tired, with bags under their eyes. He remembered their squabbling over toys in the garden, and all the empty whisky bottles in the back toilet. They reached out with such kindness and shared what time and nourishment they could in their complicated lives.

Drinking tea with a man who had murdered his wife. This was something he had never dreamed of. He seemed like such a nice and gentle fellow, although definitely haunted by his memories. The noise of the prison, constant clanking of iron gates, many voices echoing against very hard and unforgiving surfaces.

A young property tycoon who was on the edge of a breakdown. Goodness knows where the hell he thought he was going!

'The young and the old, the rich and the poor; some happy, some sad, all doing their own little things, living in their own worlds,' thought Suñño. 'Each individual trying to fit into a particular mould they had created for themselves.' His sketchbook seemed to portray a selection of images, scenes and stereotypes; all of which, when viewed flat on paper, are just that. 'Even the landscapes are my own creations,' he thought. Stereotypes seem to be so much what worldly life is all about. All beings are, even the monk. Perhaps especially the monk because in some ways he provides a reflective surface, like a mirror, against which all other images appear as they are. Empty, even including his own.

Fondly recalling the irritating photographers, he wondered how those people would relate to seeing those images again as they flip through the hundreds in their collection. Or will the wonder have already gone; the picture and the experience were never the same thing anyway.

It was clear that during the past few weeks, the Ajahn and he had touched quite profoundly upon the lives of a few. As indeed, many people had made strong imprints on Venerable Suñño. Especially the Ajahn whose guidance, skill and humble friendship revealed the beautiful potential aspect of humanity which clearly has the power to enlighten the world. Contemplating his own situation, he quite relished the idea of looking after his friend Tappassī in his new life as a Bhikkhu. Although, he was beginning to see for himself that following a monk's life itself is one thing, yet understanding the deeper direction in which it is pointing looks like something else. Apparently, certain key things have to be let go of, not just the money and stuff but the whole idea of being anyone going anywhere.

A fluff-free Andrew arrived with blood trickling down the back of his head. Suñño recognised immediately that it was his first attempt at shaving himself and laughed in sympathy.

"Hey Andrew, do you remember when we met in the church porch a couple of weeks ago?" asked Suñño. "I don't believe we ever exchanged a word."
"No we didn't," said Andrew. "Dad did all the talking as usual."
"So how come you became so interested?"
"I liked the positive vibes, man. Too many words do my head in. I mean words mostly obscure the meaning, don't you think? I always follow the vibes, man."
"Vibes which carry us to a contented rather than a frustrated, illusory future?"
"You have it man! Right on the head!"

"Everything is uncertain - naturally so.

Living like this we come right up to the edge...

Not knowing where we are going or if we will have any food to eat helps us focus the mind.

*Living very much here and now,
giving up control,
being open to all that arises
is peaceful.*

*Wanting this to be otherwise
isn't peaceful at all.*

*Letting go brings us into the present,
a natural contentment.*

It brings us back to the place we never left.

This is it."

Paṭisankhā yoniso piṇḍapātaṃ paṭisevāmi, neva davāya na madāya, na maṇḍanāya, na vibhūsanāya, yavadeva imassa kāyassa ṭhitiya, yāpanāya, vihiṃsuparatiyā, bramhacariyānuggahāya, iti purāṇañca vedanaṃ paṭihaṅkhāmi, navañca vedanaṃ na uppādessāmi, yātrā ca me bhavissati anavajjatā ca phāsuvihāro cā 'ti.

Wisely reflecting, I use alms-food; not for fun, not for pleasure, not for fattening, not for beautification, only for the maintenance and nourishment of this body, for keeping it healthy, for helping with the Holy Life; thinking thus, 'I will allay hunger without overeating, so that I may continue to live blamelessly and at ease.'

"No shoes?" said a figure at the door of the chapel.

"Being locked up in a deluded mind... it's much more difficult to escape from there, even if you have the key."

"He described it as if being pushed along a tightrope over a bottomless pit by a mad axe man..."

The monks disappeared down the footpath
which hugged the hedge at the edge of the field.

Suñño was very much aware that she had come closer, a lot closer,
but he did not respond.